S0-AER-003

# Bad Girls of the Arab World

Read it Again
3630 Peachtree Pkwy, Ste 314
Suwanee, GA 30024
770-232-93
www.Read-it-Again.com

DISPLAY

EDITED BY
NADIA YAQUB
AND RULA QUAWAS

# Bad Girls of the Arab World

University of Texas Press

*Austin*

Copyright © 2017 by the University of Texas Press
All rights reserved
Printed in the United States of America
First edition, 2017

Requests for permission to reproduce material from this work should be
sent to:
Permissions
University of Texas Press
P.O. Box 7819
Austin, TX 78713-7819
http://utpress.utexas.edu/index.php/rp-form

♾ The paper used in this book meets the minimum requirements of ANSI/
NISO Z39.48-1992 (R1997) (Permanence of Paper).

**Library of Congress Cataloging-in-Publication Data**

Names: Yaqub, Nadia G., editor. | Quawas, Rula (Rula Butros Audeh),
1960–, editor.
Title: Bad girls of the Arab world / edited by Nadia Yaqub and Rula
Quawas.
Description: First edition. | Austin : University of Texas Press, 2017. |
Includes bibliographical references and index.
Identifiers: LCCN 2017009446
    ISBN 978-1-4773-1335-0 (cloth : alk. paper)
    ISBN 978-1-4773-1336-7 (pbk. : alk. paper)
    ISBN 978-1-4773-1337-4 (library e-book)
    ISBN 978-1-4773-1338-1 (nonlibrary e-book)
Subjects: LCSH: Women—Arab countries. | Feminism—Arab countries. |
Women—Arab countries—Social conditions.
Classification: LCC HQ1784 .B33 2017 | DDC 305.40917/4927—dc23
LC record available at https://lccn.loc.gov/2017009446

doi:10.7560/313350

# Contents

*For all the girls of the world: may they
grow and thrive without fear or constraint.*

On July 25, 2017, Rula Quawas passed away unexpectedly in Amman, Jordan. Rula was a committed scholar and activist, an inspiring teacher, and a dear, dear friend. She personified love. She loved life and work and people. We loved her in return.

Rula poured her heart into this book but never got to hold it in her hands. *Bad Girls of the Arab World* is dedicated to her memory. She lives forever in our hearts and in scholarship, both her own and ours.

# A Note on Transliteration and Translation

Transliteration from Modern Standard Arabic follows the *International Journal of Middle East Studies* (*IJMES*) transliteration system with the following exceptions:

1 In Abdo's chapter, the Arabic term *sīra* has been rendered *seira* to draw attention to the relationship between that word and the name of Abdo's daughter.

2 In Martin and Caillé's chapter, names of film characters are transliterated as they appear in the subtitles of the films. In a similar vein, in Fábos's chapter, the titles of music albums and songs are transliterated as they appear in albums and online files posted by the artists or their distributors.

3 We have used the spellings that living persons have chosen for themselves if they regularly write their names in Latin characters. For the names of individuals who do not appear to have a preferred spelling in Latin characters, we have used *IJMES* transliteration for standard Arabic without diacritics except ayn and hamza.

4 We follow the transliterations that news organizations such as Al Jazeera have chosen for themselves.

5 The *IJMES* transliteration has been modified in cases of dialectal Arabic to more accurately reflect pronunciation.

We have sought to provide the reader with a translation for Arabic words and phrases that are not commonly used in contemporary English, with the exception of Diya Abdo's chapter, where Arabic phrases are intentionally left untranslated as an expression of the different relationships the author seeks to create with her Arabic and English readers.

# Foreword

How honored and delighted we are to read these excursions into bad girl representations and possibilities in the Arab world! It is a pleasure to contemplate the richness of diversity and varying approaches the contributors bring to this valuable collection. Analyzing the gendered boundaries of language, culture, and society in accessible prose, these essays take us beyond surface headlines and simple stereotypes. These stories of gender-role resistance celebrate the courage of those who deploy their voices, bodies, and knowledge to disrupt the status quo yet also empathize with those who reluctantly find themselves pushed into the spotlight. All reveal the dark side of standing at the center of controversy, becoming the bad girl target that incites heated debate over a range of issues, from class, gender, and propriety to the meanings of democracy, national identity, and religion.

In taking on the shifting definitions of bad girls and good, the contributors to *Bad Girls of the Arab World* argue that such representations cannot be separated from a specific time and place, explicating their valences in local and global conversations. The authors show how and why such representations are open to multiple interpretations and negotiations, whether discussed in family conversations around the dinner table or transmitted widely and instantly through electronic media. Tracing dynamic pathways opened by memoirs, photographs, performances, and activism, the authors find common ground among these bad girls but, wisely, do not presume unanimity of intent among them. Even self-selected bad girls may well not agree about what constitutes transgression and what should or should not be transgressed.

Bad girls expose the borders of social normativities and thereby transform what it means to be a woman in the Arab world. The bad girl tells us where the boundaries are for good girls, to make the contours of the good girl visible. Bad girl representations do not necessarily reflect progressive images, but they push us to ponder image creation itself. How are bad girl images deployed, circulated, and interpreted? How does this circulation give them tangibility as well as a power that extends beyond a single individual?

Bad girls also provoke us to ask about the subversive potential of girlhood. What dangerous possibility does girlhood hold as a period of dramatic psychological and physiological change? Why do authorities around the globe devote such attention and scrutiny to the girl, debating her proper education and future role in society?

As *Bad Girls of the Arab World* makes clear, both good girls and bad girls pay a high price for living in a patriarchal society. Bad girls show us how stepping outside the good girl script has consequences but that being a good girl is exhausting work in its own way. To have to be the custodians of virtue, purity, piety, responsibility, and submission must take time out of one's day. What mental bandwidth remains for one's own creativity and interests?

Writing about bad girls is an act of bravery in itself. There is always the risk of reinforcing the misogyny the writer seeks to undercut. There is risk, too, in provoking sanction and pushback on a topic already the target of volatile sentiment. We admire the editors and authors of *Bad Girls of the Arab World* for their fearless scholarship.

Laura Miller and Jan Bardsley
Editors, *Bad Girls of Japan*

# Acknowledgments

First, I would like to extend my sincere thanks and warm appreciation to my gifted and passionate students, who always inspire me to be a better teacher and human being. I appreciate and acknowledge their contributions and their unstinting support over my twenty years of teaching. Without them in my life, I would not be able to rekindle my mind and heart and to grow intellectually and spiritually.

I am also grateful to my friends and colleagues in Jordan and abroad who always create intellectual spaces for vibrant and robust feminist conversations that help me not only to look at happenstances through different lenses but also to locate embedded meanings that hide in nooks and crannies. I am forever grateful for their feedback and valuable comments.

Also, thanks to my beautiful mom, Umm Audeh, who brightens our home and is my source of daily inspiration. Her weaving patterns of love, healing, and hope, which are voices that speak and sing, are central to the interweavings of my feminist mind and heart. Her warrior spirit is well and alive in me. Thank you, Mamma.

Rula Quawas

*B*ad Girls of the Arab World has many invisible contributors. Jan Bardsley was there every step of the way, participating in brainstorming sessions and walking meetings. She patiently read multiple drafts of the introduction and offered invaluable feedback. One cannot wish for a more generous colleague and "femtor," to use one of Rula's favorite words, than Jan. Frances Hasso was also a mainstay of my support from start to finish. *Bad Girls* was the topic of many of our weekend speed walks. I learned a great deal, too, from coteaching with Frances and participating in her Geographies of Gender in the Arab World workshop at Duke University. Rula and I would not have embarked on this project if it weren't for the urging of Elizabeth Bishop. Elizabeth began this project with us, infusing our many Skype meetings with her enthusiasm and creativity. Although she was not able to see the project to its end, the book is shaped in part by her contribution to early conversations. I am grateful to Karen Booth and Elyse Crystall for the valuable feedback they gave me on the draft introduction. I also benefited greatly from other conversations with these women and many others. Our anonymous reviewers provided insightful feedback that has made the volume far stronger than it otherwise would have been. Any remaining weaknesses are, of course, our own responsibility.

I have been sustained intellectually over the years by conversations with a number of friends and colleagues. We didn't always talk about *Bad Girls*, but I have learned and grown through my interactions with them in ways that have affected the book. They include Sahar Amar, Martine Antle, miriam cooke, Doria Elkerdany, Banu Gokariksel, Zeina Halabi, Ellen McLarney, Rosemary Sayigh, and Rebecca Stein. I was also supported intellectually by writing and fellowship groups at the University of North Carolina and am grateful to their organizers and participants: Sohini Sengupta, Pat Parker, Morgan Pitelka, Rachel Pollack, Michele Robinson, Michele Berger, Oswaldo Estrada, Sabine Gruffat, Juliane Hammer, Mariska Leunnisen, Elliot Moreton, Andy Perrin, Jessica Tanner, and Dorothy Verkerk. I am grateful as well to my colleagues in the UNC Department of Asian Studies for the congenial and supportive work environment they create together, and in particular to Robin Visser, Li-ling Hsiao, Wendan Li, and Morgan Pitelka, who accepted additional administrative duties so that I could take a research leave. If there is any one person in Asian Studies who is indispensable to its functioning, it would be Lori Harris. We all rely on her for our research and teaching; *Bad Girls* would not have been possible without her.

I am grateful to all the contributors to *Bad Girls*, who have stayed with the project through the long and convoluted journey from conception to publication. This book is first and foremost their work. Indispensable funding for research and writing was provided by the University of North Carolina at Chapel Hill and in particular the Institute for the Arts and Humanities. Thea Galli supplied much-appreciated last-minute research assistance, and Emma Galli offered much-needed graphic design assistance on other projects when I was in a pinch. Her work allowed me to focus on *Bad Girls* and submit the manuscript on time. It has been a pleasure to work with Jim Burr, our editor at University of Texas Press. He has fielded our innumerable drafts, questions, and suggestions with patience, wisdom, and humor.

Thinking, editing, and writing require time, space, and solitude. But they are also sustained by intimate companionship—relationships that encompass conversation and silence, sharing and privacy, support and independence. I am fortunate to find such companionship with Christof. This book, like my other projects, would not have been possible without him.

Nadia Yaqub

# Introduction

NADIA YAQUB

Among the memorable images that emerged early from the Arab Spring uprisings of 2011 were two provocative photographs of Egyptian women. In the first, Aliaa Elmahdy, at the time a student at the American University in Cairo, posted a nude photo of herself on her blog on October 23, 2011. In the photo she stands facing the camera entirely naked except for a pair of black stockings and red shoes. Her body is square with the camera, as is her gaze. She hides nothing from viewers and by resting one foot on the rung of a nearby chair, hints at the female genitalia that would otherwise not be visible.[1] In the second, which appeared during clashes between the military and police in Cairo in December 2011, a woman is being dragged away by her arms by two soldiers in helmets and armed with batons. She is on her back with her arms pulled over her head. Her abaya is hiked up above her shoulders, revealing her jeans, blue bra, and bare midriff. A third soldier appears poised to stomp on her belly.[2]

There is much to say about these two images, the circumstances under which they were created and circulated, the responses they garnered when they first appeared, and the discussions they have elicited in the Arab world and beyond. I mention them here because they neatly illustrate two very different types of Arab women's transgressive actions. Elmahdy is intentionally defiant, fearlessly and publicly contravening accepted norms of behavior, and doing so in the expected realm of body politics. In a society in which the vast majority of women wear the hijab and where the visibility of women's bodies in public spaces has been (and continues to be) hotly contested both physically and discursively, she chose to transgress those norms in a deliberately provocative manner. She did not engage in the polite if often heated conversations about veiling and modest dress that have taken place in academic and popular venues and publications. She chose not to debate, cajole, or convince potential interlocutors. Rather, she staked out a defiant position and irrevocably committed herself to it with a bodily act that she then immortalized through digital media.

Elmahdy engaged in what Zakia Salime terms a "microrebellion" through which she inserted a woman's body and sexuality into the visual archive of the uprisings, and transgressed older collective-oriented forms of feminist practice in the region (Salime 2014, 15–16). Her transgression was shocking not just because she contravened accepted behavior but because it revealed the constructed and fragile nature of gendered boundaries. It took just a few clicks of a camera and computer mouse to create and disseminate those images. Millions of Egyptian women could have followed suit, thereby destroying accepted dress codes and perhaps at the same time codes of modest behavior and gender separation that those dress codes represent and support. Millions of Egyptians did look at her photo, and its dissemination became an occasion to revisit debates—and to largely reaffirm received wisdom—about the place of gender and sexuality within national movements for change (Mourad 2014, 67–70).

Unlike Elmahdy, the woman in the second photo, known in Arabic as Sitt al-Banāt, did not intend to transgress social norms.[3] She never chose to expose her body. She came to Tahrir Square modestly dressed to engage in the mode of nonviolent protest that had become integral to the dynamic politics of the first year of the Egyptian uprisings. ʿAzza Hilal, who also can be seen being beaten by soldiers in the video from which the photo was taken, and other activists have publicly protested their treatment at the hands of the military, police, or street thugs. The woman in this photo has chosen to remain anonymous. Nonetheless, her image incited intense debate. Her treatment sparked a large protest in which women carried signs depicting her not as a beaten and disrobed victim but as a ninja kicking a soldier in the face (Hafez 2014, 26). Many in Egypt were outraged by the evidence her image offered of the brutality with which the military treated the demonstrators and of the violation of her modesty. Others criticized the woman and her guardians, arguing that the square was no place for upstanding women and that she should have been kept safely at home.

We cannot know for sure what motivated this woman to participate in a demonstration but shun any role in the debates surrounding gender and violence in Tahrir Square that preceded and followed it. The incident occurred within the context of widespread gendered violence that was designed to end the new, peaceful comingling of men and women in Tahrir Square that had emerged in January 2011, including the return of virulent sexual harassment and sexual assault by thugs, police, and the military, as well as virginity tests by military officials.[4] Sitt al-Banāt likely did not expect her protest to lead to the beating and stripping that made her an anonymous icon. She did not choose to open up a conversation about rights, modesty, gender, or violence.

Elmahdy and Sitt al-Banāt were warmly received in some Western circles. Islamophobic activists in the West embraced Elmahdy, who left Egypt for Europe under threats of violence in March 2012 and joined the controversial feminist group Femen. She went on to disseminate provocative anti-Islamist images of her own naked body, including one in which she and another woman are shown menstruating and defecating on the flag of the Islamic State. The photo of Sitt al-Banāt was widely circulated in social media, becoming a global spectacle. Commenters discussed the image as evidence of the excessive violence being exercised by the military and, in specifically gendered terms, its goal of keeping women out of the public square. Western discussions complicated these Egyptian stories because they were largely based on an assumption that the patriarchal structures that the images revealed were particular to the Arab Islamic world. The narratives in the West were sometimes problematically simplistic. In one case the narrative accentuated the wholesale rejection of Arab Islamic cultures and traditions, and in the other it presented a portrait of gendered victimization that was similarly totalizing. The images and the discussions surrounding them occurred in a global and transnational context that affected how they were received and discussed locally.

I begin with these two images because they illustrate many of the themes addressed in this volume: that women may choose to transgress social norms, or transgression may be thrust upon them; that the intentions of women who appear to transgress cannot always be known; that transgression occurs within global as well as local discourses that shape decisions, actions, and consequences; and that the line separating acceptable from transgressive acts is fluid. In sum, many acts of transgression are multivalent and open to interpretation. Transgression is almost always embodied in its effects, even when it happens in virtual spaces. It either leaves its mark on bodies or delimits embodied mobility.

*Bad Girls of the Arab World* addresses the phenomenon of women whose transgressive behaviors and perspectives challenge societal norms in the Arab world, giving rise to anxiety and public debate. Our volume was inspired by the seminal collection *Bad Girls of Japan* (2005). In their introduction to that book, Laura Miller and Jan Bardsley argue that women's acts of transgression make manifest social and cultural constructs defining the borders between proper and improper behavior, as well as the social and political policing of gender, racial, and class divisions. Our book makes a similar argument about transgression in relation to Arab women. In transgressing borders, women make them apparent and often move them, demonstrating that norms are socially produced and performed. At the same time, in periods of anxiety and change, new restrictions are often imposed on women's behavior in an effort to control them. Public attention to "bad girls" can redirect scrutiny from other social ills. Because they draw attention to the fragile nature of gendered boundaries, bad girls can excite the imagination. There are, of course, significant differences between Japan of the early 2000s and the Arab world today, as the contributions in our volume illustrate. Transnational forces such as media discourses and whether and how women can move, as well as the legacy of colonialism in the region, appear to shape Arab women's badness more than that of their Japanese counterparts.

The works collected here cover a range of perspectives, experiences, geographies, and disciplines. They include short pieces by Arab women who reflect on their own experiences with transgression; an artistic intervention; and academic articles about performance, representation, activism, history, and social conditions. They address the experiences of young and old women from a range of class and educational backgrounds living in the Arab world and beyond. In the opening piece, "Inciting Critique in the Feminist Classroom," Rula Quawas reflects on her experiences teaching feminism to students at the University of Jordan in Amman as it relates to a controversial video her students produced about sexual harassment on campus. This is followed by "'And Is It Impossible to Be Good Everywhere?' Love and Badness in America and the Arab World," a brief memoir by Diya Abdo about her experiences as an American-trained academic who returns to live and work in Jordan, and as an Arab woman living in the United States.

In chapter 3, "Suspicious Bodies: Madame Bomba Performs against Death in Lebanon," Rima Najdi describes and extends a work of performance art she conducted in Beirut in response to frequent suicide bombings there, as well as describing the tremendously varied reactions that her Madame Bomba character elicited. In Randa Kayyali's chapter, "'Jihad Jane' as Good American Patriot and Bad Arab Girl: The Case of Nada Prouty after 9/11," she analyzes Prouty's memoir about her experiences as an Arab immigrant, a CIA agent, and the target of an Islamophobic campaign. In the next chapter, "Paying for Her Father's Sins: Yasmin as a Daughter of Unknown Lineage," Rawan Ibrahim offers a detailed case study of a Jordanian orphan's experiences after she ages out of institutional care and finds herself trapped in exploitative contexts that impinge on her ability to conform to normative gendered behavior.

In chapter 6, "The Making of Bad Palestinian Mothers during the Second Intifada," Adania Shibli carefully traces the construction and dissemination of the trope of the bad Palestinian mother in Israeli and Western media at the beginning of the Second Intifada in 2000. Such media accounts succeeded in shifting attention away from Israeli violence against Palestinian children to focus on the supposed willingness of Palestinians to sacrifice their children in conflicts with the Israeli military. In chapter 7, "'They are Not Like Your Daughters or Mine': Spectacles of Bad Women from the Arab Spring," Amal Amireh also draws attention to the media, in this case through a discussion of two widely reported incidents from the Arab uprisings—those of Fayda Hamdi of Tunisia and Iman al-Obeidi of Libya—demonstrating how the bodily effects of these women's encounters with discursive and physical violence was masked in the news coverage of their stories. In the chapter "'Fuck Your Morals': The Body Activism of Amina Sboui," Anne Marie Butler offers detailed readings of the topless self-portraits posted by the Tunisian social media activist Amina Sboui and traces Sboui's maturation as an artist and feminist.

In "Syrian Bad Girl Samar Yazbek: Refusing Burial," Hanadi al-Samman demonstrates how the writer Samar Yazbek effectively deploys her literary, religious, and mythic heritage in her memoirs to lend credence to her transgressive political positions. In chapter 10, "Reel Bad Maghrebi Women," Florence Martin and Patricia Caillé draw attention to the transnational context of Arab women's transgression through an analysis of films by women Maghrebi directors who transcend the expectations of national and transnational funders and audiences with narratives of dissident protagonists inhabiting complex worlds structured by local traditions, transnational cultural developments, and global neoliberalism. In chapter 11, "New Bad Girls of Sudan: Women Singers in the Sudanese Diaspora," Anita Fábos focuses on three women performers who live abroad but whose music continues to play a role in Sudanese national politics. In the final chapter, "Being a Revolutionary and Writerly Rebel," Suhair al-Tal takes us back to Jordan, where our volume began, and to an earlier period—the 1970s and 1980s—in a brief memoir about her childhood and work as an activist and journalist.

## Why Bad Girls?

Bad girls engage in or are accused of transgression, but whether an act counts as a transgression is not always clear. The institutions and communities that govern a woman's life—the family, state, religious institutions, and so forth—may have competing expectations regarding her behavior. Moreover, what was transgressive in one time may be acceptable in another. Even within a group there may be disagreement over whether an act is transgressive. In other words, transgression always involves dynamic interaction between individuals and the communities and structures that shape their lives. This focus on interaction shapes our volume in fundamental ways. Most importantly, it allows us to sidestep fraught questions surrounding agency and instead direct attention to how women negotiate the structures in which they are embedded with varying degrees of freedom and constraint.

The nature of agency and when and where it is exercised is at heart a philosophical question that hinges on a range of factors, including the formation of the subject and her desires, her capacities, and the consequences of her choices. In *The Politics of Piety* Saba Mahmood explores the nature of agency by urging feminist scholars to look beyond notions of resistance to consider how and why women might choose to submit to religious structures, inhabit rather than subvert their norms, and value practices of discipline. While her work is valuable in explaining the choices of the mosque women she has studied, Mahmood does not resolve what Linda Zerilli calls "the vicious circle of agency," whereby the agent who is seen to act solely according to free will and individual desire cannot exist (2005, 12).

The docility, submission to authority, and conformity that Mahmood describes by themselves can only perpetuate the status quo. Self-cultivation alone cannot explain the rise of the mosque movement (Mahmood 2005, 3), the diversity of practice and debate within the movement (102–104), or the rise and spread of practices of docile piety that conflict with Egyptian liberal discourses[5] and Islamic orthodoxy (15, 34).[6] Each of these developments required some type of transgression on the part of the women involved. Framing *Bad Girls of the Arab World* around questions of transgression rather than agency allows us to focus on gendered dynamics in the contemporary Arab world within the complex limits and possibilities offered by personal, historical, and social context.

At the same time, our focus on transgression is not simply another way of describing resistance, although resistance is certainly a factor in many of the cases we discuss. Transgression can also include acts of negotiation and naming. Al-Tal's memoir in chapter 11, for instance, may at first glance appear to be a straightforward story of an individual woman battling family, tribe, political organization, and state, but it also reveals the imbricated nature of relationships between the individual and those institutions as well as the need at times to muster support from one in conflict with another. Both the student video on sexual harassment that Quawas describes in chapter 1 and the use of the trope of *wa'd*, the pre-Islamic practice of burying infant girls alive, which al-Samman analyzes in chapter 8, do not so much resist these virulent practices as name them. Identified, they are brought into language where they can be discussed for what they are.

We also acknowledge reluctant bad girls—Yasmin, the Jordanian orphan described by Ibrahim in chapter 5, and the Palestinian mothers Shibli discusses in chapter 6—whose badness is constituted by social norms and media coverage, not by their own actions. Their situations make especially clear how limited women's control of their own representations can be. While some Arab women may lay claim to the "bad girl" label, reappropriating the term from their critics as a means of undermining taken-for-granted norms, many of the Arab women in this volume do not choose to be bad girls. Like Suhair al-Tal, they may be reluctant to embrace the term, refusing to cede a moral high ground to their critics, or they may have pushed boundaries created by shifting ground, as illustrated by Diya Abdo's memoir in chapter 2. Resistance does not encompass all of these practices. If Aliaa' Elmahdy embodies the deliberate and visible Arab bad girl, Sitt al-Banāt was protesting on ground that violently shifted as she marched and within power dynamics that worked themselves out on her body. The experiences of women in our volume encompass these apparently contradictory perspectives.

Like Miller and Bardsley, we use the term "girls" rather than "women" for the qualities of liminality and change it connotes. The use of "girls" to refer to adult women was rejected by US feminists in the 1970s because it suggests permanent immaturity, particularly when adult males are referred to as "men" rather than "boys." Moreover, the revival of the term "girl" in the 1990s within the concept of "girl power" was controversial for its association with antifeminism, individualism, and consumerism (Gonick 2006, 2; Taft 2004, 70). Nonetheless, the term "girls" offers several advantages. Girlhood, as Miller and Bardsley use the term, is a period between childhood and womanhood. It is characterized by danger, in-betweenness, and change that neatly bring to mind the liminal qualities we wish to explore in this volume. It also evokes a permanent state of coming into being. Women continually create, reinforce, and change themselves and their relations with others through their feelings, thoughts, speech, and actions. Every iteration of a practice or thought opens up a tiny space of danger and possibility in which something might change (Butler 1990). Girlhood, as a period of dramatic psychological and physiological change, evokes these dangerous possibilities of badness.

## Refusing Silence, Using Silence

The chapters by Quawas and al-Tal that bookend our book thematize both the silencing of women's voices and women's strategic uses of speech and silence to further their own work. Living and working in Jordan, both women make strategic choices regarding their writing and activism as they navigate local and transnational discourses around Arab or Muslim women's transgressions while remaining relevant on the ground. Such women recognize how the pioneering work of Western feminists to uncover the constructed nature of gender and patriarchy has shaped their own lives and can potentially shape the lives of others, particularly young women, but they also recognize the importance of distinguishing between the contexts in which such texts were first written and those in which they seek to apply them. For Quawas, ideas surrounding voice, subjecthood/objecthood, and the gaze that she first encountered within Western feminism apply to patriarchal structures everywhere. She shares with her students in Jordan the texts that informed her own awakening as a feminist. When viewed within the context of Orientalism and relations between the Arab world and the West, the work of Quawas is doubly transgressive—first through the controversial act of teaching feminism and supervising her students' creation, dissemination, and defense of a controversial video on sexual harassment and second by insisting that a feminist education in the Arab world should include engagement with the seminal works from the West.

Quawas transgresses a local political correctness that reflexively rejects "Westoxification." The failure of Western models of modernization and the rise of political Islam have led to pervasive indigenous critique of the application of Western ideas to the Arab world. Indeed, much of the writing in the Arab press about Aliaa' Elmahdy's photograph took this position (Mourad 2014). Quawas's chapter can be read as a response to such work. She, like Penny Johnson (2008) writing from the context of women's studies in Palestine, raises the question of how one can critically engage in conversations around gender on the ground in the Arab world, where women—like their sisters around the world—face gender-based inequities, harassment, and violence that should not be brushed aside despite the neocolonialist contexts in which they occur.

The video Quawas's students created about sexual harassment raises additional complexities surrounding women's speech. After being posted to YouTube, its notoriety and the intense backlash its creators faced led Quawas and her students to further assess the parameters within which they can speak and act. The video and its consequences raise a theme that obliquely informs other chapters, such as Diya Abdo's memoir, namely the role of silence in defining and maintaining the borders of acceptable behavior that women are not supposed to cross. The transgression of Quawas's students lies less in creating the video than in the fact that by doing so they brought into language a practice that everyone knew was taking place, sexual harassment, but about which polite people do not speak. By publicly displaying the words many young women have heard as they walk through campus, the students forced open a conversation that would not otherwise have taken place. Such acts have the potential to reshape language itself; phrases like "juicy bottom" and "strawberry lips" are altered when they are removed from the normative context of young men muttering at passing women and displayed on placards by young women.

A strategic use of silence and both veiled and direct speech in relation to institutions of support and control, as well as an awareness of the dynamic nature of the political field in which they operate, has facilitated al-Tal's and Quawas's work. In Jordan, the degree to which women can participate in public politics or speak out on gender issues has ebbed and flowed throughout the past century. State feminism has been used to control women's movements as well as to facilitate their development.[7] In addition, lines of control are often tacit. It is understood but not openly stated, for instance, that al-Tal is prohibited from teaching at the university level in Jordan. This tacitness serves important political purposes by allowing Jordan to project a more progressive image internationally, maintain institutional flexibility with regard to gender issues, and encourage women to police their own speech and behavior since what is acceptable one day may be censured as dishonorable or even criminal another.

Recourse to veiled speech and silence is also evident in the way Quawas and al-Tal have written their chapters for this volume. Quawas walks a fine line to give her students credit for their courage in creating their video and confronting the controversy that followed its public dissemination while simultaneously protecting them from further reprisal. Committed to the feminist practice of maintaining the classroom as a safe space for frank discussion, Quawas cannot reveal to us the details of what is said within that safe space. For al-Tal, allusive speech in some contexts is a tool for negotiating relationships with her family and tribe that allow her to speak frankly in other contexts. Al-Tal refuses to include a joke Yasir Arafat once made at her expense in her chapter, for instance, to avoid reigniting a political firestorm.[8] For some readers this allusiveness may at times seem frustratingly vague, but it must also be understood as a symptom of the unstable conditions in which the authors operate.

Rima Najdi engages with a different type of silence, one surrounding political violence within the tenuous conditions of post–civil war Lebanon. Through her performance piece in which she walked through the streets of Beirut dressed as a suicide bomber and subsequent manipulation of and reflection on the responses she received to it, Najdi intervenes in a silence that has troubled many Lebanese artists and writers — how to come to terms with the sectarian violence that has plagued the country throughout its modern history. Najdi's initial project aroused a tremendous range of language — emotional, analytical, thoughtful, reactionary, derogatory, and more. Some of the speech is offensive or inflammatory, and some surely reflects the artists' own anxieties about the role art can play in relation to violent contexts.

Bad Arab girls are adept at using the tools of their linguistic and cultural heritage to challenge attempts to silence them, as al-Samman demonstrates in her chapter on the manipulation of the Arabic literary and cultural tradition by Syrian activist and writer Samar Yazbek. Language is not just the medium through which Arab women's gendered selves are constructed and maintained, although Abdo's memoir beautifully illustrates this process. It is also the receptacle for cultural heritage, a treasure trove of narratives and tropes that can be used by women to deconstruct or amend gendered expectations. A woman skilled with that heritage can deploy it to lend credence to women's transgressions. By reading Yazbek's memoir and her experiences with violence and erasure as multiple acts of *wa'd*, which was outlawed in Islam, al-Samman demonstrates how Yazbek educes a shared religious heritage while writing about prisoners of the Syrian regime. Yazbek's use of language makes it more difficult for the regime to suppress or challenge what she has to say, since to do so would require challenging the Qur'an itself.

## Performing Badness

Arab women transgress through public performance as well. When women choose to use their bodies in "bad" ways, they lay bare unspoken taboos and draw attention to the effects of control on those bodies. Three of our chapters—Rima Najdi's on her Madame Bomba persona, Anne Marie Butler's on Amina Sboui's topless self-portraits, and Anita Fábos's on Sudanese singers—focus on women's public performance. While the performances differ fundamentally in subject (sectarian violence, gender and politics, and Sudanese identity) and form (performance art, social media posting, and concerts and musical albums), transgression occurs not just through the subject matter but also in the visibility of the women's bodies.

Najdi's Madame Bomba project is centered on questions of violence and forgetting in relation to Lebanese and regional politics; it is also infused with considerations of gender and sexuality. She draws attention to links between violence, strangerhood, and desire, and when she outlines her fantasy for a "normal" Beirut, she imagines her own invisibility as well as an absence of construction, sexual harassment, plastic surgery, and honking taxis. There is in this artistic intervention an implicit link between the suicide bomber and the sex bomb, Lebanon's hyper-laissez-faire capitalism, and the degradation of city life. As Anne Marie Butler's analysis demonstrates, Amina Sboui's self-portraits illustrate that it is not the public display of women's naked bodies that is transgressive but the accompaniment of such bodies by political speech. In all three cases, women have selected the sites and content of their transgressive performances to engage with their communities at home, not to critique from afar. This decision affects the transgressive nature of their performances, igniting debate within the community these women seek to change.

The Internet is a crucial site for public performance today. Amina Sboui's campaign, like that of Aliaa Elmahdy before her, began with a posting of a self-portrait on social media. As such, it is very much a product of the rise and rapid spread of social media across the globe since the mid-2000s. While our volume is not the place to stake out a position in the ongoing debate surrounding social media and political change, several chapters do note how the Internet and social media have altered the dynamics of Arab women's transgressions.[9] By furthering the spread of discourses on consumer capitalism and global Islam and creating new spaces of interaction that are separate from family and other local institutions, new media have facilitated the development of individualism (Hasso 2011, 100–101, 121), which in turn can enable new forms of transgression. At the same time, institutions have been quick to learn the linguistic and visual norms of social media in order to exploit them for their own corporatist ends.[10]

## Opportunities, Limits, and Support for Bad Girls

In her brief memoir, Suhair al-Tal locates her own transgression within the heart of her being. She recalls feeling and acting differently from other children, especially female children, from a very early age. The troubling (for others) attributes of her body and mind accompany her throughout her engagement with journalism and politics. Al-Tal's narrative is familiar, echoing the biographies of other extraordinary women who have known from an early age that accepted gender roles were not for them. However, her memoir is more complex than it first seems. What appears to be a straightforward story of an individual woman battling family, tribe, political organization, and the state actually reveals the imbricated nature of the relationships between the individual and those institutions, a theme that also arises in a number of other chapters. Al-Tal's transgressions were possible not only because of her own fierce strength but also because of the support she could muster from key figures in her own family. A political rupture within her tribe and her parents' history of political resistance helped to enable her own dissidence. In addition, the strength of al-Tal's tribe has at times facilitated her controversial work in Jordan and abroad even as it has served as a constraining force in her life.[11]

Other contributions to the volume, such as Abdo's personal memoir about work and family life in Jordan and the United States, and Ibrahim's study of a Jordanian orphan after she leaves institutional care, reveal that the functionalist advantages that families and communities provide are not the only reasons women do not lightly choose to transgress against them. When webs of relationships are important assets, individuals learn throughout their lives to desire what is good for themselves but also for those in close relation to them (Joseph 2005, 80–81). In other words, what women want is often precisely what keeps families and other intimate institutions strong. Even when they are hierarchical in gendered ways, many women cherish the families and close networks of affiliation in which they are cultivated and sustained. Such concerns often limit the degree and types of transgressions women, particularly marginalized women, will undertake.

Similarly, Amireh's analysis of women caught up in narratives of the unfolding Arab Spring in Tunisia (Fayda Hamdi) and Libya (Iman al-Obeidi) underscores women's complex relationships with family, community, and the state. Hamdi and al-Obeidi relied heavily on family support as they navigated legal and media challenges. In other words, whether or not they are intentionally transgressive, women must operate between and among various levels of structure, confinement, and support. Women's transgressions, whether chosen or imposed, can at times lie within the tensions created where these different levels of structure intersect.

Still, many of the women in our volume do break definitively with their families or communities, either by choice or out of personal necessity. Syrian activist and writer Samar Yazbek and CIA agent Nada Prouty chose to break with their natal communities, and Prouty explicitly embraced an identity as part of another community. Such malleability requires a strong sense of oneself as an independent agent. There is no question that the Arab world in general is experiencing greater individualism, but this development produces anxieties that are processed in imaginative texts. The allure and danger of individualism are themes running through the Maghrebi films that Florence Martin and Patricia Caillé discuss.

## Bad Girls between the Arab World and the West

Concerns like these, about community, identity, and individualism, are further complicated and enabled by the postcolonial conditions that mark relations between the Arab world and the West. Orientalist understandings of gender in the Arab Islamic world situate the oppression of Arab women in misogynist beliefs that are thought to be fundamental to Islam and Arab societies. Such culturalist analyses ignore how patriarchy as practiced in the Arab world today has grown out of colonial and neocolonial encounters with the West and the particular forms of modernity that have resulted from those encounters (Abu Lughod 1998). Those analyses ignore the pressures that neoliberal capitalism and globalization exert on economic and political structures in the Arab world today, pressures that have directly affected gender relations and the lived experiences of Arab women.

Many of the women in our volume are uncomfortable with narratives that situate their oppression within the cultural frames in which they have developed as individual selves and community members and that have structured their own worldviews. They may find narratives calling for the liberation of Arab women hypocritical within the Islamophobic and anti-Arab contexts in which Arab and Muslim men—fathers, brothers, husbands, and sons—can be imprisoned, tortured, and killed with impunity. They are particularly uncomfortable with paternalistic narratives about saving Arab or Muslim women from Arab men that do not take into consideration the economically and politically privileged position from which such narratives emerge and the complicity of Western powers in creating the conditions that contribute to Arab women's oppression, narratives that are tone-deaf to the paternalistic and vicitimizing nature of such perspectives (Abu Lughod 2013; al-Ali and Pratt 2010). This issue is addressed most directly by Anne Marie Butler in her analysis of the semi-nude self-portraits of Tunisian activist and artist Amina Sboui. Sboui, like most of the women discussed in our volume, is not interested in a whole-sale rejection of her culture, community, and heritage. Like Quawas, she does not draw a bright line between liberal Western feminism and the Tunisian context in which she works. Through the stance she assumes before the camera and the writing in Arabic and English she emblazons across her torso, Sboui reappropriates the figure of the brown female nude and queers it within the context of art history and within the contemporary Islamophobic politics of groups like Femen. In this regard, her work is a pointed example of pushing the representational boundaries emanating from local and transnational or Western contexts.

Transnational circuits—in the case of our women, the movement of people, words, and images across national borders—affect women's transgressions. Travel and residency in multiple countries have facilitated the transgression of many of the women in our volume. For the Maghrebi filmmakers discussed by Florence Martin and Patricia Caillé, transnational funding and global distribution have freed Maghrebi directors from the constraints that national film industries may impose, but they have also traditionally limited the types of stories filmmakers can tell to those that are likely to enjoy broad international appeal. However, as Martin and Caillé note, such structures are not impervious, and Maghrebi women directors create narratives that acknowledge oppression but complicate the impulse to pity or save Arab or Muslim women. Maghrebi women directors continue the work of their groundbreaking sisters of the 1970s by writing themselves into national narratives that have traditionally excluded their experiences.

Transnational networks have been key to the careers of the Sudanese pop musicians profiled by Anita Fábos in chapter 11. While their movement into the diaspora is motivated in large part by new controls by the state of Sudan on women's public performances, the singers maintain their relevance within conversations about Sudanese identity by performing for communities of Sudanese in the diaspora and distributing their music to audiences within and outside Sudan through YouTube. Their music may be shaped to varying degrees by musical traditions in their countries of residence and the global market for world music, but their continued relevance within the Sudanese context is evident in the gendered and racial debates their videos spark online. Through online music, then, these artists transgress the cultural and gendered norms of religious and cultural purity that conservative Sudanese forces seek to impose. As a result, they lay bare the fiction behind such claims to purity in a region that historically has been characterized by cultural and religious diversity and where Islamist political movements owe as much to global flows as does popular music.

## Scapegoats and Survivors

Women do not actually have to do or say anything to be labeled "bad." They still serve as scapegoats, burdened with the responsibility for social or political ills that are not of their making. Class, ethnicity, and citizenship status can all play significant roles in this regard. Rawan Ibrahim's description of Yasmin's transition from institutional care in a Jordanian orphanage to independent living paints a picture of an entire sector of society—children who are not legally recognized by their fathers—with no stable footing in the social and legal structures of Jordan. Because families play a powerful role not just in policing women's behavior but also in providing all their members, male and female, with a social safety net that the state cannot offer, women who lack families face particular hurdles. Yasmin, and others like her, do not choose to transgress against state or family; born to unwed mothers, they breach social norms by their personal legal status and so are vulnerable to economic and sexual exploitation. Many, like Yasmin, crave the normative structures of family life that could have offered guidance and protection.

The care that the state provides for orphans is substantive and cannot be discounted in any consideration of how women relate to it, but both state and society fail Yasmin and others raised in group homes by holding them responsible for the potential for social disorder—such as by being available, even if against their will, for extramarital sex and by giving birth to children out of wedlock—that arises out of their vulnerable condition. Adania Shibli's chapter also demonstrates how groups of women are defined as inherently transgressive by others. An Israeli media campaign of mother blaming is used to dehumanize Palestinians and deflect responsibility for the murder of children away from the soldiers who do the shooting. In these ways and others, women become scapegoats for larger social and political ills, such as the lack of an adequate social safety network, sexual and economic predation, patriarchal family structures in Jordan, and racist violence upon which Israel's settler colonial project is built.

While many women in Yasmin's position have internalized the "bad" label that social norms in Jordan impose upon them, there has been a movement in recent years calling for a reassessment of the personal status laws that scapegoat children. Since 2012 Jordanian women married to foreign men have been engaged in a sustained protest movement to demand citizenship rights for their children in Jordan. Theoretically, such a movement could eventually include the rights of children whose fathers do not acknowledge them. The Palestinian mothers discussed by Shibli, on the other hand, do not accept Israeli and Western media constructions of them as lacking the maternal love that would keep their children safe. However, it is difficult to imagine a path whereby Palestinian mothers might affect their representations by others. As complete outsiders to these media discourses, Palestinian mothers have no control over such representations. Shibli's analysis reminds us of some of the limits to the effectiveness of women's silence, speech, actions, and performances, however strategic they may be.

As Amireh demonstrates in her chapter about Fayda Hamdi and Iman al-Obeidi, two women who gained notoriety during the 2011 Arab Spring uprisings, the scapegoating of Arab women also occurs when their lived experiences are erased, transformed, and/or abstracted in order to maintain the cohesion of larger narratives or conceptions of collective identity and experience. Such scapegoating is not just the purview of oppressive states. Like Palestinian mothers, there is little that Hamdi or al-Obeidi can do to change the narratives that others have created for them. By asking readers to consider how their injured, flesh-and-blood bodies interact with the discursive bodies constructed through narratives that circulate about them, Amireh illustrates this point while she also challenges the erasure itself.

Nada Prouty, the Arab American CIA agent, is an important addition to our volume because her story, as told by Randa Kayyali, illustrates just how bad a bad girl can be. Most of the bad women in our volume transgress gender-related taboos or constraints, often helping to redefine boundaries as a result. Prouty's transgressions, on the other hand, include betrayal; her strategic maneuvering between Arabness and Americanness, like that of Badia, the protagonist of the film *Sur la planche* that is analyzed by Martin and Caillé in chapter 10, may appear self-serving, but this too is part of the landscape of badness. When a woman faces abuse within her family and community and racism in her adopted country, whose interest, other than her own, can she be expected to serve? For her, transgression may serve as a survival tactic.

## Conclusion

What do we learn by focusing on Arab women's transgressions in the diverse conditions, forms, and sites in which they occur? Dramatic developments in recent decades, notably the rise of social media, new political movements in the Arab world, transnationalism, and a growing sense of individualism across the region, have led to new forms of transgression in new geographic and discursive contexts, involving different deployments of gendered bodies. Women across the region are expressing new subjectivities and challenging long-standing taboos in their creative and activist endeavors. Through their transgressions, Arab women engage in actively shaping their communities. At the same time, increasing economic and environmental precariousness and continued violence and other stresses have led to political and social pressures that often come at the expense of women in ways that are depressingly familiar. Old shibboleths such as honor codes and mother blaming retain their potent force, particularly for the most marginalized but also for relatively privileged women who must be strategic in their activism.

## Notes

1. This is Elmahdy's pose in this particular image, the most widely circulated. In other photos she posted, she fully reveals her genitalia.

2. The photograph is a still from a short video shot by a bystander. The video is, if anything, even more shocking than the photograph, revealing how the woman was dragged and kicked by soldiers in addition to being disrobed.

3. *Sitt al-banāt* loosely translates as "a queen among girls" and is used as a term of respect.

4. In March 2011 demonstrations, eighteen women were arrested while protesting in Tahrir Square and taken to a military facility, where many of them were forced to strip and undergo virginity tests. The image and narrative of one of those women, Samira Ibrahim, also became the subject of widespread controversy in Egypt. Ibrahim challenged the military in court over the incident. In a famous work of graffiti, Elmahdy's and Ibrahim's images are juxtaposed and Egyptians are chided for paying more attention to Elmahdy's nude photo than to Ibrahim's violated body; Mourad 2014, 66.

5. Mahmood notes how the discourse of the piety movement has incorporated some aspects of liberalism and in particular the discourse of rights; 2005, 25. This is a point that Sherine Hafez elaborates more fully in *An Islam of Her Own* (2011). Zakia Salime has examined the issue for Morocco in *Between Feminism and Islam* (2011). Lara Deeb, who focuses on Shia women in Lebanon in her book *An Enchanted Modern* (2006), focuses on the new practices of piety that are imbricated with modernity.

6. To give just one example, when Hajja Faiza, one of the women Mahmood discusses, defends her right to lead prayer against the critique of this practice from a prominent Egyptian sheikh, she locates her defense in the same canonical texts that he uses as a form of submission to a higher authority, but her engagement in debate with him is also a challenge, however politely delivered, to another, worldly authority. Her leading of prayer when a male imam is present is a transgressive practice in Cairo, where she is the only woman to do so in a major mosque (Mahmood 2005, 86–87), even if it is sanctioned in three out of four of the Islamic schools of thought.

7. Women have made political gains during times of crisis, such as in Jordan during the periods of social and political upheaval following the 1948 and 1967 Arab-Israeli wars, but the gains made during these times are fragile. In the crackdown following the 1970 Jordanian civil war, so-called honor was used by the regime as a weapon against women's participation in the Palestinian movement. In addition, the regime tolerated the rise of the Muslim Brotherhood in Jordan as a counterweight to the leftist and Palestinian organizations it sought to suppress, a move that adversely affected women's struggle for gender equality; Pratt 2015. Nonetheless, while the many shortcomings of Arab states vis-à-vis women's needs are easy to see, Frances Hasso reminds us that states in the Middle East and North Africa "support women in their family policies and politics more often than is recognized by feminist scholarship"; 2011, 171.

8. When the joke was first made in the 1980s, members of al-Tal's tribe understood it as an attack on their honor. Bringing the joke back to public attention today has the potential of reigniting that furor.

9. See Gheytanchi and Moghadam (2014) and Skalli (2014) for more on women and social media in the Arab Islamic world.

10. Hasso discusses how the consumerist basis of the individualism of such media furthers the exploitative nature of global capitalism; 2011, 101. See also the work of

Adi Kuntsman and Rebecca Stein (2015) on the digital media campaign of the Israeli Defense Force. While these technologies have been celebrated for facilitating resistance protest movements in the region, they are also powerful tools for institutions that seek to crush resistance. See Nouraie-Simone (2014) for writings about Muslim women and the Internet.

11. Al-Tal's tribal affiliation facilitated her brief residency in Kuwait when she left Lebanon in the wake of the Israeli invasion of 1982. It has also allowed her to speak relatively frankly about gender issues in conservative communities in Jordan; al-Tal 2015.

## References

Abu-Lughod, Lila. 1998. "Introduction: Feminist Longings and Postcolonial Conditions." In *Remaking Women: Feminism and Modernity in the Middle East*, edited by Lila Abu-Lughod, 3–32. Princeton, NJ: Princeton University Press.

———. 2013. *Do Muslim Women Need Saving?* Cambridge, MA: Harvard University Press.

Ali, Nadje al-, and Nicola Pratt. 2010. *What Kind of Liberation? Women and the Occupation of Iraq*. Berkeley: University of California Press.

Deeb, Lara. 2006. *An Enchanted Modern: Gender and Public Piety in Shiʿi Lebanon*. Princeton, NJ: Princeton University Press.

Gheytanchi, Elham, and Valentine Moghadam. 2014. "Women, Social Protest, and the New Media Activism in the Middle East and North Africa." *International Review of Modern Sociology* 40, no. 1:1–26.

Gonick, Marnina. 2006. "'Girl Power' and 'Reviving Ophelia': Constituting the Neoliberal Girl Subject." *NWSA Journal* 18, no. 2:1–23.

Hafez, Sherine. 2011. *An Islam of Her Own: Reconsidering Religion and Secularism in Women's Islamic Movements*. New York: New York University Press.

———. 2014. "Bodies that Protest: The Girl in the Blue Bra, Sexuality and State Violence in Revolutionary Egypt. *Signs: Journal of Women in Culture and Society* 40, no. 1:20–28.

Hasso, Frances. 2011. *Consuming Desires: Family Crisis and the State in the Middle East*. Stanford, CA: Stanford University Press.

Johnson, Penny. 2008. "'Violence All Around Us': Dilemmas of Global and Local Agendas Addressing Violence against Palestinian Women: An Initial Intervention." *Cultural Dynamics* 20, no. 2:119–132.

Joseph, Suad. 2005. "Learning Desire: Relational Pedagogies and the Desiring Female Subject in Lebanon." *Journal of Middle East Women's Studies* 1, no. 1:79–109.

Kuntsman, Adi, and Rebecca Stein. 2015. *Digital Militarism: Israel's Occupation in the Social Media Age*. Stanford, CA: Stanford University Press.

Mahmood, Saba. 2005. *The Politics of Piety: The Islamic Revival and the Feminist Subject*. Princeton, NJ: Princeton University Press.

Miller, Laura, and Jan Bardsley, eds. 2005. *Bad Girls of Japan*. New York: Palgrave Macmillan.

————. Introduction to *Bad Girls of Japan*, edited by Miller and Bardsley, 1–14.

Mourad, Sara. 2014. "The Naked Body of Alia: Gender, Citizenship, and the Egyptian Body Politic." *Journal of Communication Inquiry* 38, no. 1:62–78.

Nouraie-Simone, Fereshteh. 2014. *On Shifting Ground: Muslim Women in the Global Era*. New York: Feminist Press.

Pratt, Nicola. 2015. "A History of Women's Activism in Jordan: 1949–1989." 7iber .com, May 26. http://7iber.com/society/a-history-of-womens-activism-in-jordan -1946-1989/#.V6aBgOgrKVM.

Salime, Zakia. 2011. *Between Feminism and Islam: Human Rights and Sharia Law in Morocco*. Minneapolis: University of Minnesota Press.

————. 2014. "New Feminism as 'Personal Revolutions': Micro-Rebellious Bodies." *Signs: Journal of Women in Culture and Society* 40, no. 1:14–20.

Skalli, Loubna. 2014. "Defying Marginality: Young Women's Politics and Social Media in the Middle East." *On Shifting Ground: Muslim Women in the Global Era*, edited by Fereshteh Houraie-Simone, 51–66. New York: Feminist Press.

Taft, Jessica K. 2004. "Girl Power Politics: Pop-Culture Barriers and Organizational Resistance." In *All About the Girl: Culture, Power, and Identity*, edited by Anita Harris, 69–78. London: Routledge.

Tal, Suhair al-. 2015. *Tarikh al-ḥaraka al-nisaʾiyya al-urduniyya, 1944–2008* [History of the Jordanian women's movement, 1944–2008]. Amman: Dār al-azmina li-l-nashr wa-l-tawzīʿ.

Zerilli, Linda. 2005. *Feminism and the Abyss of Freedom*. Chicago: University of Chicago Press.

## ONE

# Inciting Critique in the Feminist Classroom

RULA QUAWAS

W ho or what are Arab "bad girls"? No simple definition suffices since the meaning of badness varies according to cultural, social, and individual contexts. Badness can describe a variety of women's behaviors and can include any deviation from traditionally accepted social and cultural norms. Badness implies a lack of morality or ethics. It is thought to be an essential property of a woman's character in determining her behavior. It is not unusual for Arab women to find their nonconformist thinking or behavior labeled "bad." In Jordan today there is a binding system that I call "badnessism" to circumscribe the socially and culturally unacceptable behavior of women. Badnessism is a cultural artifact invested with a libidinal dynamic and shaped by misogyny, masculinism, sexism, and social injustice. It often projects a political dimension in the form of oppression and subjugation. Through this system, accusations of badness are deployed to assert power over women. However, badness is an artificially constructed category, construed to delineate arbitrary social rules surrounding gender and sexuality and to inscribe Arab women as objects rather than subjects. Sexual harassment is a prime example of such objectification.

Sexual harassment is far more prevalent in Jordan than most people may realize, occurring on streets, at bus stations, and on university campuses, to name only a few places. And yet scant research has been done on this socially corrosive practice. On the basis of a short field study of sexual harassment at the University of Jordan, four women undergraduate students enrolled in my Feminist Theory class in fall 2011 confirmed its ubiquitous presence on campus. Through documenting male students' misogynistic slurs and sexist language, the students found that sexual harassment is normative and that mechanisms to keep it in check are minimal at best.

University campuses in particular should be safe environments where all students, regardless of gender, feel welcome and secure. Campuses should be off-limits to those who engage in sexual harassment as well as to those who accept it and contribute to its normalization. Sexual harassment is a serious challenge to women's participation in campus life. Until university administrators acknowledge its existence on campus, take its presence seriously, and devise intervention strategies to stop it, women will continue to find their ability to engage fully with the university and work to their full potential curtailed.

Performing a brave act as a group, four young Jordanian women students from my class made a video on the sexual harassment they had experienced themselves. Titled *Hadhihi khususati, hadhihi hurriyati* (This is my privacy, this is my freedom),[1] they disrupted higher education and its stringent culture, foregrounding the sites and instances of their oppression. The video is not only an encounter with my four students' harsh reality on campus; it is also a moment of explosive revelation about the silencing of their voices. Through their brave video, the students unfold a painful truth that does not comply with expectations. Their desire to confront the unexpected and resist societal and cultural expectations or assumptions about campus life has become a source of courage and self-determination for others. Yet, to most people within their communities in Jordan, such courage looks monstrous, ugly, unacceptable, and even morally offensive. In this chapter I situate the students' video and responses to it in the context of my experiences of teaching feminist theory at the University of Jordan in the 2010s.

## The Video

The students' video is simple but conceptually powerful, consisting mostly of a series of still shots of young women holding handmade signs. Each sign quotes a sexually charged word or phrase that the woman personally heard or documented as she walked through the public spaces of the university: "Strawberry lips," "Can I take you home?" and "Humps." The video ultimately makes visible the existence of sexual harassment that few dare to acknowledge or discuss openly. By directly addressing the harassment that constrains their presence on campus, these women's video confronts sexual harassment and names it as male consumerism. It also reclaims the grounds of the university as a women's space as well as a men's space.

In June 2012, someone (neither I nor the students know who) posted it to YouTube, where it became the subject of intense controversy. The backlash was immediate and enormous. As soon as it was uploaded, the students and I were bombarded with a litany of criticism that bordered on emotional and psychological abuse. Within a few hours the video received more than a half-million hits and became prominent on social media. Jordanians were divided in their opinions. Some held the video in contempt and labeled the video makers and me "bad girls" who had transgressed social norms. Others celebrated the video and applauded it as a courageous act. I still remember students and faculty members pointing their fingers at me as I walked on campus, some in condemnation and others in commendation.

My students braved the denunciation of relatives, friends, acquaintances, and strangers who filled the newspapers and their Facebook accounts with acidic remarks and insults. The commenters often attempted to draw attention away from the video and its contents to focus negatively on the morality of its makers. They labeled the students "bad girls," emotionally unstable, evildoers, harlots, male bashers, un-Islamic, and bitchy. Some called them witches who should be burned at the stake. Groups on campus were incited to protest the video by a professor in the faculty of Sharia (Islamic law) who initiated a campaign to uphold women's modesty and chastity at the university. Leaflets were distributed throughout the campus encouraging men to file lawsuits against the four students and their teacher, whom they sought to ban from teaching. The leaflets demanded immediate action against me, their teacher, for promoting "Westoxification" and being an agent of the West. My life was actually threatened.

Jordanians and commenters from across the Arab world accused the women of being bad students who had defied the system and transgressed the borders of propriety. They were called "devils" who needed to be disciplined, for they were a threat to domestic stability and Arab culture. But the video elicited another kind of conversation as well. It allowed Jordanians and others from around the world to consider the silences and omissions that exist in national and international discourses on gender and feminism with regard to sexual harassment. A website was created to sup-

**Figure 1.1.** Juicy bottom

**Figure 1.2.** Ridden like a pillow

port the students and their professor.[2] Two petitions were created to raise awareness of the issue.[3] The students' activism, it turned out, launched a burgeoning movement to create a different social reality in Jordan and a more just and equitable society on and off campus. Through public discussions about the video on campus, and stories in the news and on social media, the genie was released from the bottle; sexual harassment at the university is no longer protected by silence. It is, rather, the subject of intense and continuing debate.

في مجال نزوح
عالبيت

Can I take you home?

**Figure 1.3.** Can I take you home?

Senior administrators at the university challenged the video, calling it a fabrication of "bad" lies created by "delusional heroes." In doing so they normalized and condoned sexual harassment, allowing a conducive environment for it to persist on campus. Rather than deny the silent epidemic and claim that sexual harassment on our campuses does not exist, some genuine work is needed to end this violation of women's human rights. Clearly, the more constructive response would have been a commitment to punish male students who assume a sense of entitlement and reduce women students to sex objects or "human furniture," to use Henry James's memorable phrase from *The Golden Bowl* (1966, 541). It is time to acknowledge the issue and criminalize sexual harassment on our campuses. In the absence of such a response, the continued teaching of feminist theory at the University of Jordan becomes even more urgent.

Through the process of making the video and enduring community reactions to their activist project and the intense public debate about the conditions of Arab women's lives that it inspired, my students created discomfort at their academic institution by challenging administration, faculty, and students to rethink how women are expected to fit into dichotomous categories of goodness and badness, which rest on assumptions related to social and cultural expectations regarding how women think and behave, the forces that define their roles in society, and their sense of duty in terms of obedience and loyalty. These four students refuse to accept the adequacy of a system of "categorizable" women who are good, bad, right, or wrong. They problematize categories and evaluations and negotiate gendered boundaries regarding speech and behavior. They push limits and learn experientially that the label "bad girls" that has been assigned to them can offer a replenishing and provocative force when women do not fear it. In a nutshell, they used their emerging critical-thinking skills to put feminist theory into practice.

## The Jordanian Feminist Classroom: Bad Girls?

Education is one of the necessary sources of a full life that women, like men, need and deserve. Education means "being able to use the senses, to imagine, think, and reason—and to do these things in a 'truly human' way" (Nussbaum 1999, 78–79). Moroccan sociologist Fatima Mernissi contends that "it is [with] access to public space, employment, and education that women's lives have undergone the most fundamental changes. Space, employment, and education seem to be the areas where the struggles which agitate society (especially the class struggle) show up in the lives of women with the greatest clarity" (1989, 3). But education is not only about studying and learning; it also requires continuous critical thinking and self-reflection, along with the ability to imagine and articulate big questions from multiple perspectives.

Although Jordan is a young country with limited resources, one of its publicly stated priorities is to invest in its human capital, that is, its young men and women. Considerable attention is given to the education sector and to public education in particular. However, most educators serve as explicators and transmitters of information and compartmentalized bits of knowledge. The Jordanian educational system tends to be confined to an assembly-line approach to learning in which students learn by rote rather than being stretched and inspired to develop their capacities to learn, appreciate, lead, and thrive during and after their studies. Students remain restricted to educative activities and pedagogical methods that for the most part do not leave room for critical thinking or increased awareness. Engaged education, as a practice of freedom, is thus undermined or diminished in Jordan's education sector.

In Jordan, women in particular are largely conceptualized not as critically thinking, choosing, sentient beings but instead as static symbols and repositories devoid of agency or voice. Traditionally they have been regarded as cultural custodians and emblems of honor in their communities and are expected to subscribe to a public identity that demands obedience and silence from selfless keepers of virtue, submissiveness, piety, purity, and responsibility. In this light, a "good girl" in Jordan is a noble mother, a martyr, and a quiet bearer of pain and suffering. She is an angelic upholder of, or a collaborator with, the hegemony of male power and ideology, accepting the ready-made cultural script presented to her, following it to the letter. Her moral character lies in a graceful state of being rather than in any semblance of ethical practice through critical thinking.

Sadly, but not surprisingly, women who subvert and disrupt norms and prescriptions to bring about social justice and change are often defensively labeled "bad" to avoid changes that would be alarming for many people in society. Why must women students at every level of education struggle to overcome gender restrictions and expectations in Jordan? Why, despite their academic achievements, are educated, thinking women so often categorized as bad? Why does their unlearning of or challenge to dominant understandings and development of critical-thinking skills still lead to tensions and instabilities?

Badness as a moral and cultural category is intended to impugn a woman's reputation and call into question her sense of propriety and fitness as a member of the community. It is not unusual for Arab women to find their nonconformist thinking or behavior labeled "bad." Badness is often attached to critically thinking women university students in Jordan and influences their self-perceptions and behaviors as they monitor themselves to avoid the stigma. Some women continue to accept the sociocultural conditions that traditionally define relations between the sexes. They decide to be maintainers and keepers of traditional values, which they fail to recognize as arbitrary. They acquiesce and acknowledge and often internalize such values without examining them. Others, however, few in number, resist the label of "badness" or transform it into a productive space where agency resides. Given the necessary critical-thinking tools that a feminist classroom can offer, they challenge the idea that men are always subjects and women objects. By learning about their rights, analyzing contentious feminist texts, and thinking innovatively, they unlearn many damaging behavioral patterns they have been conditioned to embrace. They grow into their own intellect, strength, and freedom. Such students resist cultural assumptions and norms relating to their bodies. They contest the sexualized view of bad girls scripted for them by institutionally generated ideologies that foster oppression. They ground their own scripts in their newly forming agency and subjectivity. They appropriate and reclaim the term "bad girls" through a "dialogized heteroglossia" (Bakhtin 1981), whereby openness and a willingness to dialogue allow concepts to be transformed, dislodged, or rehabilitated. Critical lenses become inverted.

Through the critical thinking of a feminist theory class, some Jordanian students gradually learn to empower themselves and recognize their innate capacity for self-reflection, self-determination, and consciously guided action. By rebelling against conventional, deep-seated assumptions and value judgments, they acquire a new and better understanding of women's reputations and how society conceptualizes female goodness and badness. In the act of deepening self-awareness, constructing fresh mental images, and giving voice to these new visions, students who experience a Jordanian feminist classroom come to a newly crafted vision of liberation through education. And that newly liberated vision leads to a vivid articulation of a woman's right to break her silence when she believes she is right. Now she is free to take an unpopular stand grounded in her own firm beliefs. As bell hooks has put it, an ideal classroom climate inspires a transgressive teaching agenda that not only promotes excitement and pleasure but "moves against and beyond boundaries" (1994, 12).

What we see, then, is that through the critical thinking they develop in a feminist classroom, these so-called bad students are no longer inhibited by convention and constructed propriety, nor are they paralyzed by fear. They speak with confidence and refute the dominant culture of inequality. They reject the notion that female biology results in moral frailty and refuse to be assimilated into the iconography of Arab womanhood. They imagine a world that is not structured by patriarchy, a world in which women are not second-class citizens. They insist on belonging to no one but themselves. Put another way, having learned in their feminist theory class to read against the grain, they recognize and resist their social and cultural programming by acting against sexist ideologies.

## Teaching Feminist Theory

Admittedly, students who sign up for a feminist theory class are a self-selecting group, but they are not insignificant in number at the University of Jordan. In spring 2015, fifty-two students signed up for my Feminist Theory course. These students wanted to learn about feminist theory and its assumptions in relation to their own experiences. They wonder, What are the lines of convergence and divergence between Western feminisms and Arab feminisms? What is meant by Islamic feminism? Do polyvocality and heterogeneity have a place within feminism? Are biological justifications of women's social limitations valid or a mere fabrication meant to subjugate women and confine them to certain roles? How do women come to resist or celebrate the circumstances of their lives? Is it possible for unequal social and gender relations to be transformed? Does feminism grapple adequately with issues of power, conflict, and the larger social, cultural, and political contexts that frame women's abilities to resist oppression? Is there a way to reconcile religious systems and beliefs with feminism?

Like students everywhere, when Jordanian students sign up for a feminist theory class, they bring with them expectations shaped by their personal experiences, culture, knowledge, and desires. People often ask me, "What is different about a feminist theory course?" My answer is simple and to the point. In this course, I concentrate on women writers and their voices that are ignored or undervalued in other courses. I introduce my students to the forbidden topic of sexuality and sexual politics. The subjects I introduce are at times difficult to read because they are rough and disturbing, painful and depressing. However, in the end the students begin to probe feminist materials, to project and predict, to hypothesize and revise, until feminist theory coheres in their imaginations.

The feminist course I taught in 2011 focused on women writers, particularly Arab women writers who write for and about women. The course is not comprehensive, but I endeavor to ensure that students acquire sufficient vocabulary and familiarity with key texts to understand and work with feminist theory. My main objective in the course is to help the students think critically about texts and gender issues through feminist thought. I begin the semester with feminist texts that expose students to a number of concerns from a specifically female perspective: marriage, a labyrinth of social roles and conventions, the nature of female sexuality, the conventional opposition of romance and passion, the moral isolation of women in patriarchal systems, the role of female friendship and solidarity, the importance of the body and the physical world to self-realization, the ambivalence toward children and childbearing, and development of selfhood.

I use Leila Ahmad's *Women and Gender in Islam: Historical Roots of a Modern Debate* (1992) in my course since it offers a historical context to Islamic discourses on women and gender. Nawar al-Hassan Golley's "Is Feminism Relevant to Arab Women?" (2004) and Margot Badran's "Between Secular and Islamic Feminism/s: Reflections on the Middle East and Beyond" (2005) broaden the discussion to explore how patterns of male and female experiences differ and to examine women's self-concepts, experiences, and relationships to themselves and others. Students also read works by Judith Butler, Adrienne Rich, Lila Abu-Lughod, and bell hooks as an introduction to the diversity and richness of feminist theory and its applications to the social, political, and intellectual contexts of women's lives across various socioeconomic, racial, ethnic, and cultural groupings.

I use short stories and novels by Arab women writers to inspire the students to articulate their own diverse life experiences in their writings. The stories I teach demonstrate, among other things, the dynamism and strength of Arab feminists. While the stories we read differ thematically and stylistically, they share the fundamental trope that while Arab women's lives are difficult, the women continue to push through the pain to create lives that to them are worth living. The stories my students read by Nawal El Saadawi, Hanan al-Shaykh, Ahdaf Soueif, Alifa Rifaat, and others illustrate how individual Arab women navigate their existence in overtly patriarchal systems. Some are forced to bear heavy social burdens, such as restricted social roles. Others lack agency over their own bodies. They must navigate the rough waters of patriarchal society while its prevailing social structures seek to control and subjugate them as they cling to their identity. Yet, in their literature we find Arab women who manage to resist the oppressive systems in which they live. No matter how small their acts of resistance, they are vital for understanding the unique manifestations of patriarchy and may inspire others to resist oppression and subjugation as well.

Through engaged readings and reflective writings, students discuss women's stories and question what has been left in the margins. They offer alternative ways of thinking and feeling about beliefs or concepts once taken for granted. They learn that they can present their dreams, desires, anger, and disappointments in their own words freely and openly. For them, the texts are not only there to be analyzed; they are reflections of what they experience and feel. As one student remarked, "Reading women's stories is not so much a record of a life lived. It is a means to more fully experience my own life; the reading of a woman's story transforms my life." Another reported that women's stories make her aware of the emotions centered in her body and mind. She says, "As I experience each moment in a text, I am willing to feel deeply and to participate in life rather than merely observe it." She can imagine change and feels she can make it happen.

The experiences of women, often considered too personal, private, or unimportant within the confines of traditions and culture, are no longer hidden. Examined openly in the feminist classroom, they are understood as noteworthy and useful in clarifying life's intricacies and complexities. They elaborate a reality that is broader and deeper for women than what is presented in other classes, a reality that weaves a context from which students wrest back some control over their sexuality and finally emerge as women committed to civic engagement in pursuit of a more equitable society. In a context of limited political power, students emerge from a feminist theory class ready to meet the challenges of an arid patriarchal society. They discover that some challenges that seem intractable can be confronted if they act together and mobilize others for the common good. In the words of one student, "I can brave the horizon now."

After fifteen years of teaching feminist theory courses to undergraduate students, I have yet to meet a class that is not enthusiastic about investigating feminist stories. They empathize with their female protagonists. As a teacher, I constantly seek ways to validate the reading experience and to open up a conscious process that empowers the readers. In my experience, Jordanian students immediately respond to the female protagonists' pursuit of freedom and identity. They regard the powerful imagery of repression and liberation as a mirror of the conditions facing them and other women in their social and cultural milieus. Arab women writers have always seemed easy to teach precisely because they elicit various and often passionate responses.

Gradually students begin to see that the road to equality for Arab women is a difficult one, filled with the obstacles of tradition and expectation. Its destination seems distant but can be reached. In this way, feminist literature is like any good literature but with one major difference: it foregrounds female characters and their plight. It not only allows for tangible criticism of society; it also allows the reader to identify with the characters' oppression and pain. The protagonists of the short stories we read are often robbed of innocence, choice, and agency, but they also offer powerful indigenous examples of female agency. Merely exposing students to feminist stories is an act of revolution when women's oppression is concealed or justified. In the stories we read, the students see women who carry the potential to resist injustice and thus display the seeds of autonomy. Those seeds do not always germinate within the fictional world, but they may germinate in the minds and hearts of the students who read them in a feminist class.

My students quickly become involved with the feminist stories they read. They are left with piercing and resonant representations that often inspire tolerance, empathy, confidence, and understanding. Together we analyze stories so that students can capture the fictional women's process of reflection and life-altering action. Such readings can produce transformation, inspiring some, like the students who made the video, to action. They find they are no longer inclined to forgive, overlook, or accept oppressive norms. They choose to fight back through concrete action.

Every day in the Arab world, women like the protagonist in Alifa Rifaat's story "Bahiyya's Eyes" attempt to "live really and truly as a woman," as the sexual and powerful beings they are (1983, 11). Going beyond gendered boundaries is never easy. But one must be willing to go beyond established boundaries and negotiate new, more relevant ones. The woman who dares to trample societal boundaries she had no part in creating in order to reclaim the power of her mind is likely to be labeled a "bad girl," improper and transgressive. Such transgressions require inner strength, a support system, and a desire to be free. Beyond their gendered boundaries, women may see equity, reconciliation, justice, and hope. Those who express themselves, refusing to be silenced, clear the way to equality and justice for others. They set a higher standard for what is acceptable.

My students use the feminist classroom as a platform from which to challenge prevailing political and religious orthodoxies and accepted opinions regarding their treatment. Students learn to break the deafening silence around issues of gender and female sexuality in a society that assumes male power and childbearing heterosexuality for women as normative. They question behavior that reinforces women's subordination. They are highly critical of sexual objectification and sexual exploitation and suggest that gender differences are produced by cultural practices, social expectations, and religious misinterpretations. They call for unlearning social roles and providing reinterpretations of some religious texts.

In my Feminist Theory classroom, theory and practice come together in a vital way. Students who think critically begin to understand how gender norms function to restrain them. They are empowered to question, contest, and overcome newly recognized binding restraints on their thoughts and behavior as they begin to unpack assumptions and perceptions they have taken for granted with regard to women and men in society. A safe yet liberating brave space is created where students feel free to engage in an intellectual exchange about the politics of gender and established cultural boundaries. This space enables rethinking of core concepts that can defeat inertia. Students speak about their own experiences with sexual harassment and the debilitating lack of conversations about it. By going further and recounting their struggles against sexual harassment on campus in a video, four students, informed by feminist thought, were able to link increased awareness to action.

Through their video these students used their heightened awareness of objectification to reposition themselves as women who challenge representations of sexuality and enhance their sense of self and ontological security. They reverse the gendered gaze and reclaim campus space by writing themselves large and legitimate upon that space. Their newly formed feminist awareness, a product of their reflections on feminist theory and Arab women's literature, prompted their subversive but liberating action even though the effects of their bold action may be uncertain. Nowhere are women "readily victims," in Alcoff's words. They respond to and work against oppressive behavior in order to have agency over their own lives (Alcoff 1996, 13–26). They act as change agents in the hope that their discourse will be instrumental in changing the taboos embedded in the consciousness of their culture. By resisting the philosophy of coverture and inscription from within, they reclaim themselves as full, free, autonomous human beings. They use mind and body as vehicles for their own self-inscription and self-expression to inspire others.

## On the Wings of a Feminist Classroom

The feminist classroom can serve as a proving ground for conceptualizations of badness and Arab womanhood. The conventional script of womanhood forged by Jordanian society was disrupted by ostensibly bad Jordanian students who chose to defy the status quo and redefine the social order. For these women, a feminist classroom is a springboard for subversive thought. By using their voices and creativity and speaking truth to power in relation to sexual harassment on campus, four Jordanian women transformed themselves from victims into agents. It remains indisputable that Arab women's lives are largely dictated by a prevailing system of patriarchy upheld through unjust laws, traditions, religious teachings, and family structures. While those reaping the benefits of this system are usually men, women often work to perpetuate and reinforce it. This makes more significant the work of the four Jordanian students who expressed themselves so daringly. They challenged the construction of badness in masculinist discourse and demonstrated how an active feminist classroom can have a profound social impact.

Adrienne Rich asserts in "Claiming an Education" (1977), "Responsibility to yourself means refusing to let others do your thinking, talking, and naming for you; it means learning to respect and use your own brains and instincts." While some Jordanian students in feminist classes have developed a series of speaking platforms for themselves and their audiences, most women live and operate passively in the shadows. The call to end women's oppression and foster women's liberation is, as Juliet Mitchell once termed it, "the longest revolution" (1984). It cannot be achieved overnight. Within feminist classrooms, bad girls effect significant change. They learn to speak in their own authentic voices. They use the feminist classroom as a venue to address differences of opinion and engage with scathing dissent. They learn to push back boundaries and embrace bad-girlness as part of the process of becoming women.

Women's intellectual and political emancipation requires breaking away from the patriarchal order that cloisters women and renders them unwelcome in public spaces. Increasingly at universities in Jordan, women students who engage in feminist classrooms are aware and critical of the prevalence of sexism on their campuses. They often choose to step out of sociocultural roles that require acquiescing to humiliating and insulting behaviors. They use their voices, pens, and cameras to shatter the stigma of harassment. They become active change agents who foster other women's agency when they speak back to the gaze of the voyeur and say "No" to Eve-teasing and catcalls. They reclaim their bodies, wills, and spirits, in the process generating a more confident consciousness.

I want to share a poem I wrote in English about teaching feminist theory courses over the years. This poem is sown from my students' seeds of challenge and change and from their budding words that flow, connect, suggest, and share. Within the space of my feminist theory class, I make room for myself and my students, a speaking space of agency within ourselves. It is simple. It is also radical.

In a feminist classroom, we have a room of our own,
a room decorated with critical thinking and words,
laced with pearly light, a room inspired by our stories
and our memories, infused with writing and with white ink,

a room refurbished with our questions and exclamation points,
swirling with *za'tar* (thyme), mint and sage.

Our own dreams are no longer crinkled, wrinkled secrets
to be enfolded between select book pages, shrouded in silence,
or entwined by tradition and long-standing social mores.
We weave and voice dreams. We paint them with unimaginable colors.
We reposition time, reveal our voices, walk naked under
the marble of our reign in a whirlpool of light.

We have wakened from the fetters of death, denied the murderous dust
that has silenced our tongues. We have released and restored ourselves.
We have journeyed toward a palm tree, an oasis welded to the earth,
We have walked toward a forest of trees standing tall,
rising assertively, our strong branches fanning out
in the soul and body, like emblems and shining symbols.

We are "bad girls." Active speech peppers our dialogue,
our dawn; the words we speak, assurance of a world that is our own.
Here we will stay. Jordanian women, uncovering the veils of ignorance,
Removing them from our souls, emerging as a fountain of hope,
and holding the sun in our hands. Singing a song of freedom,
of birth, of wings, of fertility and greenness, of visions of love and dreams
    of peace.

Come, come Jordanian "bad girls." Let us knit our songs and sing in the
    Arab night.
Come let us traverse the plains as butterflies do, free and light.
Let us move on and pass through to the future, for we are the poets,
speaking and writing the language of history, with love.

## Notes

1. The students' short video (2:33) was posted to YouTube as *Sexual Harassment: A Project for Fall 2011 Feminist Theory Class* (University of Jordan, Amman) on November 25, 2012, by "fastervids," at https://www.youtube.com/watch?v=Vzj8iy8b_fk.

2. The website Supporting Rula Quawas and Academic Freedom is at http://www.fortheloveoffreedom.wordpress.com.

3. One petition was started by Fuad Bajjali, with 477 supporters, and another by Jessica Asay, with 243 supporters.

# References

Alcoff, Linda. 1996. "Feminist Theory and Social Science: New Knowledges, New Epistemologies." In *BodySpace: Destabilizing Geographies of Gender and Sexuality*, edited by Nancy Duncan, 13–26. London: Routledge.

Badran, Margot. 2005. "Between Secular and Islamic Feminism/s: Reflections on the Middle East and Beyond." *Journal of Middle East Women's Studies* 1:6–28.

Bakhtin, Mikhail. 1981. *The Dialogic Imagination*. Translation by Caryl Emerson and Michael Holquist. Austin: University of Texas Press.

Golley, Nawar al-Hassan. 2004. "Is Feminism Relevant to Arab Women?" *Third World Quarterly* 25:521–536.

hooks, bell. 1994. *Teaching to Transgress: Education as the Practice of Freedom*. New York: Routledge.

James, Henry. 1966. *The Golden Bowl*. Harmondsworth, England: Penguin.

Mernissi, Fatima. 1989. *Doing Daily Battle: Interviews with Moroccan Women*. New Brunswick, NJ: Rutgers University Press.

Mitchell, Juliet. 1984. *Women: The Longest Revolution*. New York: Pantheon Books.

Nussbaum, Martha. 1999. *Sex and Social Justice*. Oxford, England: Oxford University Press.

Rich, Adrienne. 1977. "Claiming an Education." Speech delivered at the convocation of Douglass College, Rutgers University, New Brunswick, NJ, September. http://isites.harvard.edu/fs/docs/icb.topic469725.files/Rich-Claiming%20an%20Education-1.pdf.

Rifaat, Alifa. 1983. *Distant View of a Minaret and Other Stories*. Translation by Denys Johnson-Davies. Oxford, England: Heinemann.

## "And Is It Impossible to Be Good Everywhere?"

TWO

Love and Badness in America and the Arab World

DIYA ABDO

Firstborn children are *good*.

Saturated, no doubt, with the anxiety of first-time parenthood, firstborns are rule followers, pleasers.

When I tell my firstborn, five-year-old daughter, Aidana Sabha, that she has to drink the juice covertly because the bouncy house does not allow outside food or beverages, she crouches, doubled over under the table, hiding the silver pouch underneath her arched body. Unable to go against the place's regulations, she asks to leave; she is thirsty but would rather give up playing to go home and drink than break the rules.

In Jordan, to be a firstborn female child came with added pressure—to be *m'addaleh, sitt el-banāt, btiswi thuglik dhahab*, worth your own weight in gold.

Whenever my grandmother uses this phrase to describe some woman or other, I keep a tally of the qualities she admires. When she uses it to describe my mother, though always in the past tense, it means that my mother had listened, obeyed, self-abnegated—the butter would not melt in her mouth.

When she uses it to describe my uncle's wife, her daughter-in-law, it means that daughter-in-law is content with her lot, her dirty laundry un-aired—her secrets in a well.

When she uses it to describe her neighbor, it means that the neighbor is chaste, never flirting, never yielding to men's plying compliments and denuding gazes—as pure as yogurt.

But most importantly, to be worth your weight in gold means that your *seira*, your narrative, your story, is not on every tongue. A woman like this is given the highest compliment—she is, ironically, a man (*zalameh*) or the closest approximation, the sister of men (*ukht zlām*). My grandmother was definitely worth her weight in gold—*zalameh*. An illiterate Palestinian villager, she was married at nine and divorced by sixteen. After al-Nakseh,[1] she crossed the River Jordan with two kids in tow, knit loofahs to make ends meet, made sure her children got an education, and rejected all suitors and offers of marriage. She prided herself on never once being a piece of gum, to be chewed up by gossiping mouths and spat out. *Sumʿitha dhahab*—her reputation was golden.

Growing up in Jordan, which used to be part of the British Mandate (1920–1946), almost all of what I read and studied was British and American literature. And very early on I decided I was going to teach American literature at a Jordanian university. So off I went to graduate school in New Jersey, a dedicated Americanist. It seems like another life to me now—that plane ride to the vast Midwest on a research trip and the week spent in a small, depressing, fluorescent-lit room at the University of Minnesota, poring over confessional American poet John Berryman's unpublished works, very diligently trying to decipher his abominable handwriting, made even worse by the burned pockmarks produced, no doubt, by his cigarette ashes falling on the delicate paper as he chain-smoked his way through writing about Shakespeare.

And then September 11 happened. All of a sudden, people of all sorts—professors, other PhD candidates, members of the local community—were asking me to speak about Arab and Muslim women.

Three interrelated problems presented themselves. First, I was not a spokesperson or an expert. I didn't know, could not know, and knew even less than I should have because I was the product of a highly effective colonial legacy that privileged knowledge about Europe over that of my own country. I started reading then, and I remember how hard I cried after I finished *The Story of Zahra* by Lebanese writer Hanan al-Shaykh, the first novel by an Arab woman writer I had ever read. It wasn't because of the tragic ending but because for the very first time I saw myself reflected in a literary text. This is especially odd as the novel is about a Lebanese girl who sleeps with a sniper during the Lebanese civil war and ends up being fatally shot by him. And yet, so starved was I for recognition of my image that just the fact that the names were familiar was enough to produce a deep, nostalgic yearning for home.

Second, it was never clear what this speaking entailed. Was I supposed to explain in thirty minutes the lives of millions of women across two continents and twenty-two countries whose historical, cultural, political, and social contexts were as varied as they were similar?

And third, and perhaps most painfully, I didn't know how to reconcile my feminism with my nationalism. By this point I had become deeply interested in the issues Arab and Muslim women face, but here I was, asked to expose the Arab and Muslim world's dirty laundry in an environment already primed against them. As an Arab and a Muslim, that was very hard to do. And as a woman, it was very hard not to. Algerian activist and sociologist Marie-Aimee Helie Lucas once said to a group of women gathered at a symposium in Finland, "Probably most of the women present at this symposium take for granted that they belong to a country or a nation which does not have to prove its existence. For them, the concept of nation can be transcended and criticized. This is not true for Algeria nor for other decolonized and still colonized countries at war with imperialism. For us it is much more difficult to criticize the nation, and even the State which claims to represent the nation" (1990, 108).

And indeed, I felt that at every turn, I was betraying some aspect of my identity: if I privileged my feminist concerns, I was a national traitor, and if I privileged my postcolonial identity as an Arab and Muslim, I was being an apologist.

It is a relief when I return to teach in Jordan, American husband in hand. I so desperately want to be good for my grandmother Sabha. And for five years, the return carries with it none of the forewarned (by other Arab expats in the United States or in Jordan) and anticipated dislocation, the reverse culture shock, the frustration of in-betweenness. Every day, I talk with Tētā on the phone, and every Thursday I visit her on her farm in al-Libban, outside of Amman. On her cool flagstone front porch, under the zinc awning and the fig tree, we look over groves of olive and pomegranate trees.

To her, I am a *zalameh*. I don't wear makeup, I dress modestly, I didn't stay in the West even though I am married to an American, I hold my own and interact with men like other men would—'*ad ḥālī*—I am up to the task of myself.

So how could I tell her that after years of *ghurbeh* followed by years of *'awdeh* and thinking the return was forever, I had come back from white-washed rooms carved into sloping mountains atop the blue-green waters of Santorini to an email with a foreboding, though ambiguous, title: "Official Notification"? How could I tell her what I could not have imagined? That it contained in its belly the Arab and Muslim woman academic's death blow.

> Dear Dr. Diya Abdo,
>
> I have been asked by the Director of the Jordan Branch to inform you to submit your resignation as your publications and ideas are unacceptable at Arab Open University and are not in accordance with Arab Islamic values, which are an essential part of this institution's philosophy and mission. Your emphasis on queer theory, sexual fluidity and attack on Arab/Islamic culture and values are in direct opposition to the philosophy of this institution. Thus, in order to avoid action being taken against you at Headquarters in Kuwait, we are asking you to submit your resignation as soon as possible.

I cannot tell my grandmother, the woman who raised me and was elated that I had returned to Jordan to teach, that I am being accused of anti-Islamism and behavior unbecoming a respectable woman.

They had come to this determination of my very being while I was on vacation. In a few days I was supposed to return to teach my summer classes, but those had mysteriously vanished from my schedule when I checked online from a small Internet café in Athens. At the time, I had no idea why that had happened; I thought it was simply a glitch in our online system. I realized later that they were erasing every trace of me; I am a toxic poison to be cleansed, a tumor to be excised.

The "publications" in question: a forthcoming paper titled "'Tell Me What's between Your Legs': Redefining the Warring Self through the Nation's Sexual Others." All they had available to them was that title and this abstract:

> *Carthaginians* by Irish playwright Frank McGuinness and *The Story of Zahra* by Lebanese novelist Hanan al-Shaykh delineate the ways in which political conflict (in this case the Northern Ireland conflict and the Lebanese civil war) is largely dependent on sexual inequality and oppression. I further explore the creation of a potentially transformative/alternative national and individual self through the overt and conscious gendered and sexualized performances of the nation's sexual "others." Ultimately, however, this freeing

sexual performance of the nation's "Others" (women and homosexuals) is doomed to failure. In each case, the nation is too embedded in its masculinist performances to change its ways.

Anti-Islamic views?

And then I recall bits and pieces of conversations I've had with the chair of the department, with whom I shared an office and who would later send me the death blow. I thought I was having innocent chats with a trusted friend, but she was carefully watching and keeping track: "Do you fast?" "No." "Bit'amni?" "Not really."

I loved the title—a quote from McGuinness's play. Hark, the IRA "hard man," threatened by Dido, the queer drag queen's sexuality, mocks what he perceives to be Dido's failure to live up to gendered ideals: "Tell me what's between your legs. Is there anything between your legs? Is there one between your legs?" (1988, 7–8).

To appease the administration, I remove the quote I love from the title and my university affiliation from the publication. In the final version, I am institutionally homeless. Under my name, simply "Amman, Jordan."

The shame and guilt are suffocating. More than the fear of losing my job, I fear for my reputation. How many knew about this? Is my story on every tongue? I call a trusted colleague, a former professor of this institution, who tells me to keep this as hushed as possible. To be labeled anti-Islamic is the kiss of death for the Arab woman intellectual. No university would hire me. My name had already been printed in a Jordanian newspaper decrying local scholars who had attended, presented at, or even registered for the World Congress for Middle Eastern Studies conference in Jordan; with Israeli scholars in attendance, we were expected to boycott the event. When I am interviewed by an American reporter working for a Jordanian magazine about the boycott, I blurt: "I won't be bullied out of a conference in my own country!" He likes it; he wants to quote me.

I email him later asking him to remove the quote and send him something more measured instead—something that would make me neither a traitor nor an apologist.

I don't make it into his final article.

So I had to keep my reputation clean. What I really wanted to do was to rail and challenge them publicly, to expose their bigotry and hypocrisy in some grand gesture. To say out loud, in print: "How dare an institution whose curriculum, imported from the British Open University, is the epitome of a colonial and imperial education question my loyalty to this place, this identity?"

For an Arab woman, the label of "traitor" is the easiest to cast and the hardest to shake off.

I had to keep my narrative golden.

This memory is one of the body: sitting on a leather couch, the cool drift of the air conditioner raising the tiny hairs on my forearms, a wall of windows to my left overlooking the congested street outside the main building of the Arab Open University, cars blaring and honking, their exhaust fumes rising, suffocating the jasmine on the sidewalk trellises, already wilting in the summer heat of Amman.

The president is telling me something. It takes me a while to register what he's saying. His words are out of place; they don't fit this situation, these parameters, and how I have understood what this place and my place in it mean. Now and here I sit, feeling very small, expecting to hear a lecture on "appropriate" scholarship, but what I get instead is a lecture on how to dress, how to smile, how to relate to my students, and how I have been doing these things in ways inappropriate: sleeves (too short), smiling (too much), relating (entirely too friendly). I can be embraced in the fold again, but I will have to mind my manners. I just sit there, paralyzed, mouth dry, head underwater.

Mohannad, my youngest brother (I am the oldest child), calls me on the phone. He is in the United States. I tell him about my meeting with the president. "What did you say?"

I am too embarrassed to say "Nothing."

So I say nothing.

I love the women students at the Arab Open University. Mostly older women, some my mother's age but many my own or a little older, they come back after years of caring for small children, ailing parents, chaotic homes, and overworked husbands to do a little something for themselves. And they come from all over—from 'Abdun, the Beverly Hills of Amman; from the small hillside villages scattered around Irbid, the Bride of the North, Hartha, Kufr Rahta, and Kufr Sum; from the shantytowns of downtown Amman, al-Hashmiyyeh; or the zinc-roofed refugee camp, al-Baqʿa, erected as a temporary home for the dispossessed crossing the river but now more permanent than Petra. The Open University lives up to its name; in the same classroom I have women who have just parked a Lexus on the uneven pavement outside the buildings and will return to grand homes, well-kept by Sri Lankan or Filipino maids, and women who will take three or four buses and then walk down dusty side streets to their small rooms. I love these women, and they love me. In the office I share with the chair, they sit and tell me about their families and husbands and hopes and dreams. They bring me warm hugs and kisses and chocolates. Sometimes I meet with them at the women-only café in Der-Ghbar, the one with the blind musician. He is male, but he cannot see them. This makes him almost a woman or not a man.

I ask them to call me Diya. How do I ask these women to call me Dr. Abdo? How do I erect a wall where intimacy has been carved?

I am named after a Quaker's daughter. Diya. In English, it is a slight thing, like the sound you might make absentmindedly as you shake your head in dismay over a thing annoying but not too serious. In Arabic it is heavy and gruff, with a harsh final glottal stop. And though it means "light," the first letter is a very hard "D"— al-ḍāḍ. To pronounce it, the fullness of your tongue must rise up to meet both your upper palate and your teeth, pushing gently but firmly from back to front, tip of tongue ever so slightly emerging from behind the upper front teeth. You would really have to hear an Arab pronounce it. The Arabic language is sometimes called lughat-al-ḍāḍ; there is no other language that contains this particular sound. It is uniquely Arab. But this American Quaker, a close friend of my maternal grandfather, lived in Ramallah for a time. They called him el-mukhtār because the townspeople would often go to him to resolve their conflicts. He was married to a Lebanese woman, and they had a daughter. My mother liked her name, and when she gave birth to me in the darkness of the morning, well before dawn, she thought that the light of the moon was made for me. As the Arabs say, our names are born with us. I was born under the light of the moon, but I have journeyed to this Quaker place called Guilford College. This is how it makes perfect sense (even in my body) that a first-generation Palestinian born and raised in Jordan finds a piece of home in Greensboro, North Carolina.

As it turns out, my namesake is a director at an organization that funds Palestinian youths' education in American colleges, including Guilford.

And as it turns out, she is also named after another woman, her maternal grandmother, an Arab woman whose father wanted a boy so badly that when his wife gave birth to a girl, he was so ashamed, he named her Diya, hoping that the neighboring villagers, upon hearing of his child's birth and its name, would think he was blessed with a son.

The moon and its light, *ḍiyā' ul-qamar*, are both gendered male in the Arabic language. But it is mostly women who, in being described as beautiful, are likened to the moon. A man woman.

Thrice reflected, light diluted—infinitely removed from "goodness."

In Jordan, still trying to stay in this place I love, the stigma of "anti-Islamic" looms large over me. I have to put the fire out. Often, here, if there is an infraction, tribal laws govern. When my mother ran over an elderly woman coming out of the trees in the median and killed her, the men of our tribe negotiated with the men of her tribe an *'atweh*. Blood money was paid.

So I take a man with me to this meeting of men—my maternal grandfather—to negotiate with the AOU dean of the Faculty of Language Studies. They are old friends and both PhDs in linguistics. We sit at a small table in the lobby of the Holiday Inn near the intersection of Madina and Mecca Streets. The dean comments on my attire, my short sleeves. He doesn't mind, he's very liberal, but the Arab Open University is a conservative place, you know? I smile big, talk timid, just like in that room with the president.

From the United States, Mohannad later calls me to tell me that I am his role model. How does he know that what this means, above all else, is a feeling of badness that crawls into my heart and brain and settles there to sleep? So many women academics I know already feel fraudulent. How long will it take wherever I go until they find out I am not good enough? And now, what place would even have me?

To this day, every time someone with some kind of authority over me summons me in to "talk to me about something," I shake to my very core with fear. What have I done that needs punishing, reprimanding, firing? I wrack my brain trying to figure it out. Once, the division chair at Guilford requested a meeting with me. My mouth dried instantly, my heart beat almost out of my chest. I was so nervous when I met with him. It turned out he wanted to commend me on my scholarship, my publications. Maybe I should apply for a grant and take a semester off to work on a book? The administration would totally support that.

I flinch when a hand extends itself, even in kindness.

And is it impossible to be good everywhere? To be good here, is it because I am bad elsewhere?

If I want to stay in the place I love with the people I love and the language I love, in this beloved desert, I might go thirsty, I might not be able to be the kind of teacher and scholar I want to be. I make a very difficult choice—and leave.

When Guilford flies me in for the interview, it is my first time in North Carolina. Jim Hood, then chair of the English Department, meets me at the airport. I already know what he looks like from his photo online, and somehow he recognizes me, too. His face is beaming, and we are joking with each other from the very first minute; instantly, we are like sister and brother. But on the way to Guilford, as we drive through undeveloped land, my stomach drops. And it hits me that after Amman International Airport and JFK, the GSO airport is more like a bus stop. I am an Arab city woman; I am at home in the suffocating exhaust of public buses and exhausted cars, the heat rising in visible waves off the baking asphalt, the constant hum and drone of shopkeepers inviting you into their stores, and perhaps most unshakably, the muezzin's call to prayer, rising slowly and then wailing triumphantly, several times a day.

For months after I settle in Greensboro, I still hear it at the appointed time—the phantom *azan* calling from the distance, the recesses of my mind unable to let go of this primordial sound imprinted in me in utero.

Aidana Sabha is conceived while my grandmother, Sabha, the woman who raised me, lies dying in the hospital. For years, she has been urging me to have a child. When I left Jordan, it broke her heart. Because I couldn't tell her about the death blow, did she think I wanted to leave her? They took her to the hospital a week after I left; she never returned to Palestine like she had always dreamed. "Tētā, I am pregnant." From her hospital bed: "Mabrūk, yā Dthiyāʾ, mabrūk yā ḥabibtī." The next day she died—on my birthday. The autopsy revealed a cancer, undetected and voracious; starving, it had consumed her liver.

Aidana thinks I must not love her enough because I speak to her only in Arabic. I speak to her Baba in Arabic and English. Surely it is a sign of greater love to give someone more words, different words?

"Iḥkī maʿī bil-inglīzī." Speak to me in English.

I'm sorry. I can't.

Speak to me in English.

My biggest smile ever. I'm sorry. I can't. You're too special.

Just say "Hello."

*Marḥaba.*

Just say "I love you."

And I do. So I do.

At Guilford, we are all on a first-name basis—students, faculty, staff, even the president. Quakers are so deeply anti-hierarchical; they believe titles divide and stratify. I lunch with my students on campus, have dinner with them at my home. The college pays for these expenses. The narrative we have constructed together is golden, especially in the office building I share with other outsiders.

But while Guilford is a home, some rooms are homier, warmer than others; some are not at all—like the really bright one where I am told that to make ends meet, perhaps my husband, stay-at-home parent to our two children, can work the night shift, or the really darkened room where, after I do not budge, stare power squarely in the eyes, write and protest inequities publicly, I am told I am unprofessional, ahead of myself. So in this room I sit dazed, cower, and apologize. Again, nothing.

And is it impossible to be good everywhere? And tell me, Dido, what is between your legs?

I sang to Aidana, in utero and every day thereafter at bedtime, my favorite Arabic song. It is so old that many of my Arab friends don't know it:

O violet, why do you bloom when you are such a melancholy flower?
The eye follows you and finds you
Demure and chaste.

When I first sing it to Seira, my secondborn daughter, she tilts her head, her eyes unfocused still but searching, as if she recognizes it. A distant familiar sound, a call to sleep, heard through darkness and water.

In Greensboro, with my sister here for a short while attending graduate school, we've settled into a life that reminds me of the streets of Jordan. The girls play outside her apartment with the hordes of Saudi kids who live at the complex; their fathers attend the universities and language academies nearby. In the park at the center of the buildings, the Saudi men drink coffee and chat well into the night on woven plastic mats. They've got plenty of ice cream for all the kids who might be playing outside and hand them out whenever a child, sugar-crazed (like my niece Alana) or stranger-shy (like my daughter Aidana), asks for one. The Saudi women sit on the iron table next to the small park, shelling watermelon and pumpkin seeds, drinking Saudi coffee, and fiddling with their iPhones.

I sit with my sister on the stoop of her apartment just overlooking the park, swatting away the flies, my generous thighs feeling the warmth of the brick under me, keeping a distant eye on Aidana. I rest my Seira, now eight months, in the bend of my arm, elbow digging into the soft spot above my knee, legs as far apart as possible, and nurse her. Occasionally, I yell at Aidana to watch out as the kids weave in and out of the men playing volleyball in the sand. It pleases me to think that my grandmother would have done it just like this—squatting on the ground under the olive trees, gossiping with other women, a baby on the breast and a child playing in the groves. I sit in the sun and nurse my Seira the way a good Palestinian village woman would.

But this isn't Jabal al-Mukabber. Aidana wants long blond hair like Elsa, the Icelandic Ice Queen, and tomorrow, I will go to Guilford and teach American kids how to write in English and how to analyze literature in English. Last summer I published an article I am proud of: "My Qarina, My Self: The Homoerotic as Islamic Feminism in Alifa Rifaat's 'My World of the Unknown'" in the *Journal of Lesbian Studies*.

She is much more relaxed, this secondborn, this Seira. And I am more relaxed with her. The anxiety of first-parenthood is all but gone. And already, I hold her less accountable than the firstborn, the second Sabha. I am not occupying her every waking minute with Arabic words and Arabic music and Arabic smells. We sit in prolonged silence, which, because of the Quakers, I have come to love, as I pass her one toy after another and play a game she loves, the one where I raise and lower my eyebrows, conspiracy in my eyes and a mischievous smile on my lips. She laughs hard at my expression, like we're in on a secret that only the two of us know. A fun secret—like maybe, we can be good even if we're not perfect. Maybe we can be *'ad ḥālnā* even if we falter, sometimes, at the task of being the selves that others have constructed for us, expect of us, want for us. Maybe we can go easy on ourselves.

How great the relief. How great the loss.

## Note

1. Al-Nakseh, literally "the Setback," is a commonly used epithet for the 1967 Arab-Israeli War.

## References

Abdo, Diya. 2012. "My Qarina, My Self: The Homoerotic as Islamic Feminism in Alifa Rifaat's 'My World of the Unknown.'" *Journal of Lesbian Studies: Lesbians, Sexuality, and Islam* 16, no. 4:398–415.

Helie-Lucas, Marie-Aimee. 1990. "Women, Nationalism and Religion in the Algerian Liberation Struggle." In *Opening the Gates: A Century of Arab Feminist Writing*, edited by Margot Badran and miriam cooke, 105–114. Bloomington: Indiana University Press.

McGuinness, Frank. 1988. *Carthaginians*. London: Faber and Faber.

Shaykh, Hanan al-. 1986. *The Story of Zahra*. New York: Doubleday.

# Suspicious Bodies

## THREE

Madame Bomba Performs
against Death in Lebanon

RIMA NAJDI

Madame Bomba: The TNT Project
Public intervention
January 12, 2014. Beirut, Lebanon

Costume by Rayya Kazoun
Photography by Maria Kassab

On Sunday, January 12, 2014, Rayya Kazoun — fashion designer — strapped
my chest with a big, fake, red TNT vest. Unlike previous performances, the
intervention was based on a need to act, protest, and open a conversation
about a certain anxiety and fear caused by suicide car bombings; the war in
Syria; and the bad economy, electricity and water cut-offs, traffic, domestic violence and killing, and other crises in Lebanon.

For six hours I walked through different places in Beirut, and drank
coffee, *shīshah*, and drinks in fancy cafés and pubs. For six hours I walked
by the 'Ein el-Mreiseh corniche, feeling scared and courageous, being
mocked, harassed by some men, sniffed by a dog, and prevented from
entering elitist private shopping malls. Reacting to two recent car bombings in Beirut, my motivation for the intervention was largely connected
to an anxiety and fear of stillness that I had arrived at. It was an attempt
to map the quotidian urban environment, to hear other people's reactions
and responses to suicide bombing. These two bombs, one in downtown

**Figure 3.1.** Madame Bomba: The TNT Project. Intervention documentation #1. January 12, 2014. Ein el-Mreiseh, Beirut. Photo by Maria Kassab. Courtesy of the artist.

Beirut and the other in the Dahiyeh neighborhood, killed a total of 10 and injured 136, and they left people shocked or totally indifferent to death.

During the intervention, the local press started writing about Madame Bomba: The TNT Project. For the following three weeks I received letters — hate mail whose writers considered the intervention a scandal and in general bad taste, and letters of admiration whose writers considered the intervention courageous. With messages from strangers and endless calls from local, regional, and international press offices writing stories about Madame Bomba, I started dealing with the written and audio messages as work material in and of themselves.

I consider these responses a new layer of material for the intervention.

(1)
November 19, 2013: Two suicide bombers, the Iranian cultural center in the southern suburb of Beirut. 27 dead. 160 wounded.
December 3, 2013: Two gunmen. Beirut. 1 dead.
December 27, 2013: A car bomb. Downtown Beirut. 6 people dead. 70 wounded.
January 2, 2014: A suicide bomber, Al-ʿArid Street, southern suburb of Beirut. 6 dead. 75 wounded.

January 12, 2014: A fake bomb, various streets in Beirut. Many
    wounded.
January 16, 2014: A suicide car bombing, northeastern town of Hermel.
    5 dead. 42 wounded.
January 21, 2014: A suicide bomber, Al-ʿArid Street, southern suburb of
    Beirut. 7 dead. 46 wounded.
February 1, 2014: A suicide bomber, Hermel, Beqaʿ. 7 dead. 26 wounded.
February 19, 2014: Two suicide bombers, Iranian cultural center in
    Beirut. 8 dead. 128 wounded.
February 22, 2014: A suicide car bombing, northeastern town of Hermel,
    Beqaʿ. 3 dead. 17 wounded.
March 29, 2014: A suicide car bombing. The northeastern town of Arsal,
    Beqaʿ. 3 dead. 4 wounded.
June 20, 2014: A suicide bomber. Dahr el-Beidar, east Lebanon. 1 dead.
    32 wounded.
June 24, 2014: A suicide bomber. Checkpoint in Beirut. 12 wounded.
June 27, 2014: A suicide bomber. Beirut. 11 wounded.
August 6, 2014: A homemade bomb. Tripoli, northern Lebanon. 1 dead.
    10 wounded.

(2)

*Wounded* [past participle of *wound*]: Having an injury inflicted.

*Dead* [adjective]: No longer alive. Having or displaying no emotions,
    sympathy, or sensitivity.

(3)

Madame Bomba is a persona that has a fake, red TNT bomb strapped to
her chest. The bomb cannot explode, and she cannot get rid of the bomb.
Madame Bomba only responds with questions, since she does not have
any answers. She writes full sentences only in her personal diary. Madame
Bomba's psyche is a bit complex. She believes in the effect of mystical
powers. She has obsessions about encounters with strangers and suspicious objects. She thinks about herself as an art object. She is aware that
the fake, red TNT bomb she carries evokes fear and suspicion, but she
thinks that she lives in a country where most people are familiar with such
emotions — so she decides not to hide them any more. Madame Bomba
does not like to label herself a "bad girl"; she thinks that it is very problem-
atic to be called such. Her hobbies are writing poetry, walking the streets,

and sitting in cafés to watch people. The sounds that Madame Bomba hears are dramatic and scary. They fade only to explode. They come and go.

Madame Bomba is aware of the damage she can cause. After all, she always watches the news at 8 p.m. Beirut time. She sits in a cozy place to watch the news; she gazes at familiar faces. She only gets more anxious in the coziness of the place and more tired of the news. In order to hide her anxiety, she watches silly TV shows to fall asleep. And she only sleeps when she gets absolutely tired.

Madame Bomba has mysterious powers to eject herself from her body. Her self floats while her body remains in its position. Sometimes when her self and her body get away from each other, Madame Bomba cries.

When Madame Bomba cries, she starts having thoughts about her existence in such a body. A body that carries a hidden subject. She hates the fact that it is hidden. Madame Bomba knows that you know and that you are familiar with her suspicious, ticking, red, fake TNT bomb. She doesn't mind that you might have ridiculed it, but she can't bear the thought of covering that part of her body in order to meet strangers in the city. Emotionally, she is not ready to understand why a society needs to cover its uncomfortable memories, uncomfortable wounds, uncomfortable skins.

One day she decided to walk out. To reveal herself as a ticking body that holds a bomb. That day, she heard a lot of comments, and she received various reactions. Overwhelming, she thought, but she had many euphoric emotions from the number of strangers she met in the city. She took photos with them, as they did for and with her. In photo moments, she didn't compete with any other person as to who would look better in the photo. She did not try to control the situation or defend her bomb. It seemed that there was more power in leaving strangers to gaze at her.

She knows she can't change her appearance or hide the ticking time bomb strapped to her chest. Often, when she is sitting in traffic, she starts imagining and daydreaming that everyone has a ticking bomb strapped to its chest like she does. She developed this technique of seeing other bodies as suspicious while sitting in a car, in traffic.

She has a love/hate relationship with the car. She loves to drive; it gives her a different feeling of the space around her. The road gives her some kind of a familiar freedom, a freedom that doesn't trouble her nerves. She hates red traffic lights, but she never ignores them. She hates traffic in general as well, she doesn't like to give the car to the valet, and she gets frustrated when she can't find a parking space. She also doesn't like it

**Figure 3.2.** Madame Bomba: The TNT Project. Intervention documentation #2. January 12, 2014. Ein el-Mreiseh, Beirut. Photo by Maria Kassab. Courtesy of the artist.

when someone reserves a parking space by leaving a chair in the middle of it. The car, as a structure, annoys her and makes her anxious.

Madame Bomba is still looking for her lover. The idea of suspicious strangers makes her horny. When she is horny she masturbates. She tries to discover her relationship with that stranger.

(4)
Personal diary—Madame Bomba:

1.
November 19, 2013
Dear suspicious body, I want to see you. I want to look at you. I want to touch you.

I feel you, but I don't understand you. Tell me: who do you really love?

I don't want to tell people your story, I don't want to describe it to them.

But I want to talk with them about you, I want them to feel you, like I do.

I know that when you see me you will kill me. But I can't find you. Please don't find me.

If I find you please don't kill me. I am uncomfortable with the idea of dying now.

Your invisible body makes me feel that you have power. A mysterious power.

I—like you—am obsessed with all the failure that I am living in. Failure of finding you, of seeing

you, of having a dialogue with you.

I—unlike you—am not able to appear in the society we live in.

XX

M.B.

P.S. Do you exist?

2.

December 3, 2013

One time I was waiting for the traffic light in Beirut to turn green. I think I met a terrorist crossing the road. Or so I felt. I felt some kind of terror at that intersection, waiting for the traffic light to turn green. The neighboring car in the crossroad was waiting for the red light to turn green as well. Its occupants stared suspiciously at the person passing by. But we were not sure, since he hadn't terrorized us yet. That moment I am trying to describe to you makes me emotionally confused. That was a mysterious encounter that I still cannot put into words.

3.

December 27, 2013

Today I was breathing in the taste of panic, breathing out the smell of death.

4.

January 2, 2014

I think I met with several terrorists. I think you might be one of them. You look suspicious to me. But I never recognized them as such. There was no way for me to know that they were real terrorists, and why would I make such an assumption and judge you as such if you don't look like one? How do they look, anyway? Their description has changed a lot during the last few years. They used to have less hair. Why are you growing a beard?

5.

January 12, 2014

The closer you were getting to me, the more alien I became. I tried to make you comfortable by speaking about a bomb, about death, about fear that has come to live between us. I did so for your sake. I answered with questions. The image that you took of me is an object that will store our encounter, our relation. It will satisfy you when you look back at it.

6.

January 16, 2014

The sound just got deeper. I close my eyes. My pupils are just getting larger in the dark, with words and sounds.

> A mother shouting to her daughter:
> Stay away from it!

Walk in the street, cars blocking roads—traffic!

Radio sounds escape from cars, creating a single orchestra of fear.

For an hour or so, citizens are afraid, waiting for responses, for a certain truth.

Youngsters are not here any more.

Fuck, stupid, death.

Politicians calling for *ḍabṭ al-nafs*, containment of the self.

7.

January 21, 2014

I contain your most horrible trauma in order to provoke you. I make you think that I am an object, while in fact I am breathing and watching you. I look at you with suspicion. I try to find some warmth in my gaze to you, but I can't. There is no empathy in me toward you. You become distant. You become suspicious to me. You start stimulating desires in my unconscious, desires not only about you but about other suspicious bodies in the space. I start envying your passiveness and regard it as power, a power that I can't have. I start to get jealous. I begin to hate you.

8.

February 1, 2014

Then, there, a deep sound hits my ears. A honk from a car. It wakes me up; military music is playing in the head. A mosque calling for the noon prayer behind me: "Allahu Akbar, Allahu Akbar"—God is the Greatest, its speakers shout. I am coming out. Now. I am walking and coming out in front of you. Marching, to the space where there are a lot of people. Marching toward you. Now it is my body against yours. My suspicious fears, against yours. Hip hop dancers rehearsing. Can I go and dance with them? Families sitting on benches. Do I go sit next to them? My silence grows in my throat. My tongue becomes numb, just got numb to any memory that grew in silence, in stillness, in loneliness. Toward the sea I marched. Finally I am breathing better. The sound of the waves from the sea mixes with the sound of the city, of the people, of the dancers.

9.

February 19, 2014

I have a photo of a man taking a photo, and he is smiling but not laughing. Other men are in the photo, tall blocks behind them. Men in the photo have their hands in their pockets. A few have mobile phones. One man is taking the photo, with a big smile on his face. He is looking at the smartphone that he is holding in his hand. He is taking a photo of something. Something that isn't far away from them. He and the other men in the photo. There was some subject of fear there but not only fear — something more suspicious. Something public that entertains some and leaves others with disrespectful, annoyed, and angry feelings. It intrigues me to know the level of violence in the photo. To build some sort of image thermometer to ascertain the emotional temperature. Some seemed entertained in the photo. Maybe this is how they interact with fear? Or this is how they ensure that they were there, having witnessed such a fear. But maybe fear wasn't there. I can't find any subject of fear other than the men themselves, in the photo that I have.

10.

February 22, 2014

A suspicious body: Its color is silver, and it is called Sang Yong.[1]
A suspicious body: It exists in Hamra Street.
A suspicious body: That causes danger.
Silence. Heavy silence.
A suspicious body: That causes a public panic.
A suspicious body: That requires you to hold your breath — *ḍabṭ al-nafs*.
A suspicious body: That attacks.
A suspicious body: That is loaded.
A suspicious body: Stay away from it.

11.

March 29, 2014

What is this white flower that you sent me? Is that how you bring peace to our relationship? Is it an apology? I asked you for an apology a long time ago. I sent you numerous messages, asking you to just admit that you are a stupid, ignorant, selfish fuck. Do you believe that I will walk away from you now, without anger and a desire for revenge? The now where I am sitting. It's a bit uncomfortable to sit and write to you. I am pretending that I know exactly what I am saying when I am writing. I am pretending that I am being passive-aggressive, that my emotions are indifferent toward you. But my emotions are simply aggressive toward you. I am getting angrier and more frustrated each time I look at the silly white flower. But really, I never thought you believed in peace. You always thought of yourself as a victim. You always thought it was ok to take revenge. Do you believe we will walk away from the now at ease with each other? I think you are selfish, and you are thinking I will forgive you. But I will not. It's about time for you to see yourself as I feel you. I am not asking you to make me understand your story, motivations, and the reasons behind your doing xxxx. If you continue to have such an attitude, I will try hard to hurt you.

12.

June 20, 2014

A new flag on a building that had just spit out its furniture, glass, and
    balconies.

A new flag on a building that a few seconds ago had some sort of life.

13.

June 24, 2014

Today I am tired of the questions I asked other people—I will edit them tomorrow if I am still alive:

When do you think?
Where do you think?
What do you think?
Why do you think?
Who do you think?
    (*Banal*)

When do you think I will leave the space?
Where do you think I will go next?
What is your reaction?
Why are you telling me to wear an abaya? Is that how suicide bombers dress?

Who do you think told me to wear a fake red bomb?
   (*Spectacular banal*)

When will you take the photo?
Where do you think I should stand?
What do you propose that I should do?
Who is offended by a live action?
Why do I look suspicious to you?
   (*Spectacular banal action*)

When is the dog coming to sniff me?
Where should I sit down?
What is dangerous?
Who are we calling terrorists?
Why not?
   (*Suspicious spectacular banal action*)

When will you make that decision?
Where is your lighter?
What is normal?
Who is offended by a live action?
Why are you scared of me?
   (*Suspicious political spectacular banal action*)

14.
June 27, 2014
A guy clapped for me today. He was fishing. He transformed my marching exercise into a theatrical march. He was clapping for me. I thought he was giving me credit for walking out in society. I thought he was encouraging my differences. I thought he loved my march because my body was different. I started to imagine him walking out from his anger and fear. Showing us all the suspicious covered parts strapped to his body. He didn't. He shouted, "We get the idea. Please leave now. Just get away from us."

15.
August 6, 2014
I had a dream that I was a normal person. I didn't have anything suspicious attached to my body. I was walking by and people did not notice my presence. I didn't have any fear, paranoia, or claustrophobic feelings.

People in my dream didn't have angry faces. They were smiling. The street looked more colorful. It was the first colorful dream that I have had. I always dream in black and white. No smoke in my dream. The vision was clear. The street where I was walking was not a construction site. People on the sidewalk were walking normally, not looking suspiciously at the cars passing by, at each other. There were men and women on the streets. Actually there were more women on that street. Men did not harass women. They didn't stare at their asses, boobs, or legs. And women did not harass other women for their color or their looks. Women in my dream looked normal, with no plastic surgery applied to their bodies. Nor did the men have any plastic surgeries. Taxi drivers didn't stop for every person walking on the sidewalk. Taxi drivers did not honk constantly to check if pedestrians needed a ride. Cars passed by with loud militia music playing from their speakers. No pollution, neither from the cars nor from the people. Cars and people were not suspicious of each other. All traffic lights were green. No one had a gun on the street. The military tank that used to be there on the corner didn't exist in my dream. I dreamed that the streets were safe. There were no police near the traffic light. Everyone walked in harmony, not suspicious of each other.

(5)
Madame Bomba — Monologue:
Sit home tight — don't move.
Next day, walk in the street — keep looking at people — keep looking for
    an anonymous car —
Death.
Look at the car plates — receive messages from car plates — avoid these
    cars.
Endless amounts of police men and, recently, women.
Drive in your car — a red light — a game.
Do you stop?
Red light — You have to stop.
Motionless — An explosion?
Red light — Where is the car that would carry these bombs?
Red light — Is it a car? Or a person?
Red light — Why does it matter? You are going to die anyway.
Red light — But if you can avoid it, you don't want to die.
Red light — Turn the volume up, make it louder, so you don't hear the
    explosion if it happens.

Red light—Turn the volume down; maybe you need to hear it, so you can just pass the red light.

Red light—Fuck.

Red light—Is the car next to me going to explode?

Red light—Look at the car next to you.

Red light—Eyes from neighboring car are looking suspiciously at you.

Red light—They are looking for the bomb.

Red light—Maybe it's in the cars parked by the sidewalk.

Red light—Green light.

DRIVE FAST.

Red light—You think you are going to die.

Red light—No not yet.

Red light—Does this car have a Syrian plate number?

Red light—What? I can't believe that I am thinking that way.

Red light—A bearded guy, move away! Where to?

Red light—You hate, you hate yourself.

Red light—Why do you take so long?

Red light—Smoke a cigarette.

Red light—Phone call—just tell someone where you are—a strategy.

Red light—Where is the fucking bomb?

Red light—It is not green yet.

Red light—No cars coming—just drive.

Red light—You drive.

You drive out of fear, out of panic.

Red light, fuck you, you don't want to die.

Park the car—Go see your friends.

Speak about anxiety, and notice that fear and suspicion have become collective.

Have a drink with your friends—Whiskey, wine, beer, rum are not sufficient.

Go see your parents—Speak about politics.

Politics—Who was behind the explosion? What is the truth?

Lebanese politics—SICK.

Lebanese politicians—Warlords.

Family—Walking-and-driving-around-the-city strategy.

Family politics—Try to avoid places in the city.

For yourself—But how would we know?

We are all explosives, walking and driving around.

Zero tolerance.

(6)

A stranger's monologue:

What an idiot . . . A fake cartoon bomb in an open public space . . .
No one should joke this way . . . Is this art? . . . I am already tired of the
news of death on TV and in newspapers. The situation can't handle some
tasteless art project mocking death. How could she, anyway? Is this supposed to make me want to talk about suicide bombings? Does she know
the misery that we live in? I really can't stand anyone broaching this subject any more. We are already reminded constantly of the existence of a
bomb. This "art project" looks like a joke. Even though I don't believe that
this art has any meaning or intention, why do I need to see one? What
a travesty. Would she go to the southern suburb where the real danger
lies? I think we should call the police and report her art. I think the police
should shoot her. She needs to die. Why do I need to see this art project
when all I want is to spend some time in peace? I came to sit and watch
people by the sea, not to see another art project. I don't like art anyway.
I think it is incomprehensible, and it is very expensive in the first place.
You know what? I think all artists are crazy. Maybe the insane asylum
is missing one of its patients. I never attended an art project in my life.
Sometimes some crazy artists would come and do public things here, but
not like this one. What a bitch! . . . Anyway I never heard of an art project or an artist offering a solution. I didn't. Palestine is still occupied. The
war in Syria is still ongoing and we still don't have electricity. And now
with all the bombs . . . Why is she putting herself in such a position? The
police should arrest her. Maybe she thinks she is smart, mocking all of
us. I don't like it when people think of themselves as smart. She wants to
make us afraid. I am not afraid. Are you afraid? . . . What is her message?
Does she understand death? I don't think anyone in her family died in an
explosion. I know about explosions. I don't want to remember them. And
I definitely don't want to talk about them on a Sunday. It's my only day off.
I mean, we already live in fear, in suspicion. What is her message? I don't
understand art that doesn't send a message. What will foreigners think of
us now? The Western media, do you know that they will take this "Farha"
and make her famous? I think she did this project to get famous. But she
isn't good enough. I know that good artists entertain us. Anyway, what
a waste of time. The media will talk about it for a few minutes, and then
what? What will it change? Do you know what, maybe we should go and
bomb her as an art project. That would be better than her mocking us. We
will mock her and her art project . . . Even though I don't believe that this

art has any meaning or intention. Can you understand the level of negativity attached to such a project? Maybe tomorrow a suicide bomber will dress himself like her, wait for everyone to gather around him, and then blow himself up. Maybe she will blow herself up. We need to be careful, don't approach her. Don't touch her, just look . . . She is wearing some sexy socks, though . . . UFFF! But I don't know if this will end well. I think she watches a lot of cartoons. This is why she looks so . . . Artists, how shallow. How stupid, selfish, self-centered. Maybe we kill her before other artists start to do the same. Protesting death wearing fake bombs. I don't like that she is laughing at death, I don't like that feeling she provokes, I am not provoked at all. You know? It is normal. I think maybe it would be better if she covered the bomb. If it was me, if I was the artist, I would cover the bomb. How masochistic these artists are nowadays. I think she has some perverted fantasies in scaring other people, in reviving death in their memories. Artists that like the use of pain, I don't understand them. I know pain, the pain and horror of bombs, you know? . . . That's it, I am sure now that I don't like art. It's a waste of money and time. If I were the artist, I would take that mask off. I think politics and arts shouldn't mix. Maybe in songs. Only in songs. You know what—I really don't need to see such a thing when I leave my house. I really don't know how you can call this art. I think she is a university student and she is doing this as a university project. Someone just told me that it is for a film. Look at us, she will film us and then go and get famous. How selfish these artists are. I don't find this funny, artistic, or useful. I can't understand the goal of her project. I think she is doing this for attention. What some women will do for attention! Maybe her cousin is a Muslim extremist. You know, this takes the self-effacing masochism of some Muslim women to a whole new level. She is lucky. I am sure someone will shoot her. I think she may have some psychological problems. I simply don't understand her. Obviously she is either an idiot or gay. Why don't they arrest her for being a gay idiot? I don't want to comment.

## Note

1. Sang Yong is a car company.

# "Jihad Jane" as Good American Patriot and Bad Arab Girl

FOUR

The Case of Nada Prouty after 9/11

RANDA A. KAYYALI

LOOKING DOWN THE BARREL OF THE M16 SHOVED IN MY FACE, I DID WHAT
ANY PATRIOTIC AMERICAN WOULD DO: I PROCLAIMED MY ALLEGIANCE
TO THE USA. "I'M AN AMERICAN; I'M AN AMERICAN!" I SCREAMED.

NADA PROUTY, *UNCOMPROMISED*

Nada Prouty begins her autobiography with the anecdote above, offering a full-on assertion of her American identity and patriotism. With her next sentence she reveals that the holder of the M16 is a young US Marine in Iraq who assumes she is anti-American because she has an Arabic accent and is wearing "Arab garb." At the time, Prouty was a Central Intelligence Agency (CIA) agent gathering intelligence for the US government. Originally Druze by religion, Lebanese by nationality, and a native Arabic speaker, Prouty moved to the United States to study at age nineteen, became a citizen, and later entered into government service in the Federal Bureau of Investigation (FBI) and the CIA. By 2007, however, the FBI and the Department of Justice (DOJ) in Detroit publicly accused her of being a spy for Hezbollah and an "enemy of the state."[1] Shortly afterward, her citizenship was revoked and the right-wing social media nicknamed her "Jihad Jane."

Denying the accusations and seeking to regain her US citizenship, Prouty launched a defensive campaign that included an autobiography,

*Uncompromised: The Rise, Fall, and Redemption of an Arab American Patriot in the* CIA (2011); an interview on CBS's *60 Minutes* (2010); and a *Marie Claire* article (Schlussel 2011). Prouty mobilized a campaign with a dominant narrative of gendered patriotism that painted her as both the good all-American woman and bad Arab girl. She consistently emphasized her transformation from a Lebanese Druze immigrant into an American patriot who valiantly fought for the United States in the war on terror. Refuting the charges against her, she cast herself as the victim of political wrangling by sectors of the US government, Detroit politicking, and implied racism toward Arabs and Muslims. Her efforts to clear her name through a tiered media strategy were effective—her right to reside in the United States was reinstated in late 2011.

Prouty's story reveals the inner workings and connections between dominant media frameworks of Arabs and Muslims, foreign policy, and Orientalism in the post-9/11 environment in the United States. Hers is a story of an Arab American woman that unfolds from a place of intersectional identities. Prouty begins to unpack how her own intersectional identities played a role in her case, explaining in her autobiography,

> My prosecution brought into stark relief the possibility that the politicizing of the war on terror would create similar "internal enemies" here in America. Such enemies are, more often than not, patriotic Americans who happen to have what some, in their ignorance, see as "different" names and faces. It's not overt racism in the classic sense, but rather a troubling kind of suspicion of non-white, non-ethnically Western European, and non-Christian individuals. Such suspicion promotes ignorance, which is a very real threat to American freedom and enlightened civil society. (2011, 281)

Rather than acknowledge her own identities as factors in this case, Prouty emphasizes what she was not; she was not white, western European, Christian—the archetype of a patriotic American in her mind. She felt that she was the victim of racist and Orientalist perceptions that permeate US culture due to her intersectional identity as a woman from the Middle East who was not originally Christian. However, in order to restore her name, she engages with the same Orientalist concepts of Arab Muslim woman in contrast with a narrowly conceived American feminism in an assertion of her own form of gendered patriotism. In the title of her book, she identifies as "an Arab American patriot in the CIA," and throughout the text she consistently couples "Arab American" with "patriot." At one point she explicitly supports vigilante violence against al-Qaeda and links this position to her identity as an Arab American (148). Her insecurity with regard to the politics of her ethnicity amid the war on terror is profound and leads to an overcompensating gendered patriotism.

How can the apparent contradiction between Prouty's description of the discrimination she has experienced as an Arab American woman and her adoption of a gendered patriotism rife with Orientalist underpinnings be reconciled? The Prouty affair unfolded within sociopolitical constructs of Arabs and Muslims — or more precisely, bad Muslims — as potential internal enemies within the political ecosystem of the war on terror in the United States. Orientalism and colonialism are the dominant thought structures that inform this political ecosystem. Throughout her media campaign, Prouty expressed an urgent need to be perceived as an American patriot in order to secure the broad public support necessary to have her citizenship restored. As a woman, the way in which she expressed her patriotism and loyalty was deeply gendered. For Prouty, her status as a woman affected perceived loyalties and her presentation of self as an Arab American patriot.

I propose to provide a feminist reading of Prouty's autobiography. In doing so, I demonstrate how Prouty's successful media campaign illuminates post-9/11 politics for Arab Americans and illustrates one narrative of ethnicity, gender, and immigrant status that can be sold to a general American audience.

## The Backstory

Prouty grew up during the civil war in Lebanon before she came to the United States for college. Once in the United States, she did not wish to return, so she engaged in a fake marriage to secure US citizenship. Then, American by nationality, she joined the FBI and later the CIA, serving in Iraq, Yemen, and Pakistan. From 2005 to 2010, Prouty faced investigations for illegally accessing the FBI computer databases and providing information to her brother-in-law, Talal Chahine, a Lebanese national who fled the United States after he was accused of transferring money to Hezbollah in Lebanon. In 2007 Prouty pled guilty to counts of criminal conspiracy, unauthorized computer access, and naturalization fraud. Press releases from the DOJ US Attorney's Office in Detroit kept the media informed about her case, fueling panic about the infiltration by Hezbollah in Detroit and the United States. A 2007 press release claimed, "It's hard to imagine a greater threat than someone like Nada Prouty" (in CBS News 2010). Because she had been a CIA agent, in 2008 the US Senate held a closed-door hearing about her case. The outcome of the hearing is not available, but an internal CIA investigation cleared Prouty of any wrongdoing or breach of national security.

## The Label "Jihad Jane"

Debbie Schlussel, a Michigan-based attorney, writer of opinion pieces in the *New York Post*, and widely read blogger, is a self-described "conservative political commentator, radio talk show host, columnist, and attorney." Schlussel led the media campaign against Prouty in articles in the *New York Post* and on her personal blog, in which she nicknamed Prouty "Jihad Jane."[2] Politically conservative news outlets, including Fox News, carried her story, casting Prouty as a spy and her patriotism as inauthentic because she was Arab and Muslim and broke US immigration laws. In 2011 these same commentators presented Prouty's exoneration as proof that the US government was incompetent to fight Islamic terrorism and was really pro-Muslim (Schlussel 2010).

In 2010 and 2011, Prouty chose to break her silence and publicly comment on her own case, countering the moniker "Jihad Jane." In retrospect, we can see that Prouty displayed political agency in her orchestration of a media campaign in her own defense. She sold her side of the story, and her autobiography made the best-seller lists as a hardback book in 2011 and appeared in paperback two years later. She convinced CBS to do a segment on her case by taking on the narrative of an Arab American woman and immigrant who suffered both patriarchal and anti-immigrant oppression. Prouty tapped into mass appeal by reminding audiences that she fought in support of the United States. Prouty's subjugation to the dominant narratives enabled her to become the primary actor and the narrator of her own story, strategizing to gain maximum emotional effect and sympathy for her case.

Prouty's tell-all autobiography is highly unusual for CIA agents and Arab Americans in general. It is more common for Arab American writers to critique US foreign policy in the Middle East and the war on terror.[3] Nonetheless, an analysis of her case offers insights into the complex forces that shape the lives of many Arab and Muslim Americans, particularly those with connections to US security services. I argue here that a master power narrative that accounts for the intersections of race or ethnicity and gender is necessary to understand the positioning of Arab Americans like Prouty. In the post-9/11 era, Muslim's and Arab American's allegiance to the United States is often scrutinized and questioned. Gender, however, can be deployed to play a pivotal role in countering these religious, ethnic, and racial narratives, as the Prouty affair illustrates.

## Strategic Media Recuperations

A critical cultural studies approach, as articulated by Shohat and Stam (1994) and Alsultany (2012), allows us to see that Prouty was part of a process of rehabilitation of certain Arabs and Muslims in the media. In line with the "simplified complex representations" (Alsultany 2012, 14) of Arabs and Muslims post-9/11, Prouty appears as the acceptable and exceptional Arab American who is loyal to the United States. At the beginning of the 60 Minutes piece, she is defensive, declaring, "I love the country. I believe in the country. I believe in everything that this country stands for" (CBS News 2010). By asserting her US patriotism up front, she places herself on the good side in a good/bad Muslim binary. She further plays the victim, the oppressed Arab Muslim woman who escaped her repressive culture, religion, and family to embrace an American identity and individualism. Her media strategy confirms to viewers that "Islam poses a threat to women and the West" (Alsultany 2012, 85). Robert Pelley, the narrator of the 60 Minutes segment, calls for saving Prouty from Lebanon, Islamic terrorists, and Arab men in general: "Nada Prouty was to be deported to Lebanon, but because she would likely be killed by the very terrorists she investigated, the judge blocked her deportation" (CBS News 2010).

Prouty's gendered patriotic image is tied to US military strategies and notions of empire in the greater Middle East through the tropes of the oppression of the Arab and Muslim woman at the hand of the Arab Muslim man and the potential liberation available to Arab Muslim women in the United States. On the eve of the US invasion of Afghanistan, these exact arguments were mobilized to gain support from US feminists and liberals for an occupation that was framed as a civilizing mission (Abu-Lughod 2002; Khalidi 2004). Within the context of the war on terror, the repression of women by the Taliban, Islamic State, and other Islamicists is often cited as a reason for US military actions. Prouty's approach, then, is part of "a massively popular genre of writing about the wrongs other women suffer—particularly Muslim women" (Abu-Lughod 2013, 81–82).

Her assertions about Arab patriarchy and women's oppression follow the logic of subordination that has justified Western colonialism and military occupations in the region for more than two centuries.

Prouty intentionally mobilized a racialized, engendered sexuality in combination with US structures of power and patriotic discourses. The cover of her autobiography features a photograph of Prouty holding an American flag and giving a sultry stare into the camera while hair falls over her shoulders. She entices the reader to come hither, to buy and read her book. In this picture and in the photograph that accompanies the *Marie Claire* interview, her hair is markedly visible and distinctly unveiled. Yet, even without a hijab, Prouty looks exotic. She is sexually enticing, like many of the Orientalist nineteenth-century paintings and narratives which depicted Arab/Muslim women as oppressed, submissive, exotic, and secluded (Said 2000). Prouty's posture as a weak Arab woman in need of saving and/or seduction reinforces Orientalist framings of Eastern women. Moreover, as I discuss in detail below, in the text itself Prouty echoes Orientalist critiques of the Arab woman as oppressed, submissive, and abused, emphasizing the tyrannical patriarchy within her Lebanese family. As the title of her book indicates, her "redemption" came through her becoming an American patriot.

## Good American Woman, Bad Arab Girl

In her narrative, Prouty critiques the gendered norms of her Arab heritage and conforms to American gendered and racial social norms. She opens her autobiography in Lebanon, where her father and brother subjected her to physical, verbal, and psychological abuse. According to Prouty, men from Lebanon are prone to use violence to dominate female family members. She suggests that historical circumstances may have affected gender relations by postulating that the omnipresent and vicious factionalism during the civil war of her childhood contributed to men's unconscious need to assert their power in the one arena they could control: female family members. But ultimately, she argues that culture and society are to blame for the "submissive and self-effacing behavior" of Lebanese women, including herself when she lived in Lebanon (2011, 106). For Prouty, Arab women are complicit in patriarchal gendered subordination, and Arab society oppresses females. She remains the exception to the norm because she learned to stand up for herself in the United States (91).

Prouty strategically frames herself as a bad Arab girl who rejects the control of her father and brother to become a good American female patriot who fights for her adopted country. Her decision to become an American patriot and adopt an American-style feminist perspective is presented as an act of transgression against her natal Lebanese community. Although she sees herself as an exceptional minority woman who performs her loyalty and US citizenship through her work as a CIA operative and FBI agent, in fact she reinscribes the social boundaries that discipline social actors, especially women. Through claiming exceptionalism, she replaces one image of herself (that of an oppressed Arab Muslim woman) with another (that of a liberated and independent American) but does not challenge monolithic characterizations of most Arab women as oppressed or of Arabs as potential terrorists. Even Arab Americans are complicit due to their transnational connections and identification with Arab and Muslim cultures and communities.

While Prouty explicitly rejects the patriarchal family structure of her early years, she engages uncritically with assimilationist immigrant narratives and assertions of her feminism when addressing family and patriarchy within the United States. Her loyalty to family as a concept is central to her identity transformation from a good Arab girl to a bad Arab girl and good American woman. Prouty states that in the Lebanon of her childhood, her individual identity was not developed and her only peer group was her family. If family is the most important social institution in Lebanese society (Barakat 1993), then she was a good girl for not breaking with her family, the al-Aouars, in her early years. However, her "exhilarating journey" to the United States transforms her. After six years in the country, she ceases to identify with her Lebanese family and joins the FBI in order to "do something for my new homeland" and soon begins to call the FBI her "family" (Prouty 2011, 77). Although she criticizes "the Bureau's male dominated culture" for "an endemic gender bias," she also notes that it has "good intentions" (91, 187). She gets remarried, this time to a fellow CIA officer who is non-Arab and "white," lives in a Virginia suburb, and bears two children. In other words, she constructs herself as a normal American woman who achieves freedom and independence in suburbia. Her changing associations with family mark a rejection of Arab family and society and her transition to what she describes as an American liberated, independent womanhood, all the while maintaining a claim to family values and loyalty.

Yet, these gendered strategies to insinuate herself into an ambiguous American mainstream echo discourses about good and bad Americans, particularly Muslim Americans. Post-9/11, public debates and media representations of good and bad Muslims have posited that good Muslims are those who are loyal to the United States (Mamdani 2004). Similarly, Prouty promotes herself as a good, that is, loyal, American patriot with a new American family. Recounting her performance as a gun-toting spy who fights in the war on terror is crucial to this positioning. She gathers intelligence, wears a bulletproof vest, and carries weapons in Iraq, where she serves as a CIA operative with her husband. She even serves in a combat zone while pregnant and has her flak jacket adjusted to account for her belly. This badass-girl image is actually perceived as good because it taps into US cultural gender norms and citizenship narratives in which the good American woman can have it all: family, career, and independence while she wields weapons and fights against the enemy in the name of the country.

## Strategic Religious Identities

Prouty's stated religious choices reflect racial framings that are particular to the Middle East and Islam. In the United States, Prouty converts from the Druze faith, which she did not practice, to Roman Catholicism, ostensibly to share the faith of her third husband (Prouty 2011, 6). In Lebanon, her family's proximity to Maronites had exposed her favorably to Roman Catholicism prior to her immigration. She categorically rejects that she had any connection with Islam and that she might be or have been Muslim. She describes the Druze as a Lebanese minority that is neither Muslim nor Christian (105). This strategy reflects the religious politics in the war on terror and even an Orientalist binary of East-versus-West framings in which Islam is superimposed on "East" and Christian on "West." Prouty evidently felt that her religious affiliation was significant in this story and that she had to deny any form of Muslim identity to assert an American-only loyalty. Whereas a Hispanic woman would not be expected to disavow her Roman Catholic religion in order to prove her American loyalty, Prouty appears to have felt it imperative to deny any and all Islamic affiliations.

Prouty is not alone in denying Islam to prove loyalty to the United States and support for military interventions. Post-9/11, other women, among them Ayaan Hirsi Ali (2008), Nonie Darwish (2007), and Wafa Sultan (2011), have published books explaining their disavowal of Islam and embrace of a pro-Israel and/or pro-US foreign policy. These narratives posit redemption through the rejection of Islamic identities, Arab family, and/or culture in combination with an adoption of a US identity and patriotism. Like Ali, Darwish, and Sultan, Prouty understands the war on terror's anti-Muslim bent, and as with these women, her conversion serves to emphasize her claims to patriotism within a Western context and her full support for US foreign policy in the Middle East. Her religious identity positioning reflects anti-Islamic rhetoric in popular discourses and depictions of US patriots, particularly if the subjects and advocates are formerly Muslim women.

## The "Slippery" Druze

After moving to the United States, Prouty converted to Catholicism but continued to ascribe importance to her Druze heritage. There is a contradiction in how she represents herself as Druze and not Muslim. In her autobiography Prouty asserts, "You don't lose that identification easily; it's always part of you" (10). She says her Druze inheritance made her a better CIA agent because the Druze are "more versatile than the average Joe" (10). The Druze, she says, are "slippery" and make alliances according to the situation. Prouty boasts about how her "slipperiness" and Druze heritage contribute to her qualities as a good CIA officer.

> These people [who called her a "traitor" to the United States] have little idea of what goes into being a good CIA officer. The truth is you have to be a little slippery sometimes. You have to play a role, and it helps to be a part of the world your enemy is coming from. I tell you this: the Druze are respected in the Middle East. . . . [T]hey work in sensitive offices of several Middle East governments, or they emigrate and become decorated US Marines, or they line up with their Jewish colleagues in the Israeli Defense Forces. (10)

Prouty says that the Druze can be pro-Israeli, pro-US, and pro-Arab regimes to underline that she is not unusual for her sect.

It is precisely this Druze slippery characteristic that allowed her to be a chameleon and perhaps bolstered her claim that she was a CIA officer passing as an Arab. She states that she relied on her Arab features to help her move "without raising alarms through Baghdad's spider web of streets in search of contacts" (1). She contrasts herself with the "white males" who compose the majority of the agents but are conspicuous on the streets of Baghdad, Sana, Amman, and Islamabad. American males of European descent do not—indeed cannot—pass as indigenous in Afghanistan or Iraq. In Iraq she wore a black abaya, a full-length covering that hid her gun, US government ID, and bulletproof vest. Phenotypically and culturally, she was close to contacts and subjects and so was able to utilize her Arab looks, language skills, and life experiences in "playing the cultural role" of a Muslim woman while working as a CIA agent: "I knew that Arab males generally did not want to disappoint someone playing the cultural role of a 'sister.' So I often played that role and got what I asked for when other interrogators had been refused" (195).[4]

Prouty touts her ability to be slippery and to pass, and yet in reality she is an Arabic-speaking woman of Lebanese heritage—a fact that is not lost on the insurgents in Iraq. In her story, Arabs did not think she was passing; in 2003 anti-US insurgents directed an ambush against her precisely because she was an Arab woman working for the US government (210). The politics of passing reflect gendered, racial, and religious belongings that complicate a Manichean interpretation of the war on terror as consisting of two sides—"us" versus "them"—and make the intersections of multiple gender, racial, ethnic, and religious identities visible. Prouty has to position herself as passing despite her real background because structures of domination do not allow for the combination of authentic Arab and CIA spy.

## Ethnic Politics of Detroit

Detroit was a central character in the Prouty affair. Blogger Debbie Schlussel regards Detroit as a terrorist haven and a central threat in the war on terror. Schlussel has made liberal use of derogatory terms such as "Dearbornistan" to highlight the city's large Arab and Muslim populations and "Hezbos" to refer to city leaders whom she claims are Hezbollah supporters. She accused Prouty of espionage and being a Hezbollah mole in the United States government, blogging, "She spied. She spied. She spied" (Schlussel 2010). In the right-wing media campaign against Prouty, her Druze Lebanese heritage was conflated with Arabs, Islam (in particular with Shia Islam), and, by extension, disloyalty to the United States. In her media appearances at the time, Prouty writes, she stated that the government prosecutor in her case insisted that "all Shiʿa in Detroit are supporters of Hezbollah" (2011, 255). This conflation by her prosecutors and detractors of various Lebanese religious groups and political parties contributed to Prouty's public alignment with Roman Catholicism and distancing herself from any politics associated with Islam or Druze leaders.

While Prouty acknowledges that Arab Americans have been cast as "internal enemies" within the war on terror, she stops just short of calling her experiences "overt racism" for reasons related to her desire to elicit certain emotions from her readers. To call her experiences "overt racism" would require her audience to reconsider the moral trajectories of US foreign policy. Instead, as characterized by Mohja Kahf (2011), Prouty cultivates "the neo-Orientalist Pity Committee" by portraying herself as the victim who "casts off the shackles of Muslim patriarchy. . . . Then [she] runs into the arms of the waiting West" (112).

Prouty concludes her autobiography by arguing that Arab Americans were expendable fodder for political advancement in Detroit in the post-9/11 moment. At the time, Detroit was a major focus of national attention as a site of domestic foreign policy in the war on terror because of its large Arab American community. The FBI doubled the size of its Detroit office to step up investigations of the resident Arab American populations (Youmans 2011). Prouty first moved to the United States at age nineteen to join her elder sister and attend the Detroit College of Business. While waiting tables, Nada's sister met and later married Talal Chahine, who was suspected of financing Hezbollah through his restaurant chain, La Shish, in Detroit and Dearborn. He also allegedly participated in a tax-evasion scheme with Prouty's brother in which they funneled money to Lebanon and remitted it back to the United States tax-free. Prouty claimed that her brother gave false information about her in exchange for immunity from prosecution, sparking a full-blown FBI investigation that led to the discovery of the decade-old fraudulent marriage that had secured her US citizenship. According to Prouty, the Detroit FBI office was under a great deal of pressure to find terrorists and internal enemies, domestic foreign terrorists among the Arab American population, partly due to the office's rapid growth in the immediate aftermath of the 9/11 attacks. Prouty concluded that she became a scapegoat for local politicians who wanted to prove their political effectiveness in the war on terror.

Prouty was no outsider to the intricacies of US governmental politics and hierarchies. She knew that her claim to the more powerful CIA trumped the Detroit office of the Department of Justice, and she aligned her story with the CIA headquarters in Langley, Virginia. Perhaps she gave the name of a former CIA colleague to the producers of the 60 *Minutes* segment. Regardless, a former CIA station chief came to Prouty's defense on national television. The transcript reads,

> CBS correspondent: Bob Grenier met Prouty when he was CIA station chief in Islamabad, Pakistan. He retired in 2006 as a 27-year veteran who headed the CIA's counter-terrorism center.
>
> Grenier: She was involved with virtually all the high-profile cases during those years.
>
> CBS correspondent: And became one of this country's most experienced officers in doing all these cases?
>
> Grenier: Yes, she was. And in those few years that she actually had in service, she was tremendously experienced.
>
> CBS correspondent: Did she save American lives?
>
> Grenier: I think that is fair to say, yes. (CBS News 2010)

Surely the backing of a former high-ranking CIA officer influenced the American viewing public and strengthened the support for her case. When her supervisors at the CIA came to her defense on television and perhaps in the Senate hearing, they were not just supporting a former colleague; they were also refuting accusations by the local FBI and DOJ offices in Detroit. Through political alignment with the CIA, Prouty successfully navigated the power structures in which she lived and worked.

## Conclusion

A master-power narrative that accounts for the structures of power should be juxtaposed with intersections of race or ethnicity and gender in order to understand the positioning of Arab Americans in the present moment in the United States, particularly those who are accused of disloyalty to the United States. When Nada Prouty faced deportation, she had to dig into a thought arsenal of Orientalist tropes, racial stereotypes, and framings of Islam that positioned Muslims as the enemy. In a political and social minefield, Prouty made strategic choices of images that reflected simplistic binaries in identifications and gendered cultural norms, especially the American good woman and Arab bad girl. Markers of religion and kinship accompanied these tropes. Prouty chose to portray herself as a Roman Catholic rather than the potentially disloyal Muslim, and her family as the FBI and CIA. She used her American husband's last name, Prouty, rather than that of her natal family, al-Aouar. The importance of these binaries was underlined by her claims of passing as an Arab and by the invocation of her primary loyalty to the CIA and passionate support for and participation in the war on terror.

While Prouty's description of herself may have been authentic, it also served to mobilize support for her case. The redemption in this story lies in her having been saved by the US public and living in Virginia rather than being deported to Lebanon after having experienced a past associated with the Middle East, Islam, and Arab patriarchy. In the post-9/11 era, when the national allegiance of Arab and Muslim Americans is held under a magnifying glass, Prouty's media campaign illustrates how structures of power and domination are at work as a result of the war on terror and how post-9/11 domestic politics have molded a socially acceptable public identity for good Arab Americans.

## Notes

The epigraph is quoted from Prouty 2011, 1.

1. Hezbollah is a Shia Muslim organization based in Lebanon that is on the US State Department's list of terrorist organizations.

2. Schlussel's blog is published at http://www.debbieschlussel.com. She dubbed Prouty with the nickname "Jihad Jane" prior to Colleen LaRose using that as her online name and "self-proclaimed alias" before and after she was arrested and pleaded guilty to plotting to killing a Swedish cartoonist, providing material support to terrorists, and other criminal charges; Shiffman 2012. In this article I use "Jihad Jane" to refer to Prouty. The moniker obviously references the movie *GI Jane* (1997, Hollywood Studios), in which the first female Navy SEAL trainee survives the military's toughest training camp and fights Arab terrorists in Libya. The movie presents the main character, played by Demi Moore, as "blowing up Arabs" off the Libyan coast with fellow SEALs to prove that she is a "world-class warrior"; Shaheen 2012, 212–214.

3. In best-selling books, Arab American writers, including Rashid Khalidi (2004, 2013) and the late Edward Said (1993, 2003), have been deeply critical of Orientalism, US foreign policy, and the war on terror.

4. Comparisons could be made to Asmahan, another Lebanese Druze woman, who worked for the Allied Forces in the Middle East during World War II; Zuhur 2001.

## References

Abu-Lughod, Lila. 2002. "Do Muslim Women Really Need Saving? Anthropological Reflections on Cultural Relativism and Its Others." *American Anthropologist*, New Series, 104, no. 3:783–790.

———. 2013. *Do Muslim Women Need Saving?* Cambridge, MA: Harvard University Press.

Ali, Ayaan Hirsi. 2007. *Infidel*. New York: Free Press.

Alsultany, Evelyn. 2012. *Arabs and Muslims in the Media: Race and Representation after 9/11*. New York: NYU Press.

Barakat, Halim. 1993. *The Arab World: Society, Culture, and State*. Berkeley: University of California Press.

CBS News. 2010. "The Case against Nada Prouty." *60 Minutes*, CBS News, March 26. http://www.cbsnews.com/news/the-case-against-nada-prouty-26-03-2010/.

Darwish, Nonie. 2007. *Now They Call Me Infidel: Why I Renounced Jihad for America, Israel, and the War on Terror*. New York: Sentinel Trade.

Kahf, Mohja. 2011. "The Pity Committee and the Careful Reader." In *Arab and Arab American Feminisms: Gender, Violence, and Belonging*, edited by Rabab Abdulhadi, Evelyn Alsultany, and Nadine Christine Naber, 111–123. Syracuse, NY: Syracuse University Press.

Khalidi, Rashid. 2004. *Resurrecting Empire: Western Footprints and America's Perilous Path in the Middle East*. Boston: Beacon Press.

———. 2013. *Brokers of Deceit: How the US Has Undermined Peace in the Middle East*. Boston: Beacon Press.

Mamdani, Mahmood. 2004. *Good Muslim, Bad Muslim: America, the Cold War, and the Roots of Terror*. New York: Pantheon Books.

Prouty, Nada. 2011. *Uncompromised: The Rise, Fall, and Redemption of an Arab American Patriot in the CIA*. New York: Palgrave Macmillan.

Said, Edward. 1993. *Culture and Imperialism*. New York: Knopf.

———. 2000. "Shattered Myths." In *Orientalism: A Reader*, edited by A. L. Macfie, 89–103. Edinburgh, Scotland: Edinburgh University Press.

———. 2003. "Orientalism." *Counterpunch*, August 5. http://www.counterpunch.org/2003/08/05/orientalism/.

Schlussel, Debbie. 2010. "The Documents Don't Lie: The Hezbollah Spy's Lawyer v. Me." *Debbie Schlussel*, March 30. Blog. http://www.debbieschlussel.com/19840/the-documents-dont-lie-the-hezbo-spys-lawyers-60-mins-v-me/.

———. 2011. "Women's Mag Whitewashes (& Cheers) Hezbollah Spy." *Debbie Schlussel*, November 7. Blog. http://www.debbieschlussel.com/43955/womens-mag-whitewashes-cheers-hezbollah-spy/.

Shaheen, Jack G. 2012. *Reel Bad Arabs: How Hollywood Vilifies a People*. 3rd ed. Brooklyn, NY: Olive Branch Press.

Shiffman, John. 2012. "Special Report: Jane's Jihad; Confessions, Jail, and Unwavering Faith." Reuters, December 10. http://www.reuters.com/article/2012/12/10/us-usa-jihadjane-four-idUSBRE8B90ER20121210.

Shohat, Ella, and Robert Stam. 1994. *Unthinking Eurocentrism: Multiculturalism and the Media*. London: Routledge.

Sultan, Wafa. 2011. *A God Who Hates: The Courageous Woman Who Inflamed the Muslim World Speaks Out against the Evils of Islam*. Reprint edition. New York: St. Martin's Griffin.

Youmans, William. 2011. "Domestic Foreign Policy: Arab Detroit as a Special Place in the War on Terror." In *Arab Detroit 9/11: Life in the Terror Decade*, edited by Nabeel Abraham, Sally Howell, and Andrew Shryock, 269–286. Great Lakes Books. Detroit: Wayne State University Press.

Zuhur, Sherifa. 2001. *Asmahan's Secrets: Woman, War, and Song*. Austin: Center for Middle Eastern Studies, University of Texas.

# Paying for Her Father's Sins

FIVE Yasmin as a Daughter of Unknown Lineage

RAWAN W. IBRAHIM

Yasmin was a participant in a follow-up qualitative study of a group of Jordanian young adults as they transitioned from residential care to adulthood (Ibrahim 2010; Ibrahim and Howe 2011). Yasmin's case represents the generally difficult transition to adulthood from group homes that is experienced by many of her peers, especially girls born to unmarried mothers and those who do not know their families, upon reaching the age of majority. The phenomenon occurs within conditions of patriarchy as well as stigmatization, as conceived by Erving Goffman (1963).[1] This case study demonstrates how patriarchal and cultural values can be punitive toward girls who have been abandoned by or removed from their families. When, as young women, they leave group homes and attempt to function in the everyday adult world, they are stigmatized as "daughters of sin" and find that their participation in society is hindered.

Transgression is often viewed as a choice made by courageous women who deliberately push against or challenge boundaries of accepted norms that limit women. The case of Yasmin, however, sheds light on the implications of transgressions that are thrust upon some young women not through choice but rather as a result of dynamics within a sociocultural system that allows biological fathers to relinquish paternal responsibility and leave their offspring to shoulder the lifelong consequences. How do these young women, who are labeled "transgressive" by the circumstances of their birth, navigate these conditions?

I argue that those like Yasmin who leave group homes face two hurdles. First, there is a pervasive stigma attached to anyone, particularly any female, who does not fit within the patriarchal structure of Jordanian society. Second, Yasmin's case illustrates the vulnerabilities that women outside patriarchal structures face in all aspects — economic, social, and cultural — of their lives. Some of that vulnerability arises from inadequate mechanisms for the transition of young women from group homes to lives as independent adults.

## The Context of Leaving Institutional Care

Young Jordanians who age out of group care experience many of the disadvantages and challenges faced by those in other countries, such as transitioning into society at large with poor, if any, academic qualifications (Ibrahim and Howe 2011). As is common around the world, their experiences of leaving the homes tend to be "accelerated and compressed," "extended and abrupt" (Stein 2008, 296). Their preparation for aging out of institutional care is often patchy, leaving many vulnerable as they move into an unknown adult world. Some succeed, but many struggle. Specifically and importantly, the patriarchal and collectivist culture, with its deep-rooted values based on notions of honor, has a profound impact on many of these young people of both genders, but particularly on young women of unknown family. The most salient aspects and implications delineate the setting of Yasmin's case.

There exists a wide variation in how patriarchy manifests itself in different contexts. The discussion here focuses on a particular Jordanian context. Generally speaking, patriarchy prioritizes the rights and dominance of males and older women. Gender roles and relations are predetermined based on this hierarchy. In Jordan the system is rooted in family and cultural belief systems (Kawar 2000). At the same time, collective societies require people to define and understand themselves as members of a social group rather than as individuals. This collectivist outlook is one of the most important characteristics of Arab society: "the significance of collective units; not the individual, whose intrinsic value lies in being part of a greater — indivisible — whole, such as a family or group of kin" (Cinthio and Ericsson 2006, 37).

Several other important features stem from this outlook. In much of the Arab world, families are the primary safety net socially, economically, and politically (Joseph 1996), despite the impact of socioeconomic conditions and changes (Olmsted 2005). Families are naturally interdependent practically, morally, and emotionally. Care and support are generally reciprocated and take place vertically, between generations, as well as horizontally, among siblings and extended family. Traditionally, parents are said to care for their children well into their adult lives, and children reciprocate by taking responsibility for the care of their aging parents. In fact, such responsibilities can be a source of pride (Rashad, Osman, and Roudi-Fahimi 2005, 2). Arab youths transition out of the parental home for specific reasons, such as education, employment, or marriage; moving out simply to be independent is very unusual. In more conservative communities women leave the parental home only on marrying. Due to this interdependence, when young people leave home they remain supported, even if only emotionally. Societies with collective identities often broaden their affiliations and support to include the extended family, and this, combined with religious prescriptions, may even endorse the tradition of extending support to strangers, particularly those without their own natural support networks, such as orphans. However, since this support depends on the kindness, empathy, and economic means of individual families, it is precarious and uneven.

Family members have a collective responsibility for protecting the unity and honor of the family. The actions of an individual reflect not on that person alone but the family as a whole, and therefore the reputation and needs of the collective take precedence over individual needs. Family honor "is expressed by the generosity of its members, honesty of the individuals, courage, and bravery (of its men), and through the sexual purity of females (sisters, daughters, wives, and mothers)" (Kulwicki 2002, 84). Parents and male relatives are responsible for protecting their female kin from other males and principally for "controlling the potential sexuality of their unmarried daughters, which poses the greatest threat to family honor" (Kawar 2000, 146).

While the family is the main support unit, it can also pose a threat to the individual who is perceived as dishonoring the family (Cinthio and Ericsson 2006, 39). The repercussions can vary depending on attitudes, how conservative the family is, and how close-knit the community is. Responses can include concealing the misdeed altogether, casting out and disowning the individual concerned, withdrawing support, and maintaining basic support but inflicting social isolation. Those perceived as dishonorable and bringing shame are also at risk of abuse and, in extreme cases, murder ("honor crime"), which is believed to redeem the family honor.[2]

Children born to unwed mothers or as a result of other sexual taboos are often abandoned or placed in group homes as a means of concealing dishonor, victims not just of cultural norms but also of a legal system that affords power to men at a significant cost to women and children. Women who are pregnant outside of marriage may resort to abandoning their children because their partners refuse to marry them. If found out by authorities, these women may be imprisoned under administrative detention. Moreover, it is the father's legal acknowledgement of their offspring that separates legitimate from illegitimate children. Men may therefore pressure, coax, or coerce women into sexuality but leave them to shoulder the blame and responsibility for the offspring by either caring for children alone or abandoning them to alternative care.

The Qur'an clearly states that children of absent fathers—those born to unwed mothers—are not to bear their parents' sins; their fathers are to be found, and if this is not possible, the children are to receive a good Muslim upbringing as brothers and sisters in the faith. Caring for them is a social responsibility: "Assert their relationship to their fathers; this is more equitable with Allah; but if you do not know their fathers, then they are your brethren in faith and responsibility of your care" (*Sūrat al-aḥzāb* 33:5, my translation).

Many such children are indeed viewed and treated kindly by society even when they lack their own family support networks. Despite the clear religious expectations, though, many do pay for their parents' sins, as Yasmin's case demonstrates. They are seen and treated as products of "immorality and dishonor" (*mukhill lil-sharaf*) and of "dishonorable and immoral families" (*usar fāsiqa*), and as "children of sin" (*awlād ḥarām*), and they are legally termed "illegitimate children" (*aṭfāl ghayr sharʿiyyūn*).

## Cultural Implications for Young Adults Aging Out of Care

Children end up in group care for a variety of reasons, including neglect and abuse as well as abandonment to conceal dishonor. In these cases, separation from birth families is institutionalized and the names of the birth parents are concealed. Tribal and family links are severed by giving the children ambiguous family names. While the attitudes of the families of such mothers pose a dilemma for the authorities, the current approach to managing such cases overlooks the consequences for young people leaving institutional care and fails to question these family separation strategies.

Such children are placed in homes (*dūr riʿāyat al-aṭfāl*) that are relatively separate from mainstream society. There is a stigma attached to being a resident. At any given time, there may be between 800 and 1,100 children in residential group homes (colloquially termed "orphanages," *mayātim*), mostly in Amman. Children are admitted to the homes through police or court orders. All but five of the thirty-two homes are privately run by nongovernmental organizations. Some are faith-based, both Muslim and Christian. All the homes are licensed and monitored by the Jordanian Ministry of Social Development. The majority of the children are enrolled in the public school system. While there have been shifts in policy and practice to provide community-based care for children in need of alternative care, residential group homes remain the main form of substitute care. Earlier studies found that many of the group homes do not provide adequate psychosocial services, care plans, education, and vocational support (Gearing et al. 2013; UNICEF and Allayan 2002). The combination of ongoing psychosocial difficulties and shortfall in preparation and planning renders those aging out of the system vulnerable (Ibrahim 2010).

Awareness of the plight of these adolescents and young adults is increasing. In 2013 the Ministry of Social Development established a "postcare unit." Additionally, a few organizations have been founded to support this population with housing, education, work, and general psychosocial needs. Nonetheless, when young people leave group homes for "outside society" (*al-mujtamaʿ al-khārijī*), they take various routes. Some are supported, and others are coerced by the system into culturally acceptable roles and positions. Since young women are expected to live with families or spouses, this can entail forced return to abusive families and encouragement for young women to marry. One group home that has better resources sets up women without family in student dormitories.[3] Generally, these dormitories are closed; males are not allowed to enter, and the residents have curfews and must inform managers if they intend to spend the night elsewhere. Despite the restrictions, the dormitories do provide some freedom and opportunities to improve practical and life skills as residents care for themselves, and women generally report having good experiences in them.

Overall, growing up in care without the experience of family life and all it entails places the young people at a cultural disadvantage. Their postcare survival often depends on individual enterprise; yet that very independence presents young people without family, especially women, with a major problem in a patriarchal culture. Moreover, women experience stigmatization simply for having been a child in nonfamily care. They learn to be careful about saying too much too soon about their backgrounds to new acquaintances, potential employers, or prospective landlords. Participants in the study have described experiencing different forms of stigmatization. The two most common were being labeled "children of sin" or "illegitimate children" and being vulnerable to exploitation.

One advantage for women in patriarchal societies is that their male kin are responsible for looking after them; for a woman, this shifts from her father and/or brother(s) to her husband upon marriage. Still, even married women in Jordan can ask their brothers or other male relatives for support should they need it, particularly for protection from other men. Young women of unknown family do not have this normative backup, nor is there any formal follow-up from the group homes once they have left, making them easy targets for abuse.

## Yasmin's Case

Yasmin spent her first eighteen years in this type of group home. The group home where she was sent as an infant is considered one of the better facilities in a small town in southern Jordan. Her compound had approximately seventy children who lived in smaller groups in independent houses. In our study, some of her peers discussed the advantages and their appreciation of this type of model; others criticized it (Ibrahim 2010; Ibrahim and Howe 2011). The main factor contributing to the quality of the experience was the nature of the relationships they had with their main caregivers. As a teenager, Yasmin was transferred to an all-girl youth facility in Amman, the capital. Unlike other homes, Yasmin's youth home requires the teenagers to have summer jobs as part of their preparation. If the young people are not in the school system, they participate in either vocational training or full-time employment, as Yasmin did.

During periods of employment (summer or otherwise), it is expected that the young people pay for all of their expenses as part of their preparation for independent adult life. Any pocket money previously provided by the home is stopped. Participants in the research who grew up in this group home appreciated the policy in principle, though they noted that their wages were so meager that its application did not provide the intended education with regard to budgeting or allow them to save money prior to their departure. As with many of her peers, Yasmin's material needs were met, but her description of her experience reflects the home's failure to fulfill its responsibility in loco parentis, particularly to protect her from abuse and provide emotional nurturing: "I've never thought of positive things because the negatives overshadow the positive. . . . [T]he way they treated me was bad, to the extent that I became apprehensive of sitting with a social worker. I was to blame [for any problems], not the care-giver. . . . I even used to be afraid they'd beat us" when those in charge went to their own homes at night. By the time I met Yasmin, in the first set of interviews in 2007, she was eighteen years old, had been out of care for approximately four months, and had had two jobs, one at a fast-food restaurant and the other as a hotel cleaner. She was struggling to cope with long, physically demanding hours and low pay. She had no health insurance, no social security, and no savings; in fact, she barely had money for a snack. Her focus was on the most basic level of survival: maintaining shelter and securing food. Emotionally, she appeared lost and bewildered.

Although limited in scope, the preparations in place for leaving the group home upon reaching the age of majority were appreciated. Yasmin noted that residents were educated on issues such as personal hygiene, transportation, and budgeting. She discussed learning about social matters such as how to select friends and "not going out with men."

When assessing the strengths of her position leading up to the departure phase, Yasmin described compounded vulnerability. Although she was legally an adult, her life had been spent in a very sheltered environment that did not provide the nurturing needed to equip her with skills to cope independently. She failed her secondary schooling exams and had no interest in continuing her education; group home personnel secured a minimum-wage cashier's job at a large fast-food chain for her a few months before discharging her. They also found her a room in a privately owned female dormitory and paid the first three months' rent. Still, Yasmin was not emotionally prepared to leave the only home she knew and was afraid of having to fend for herself. "I was going to leave the orphanage and end up on my own in a society different from the one that I'd gotten accustomed to, where you have to depend on yourself."

Leaving institutional care is an especially important time and event. It represents separation from significant and familiar individuals and moving into an unknown and frightening adult world. Unlike her peers in the normative wider society, Yasmin was not leaving her home for goal-oriented reasons such as pursuing a career or education. Her leaving was preordained by her reaching legal adulthood. Also, unlike peers in the wider society who move out of parental homes, she did not have the opportunity to return or have a base to resort to during times of need. Yasmin's departure from care marked the end of her support. She had no choice of when, where, or how to leave.

> It was an ordinary day. Suddenly I got a telephone call from [the home], telling me that I should ask permission to leave [work] and go back to the orphanage because we were being discharged that day. I was shocked. I was not prepared to leave; it came out of the blue. They hadn't told us or prepared us for that day, not to mention that we needed to pack our things. . . . Certainly I cried, and I got scared because I wasn't ready to leave; they didn't give us the necessary preparation. This is why I got scared.

Yasmin discussed how difficult adjusting to outside society was. She described a self-imposed state of isolation from new encounters, such as with other young women living in the student dormitory and with colleagues at work. Like others in her position, she struggled to answer the most ordinary questions about her family.

> I worked alone; I learned how to do my job, but I didn't mingle with the other girls. I used to take my break alone; I wouldn't go out with any of the girls because I was afraid they might ask me questions that I wouldn't feel comfortable answering . . . about my parents and what they did for a living. That kind of question scares me, and I hate them, and I hate to socialize with people who have families and ask me about my parents.

Yasmin's main support network was limited to the surrogate sisters with whom she had grown up in care. Although they were equally vulnerable, their continued presence in her life was important. Yasmin and others described a strong sense of camaraderie, and being there for each other during emergencies. After a difficult start to the friendship, Yasmin described being close to one friend whom she had met while still in school during her time in group homes. Her friend was from society at large; Yasmin was curious to get to know the girl and her family, as she "wanted to know what it would feel like to have a family." Yasmin believed that her friend had implied that children in institutional care are children of sin, without understanding what that meant to her and others in her situation. Despite this painful start, she attempted to correct the misconception and gained an important relationship.

> When I first met her, she invited me to lunch and upset me with something that she said; she said, "You know you care home girls . . ." and at that point she'd meant to say that we were children of sin. I couldn't take it and immediately started to cry; society looks down on us, as we don't have any family, and people think we're illegitimate. So I made sure she understood that I had had no control over my circumstances and then explained what the care home was all about and how we had to depend on ourselves. I just tried to get through to her that I wasn't [bad] and that I was something totally different [good]. The care home raised me like her family brought her up, but [she said to the girl] when I'm discharged from the orphanage I'll be on my own. This is why I stay close to her. . . . [H]er mother even asks after me and takes an active interest in my life. I feel as if she's my family. And, indeed, to this day we're very good friends, and her family as well.

About six years later, in the second set of interviews, I asked Yasmin to rate her current position on a scale of one to ten. She positioned herself at five and stated, "It's getting worse, not changing for the better." She was unemployed again. A review of her career history revealed that she had struggled to maintain work. Several changes had been due to difficulty coping in challenging circumstances, particularly when she was mistreated by employers. This was compounded by the lack of legal and other support and not knowing how to protect her rights. Yasmin struggled to stabilize her living situation; within six years of leaving institutional care she had moved nine times and was eager to move again. Her instability was dictated by her financial situation and other circumstances. Emotionally and psychologically, Yasmin was in an extremely difficult position, but she was more eager to discuss other issues and her sense that she was repeating her mother's story.

Yasmin was raped by a regular customer at work at a fast-food outlet. He was a college student who continued to have intercourse with her by threatening to inform her dormitory manager that she had slept with him.

> I met [him] through the restaurant where I used to work. . . . I saw that this girl knew this person or that person. I wanted to be like the rest of the girls. . . . I went the second time [to his house], and he did what he was looking to do. . . . [H]itting was involved. He was violent. I was confused and shocked.

I stopped going to his house and left him. He started threatening . . . that he'd tell the residence and that he'd cause a scandal and tell what had happened in detail. So I started to go to his house, against my will, of course. It was what he wanted and under threat. Finally he left me and left the country.

Another male college student with whom she became sexually involved after that informed her that the man who had raped her was his friend and had passed details about Yasmin on to him and other male students before leaving the country. Despite this disclosure Yasmin believed that the second man cared for her and wanted to marry her once he graduated. She recalls, "And he proved to me that he truly loved me. . . . He agreed that after he finished studying we'd get married. . . . I stayed with him, and when I got pregnant I told him and he denied it [was his child]. . . . So he ignored me completely when I was in my third month, and I wanted an abortion in any way possible."

This man, like the first, left the country upon completing his studies, abandoning her to cope alone. She attempted to secure an abortion, although they are illegal in Jordan. She was taken to a doctor who knew that she was not married. He agreed to conduct the procedure but for a price she could not afford—and sex. She gave up on the abortion and "left it to God—whatever happens, happens."

Yasmin isolated herself further from most of her friends to conceal her pregnancy. She had to leave the dormitory. While the dorm managers sympathized, they had received a call informing them of her situation and were concerned about being implicated in any legal issues, such as child trafficking or concealing a crime. Friends introduced her to a married couple who suggested that she become the second wife. Yasmin believed this would enable her to register the birth of her child and she would therefore be able to keep and raise her or him. This was a critical issue for Yasmin. In a patrilineal society, if the child is not claimed by the father, as Yasmin was not herself, he or she is deemed "illegitimate." The agreement was that she would live with the couple and cover her own and her child's expenses; the marriage would be only on paper.[4] It was only a matter of time before the husband started pressuring her to have sex with him and threatening her with divorce, which would mean losing her shelter and her son. She succumbed, clarifying in our interview that she was being forced: "I told him, 'I don't want this. You're forcing me!'"

Yasmin's birth mother found her during that period, and Yasmin took her son and left the couple to move in with her mother and half-siblings.

The honeymoon period with her birth family ended shortly afterward. Yasmin described her relationship with her mother as volatile and dysfunctional. Her mother was verbally abusive and sometimes beat her when they disagreed. Then, during an argument, her mother informed authorities that Yasmin had become pregnant out of wedlock. Yasmin's son was removed from her care. Yasmin blamed her mother for having left the couple and losing her son; she did not want to live with her mother under these difficult circumstances. Nor did she want to be without a family again. Worst of all, she was preoccupied with repeating her mother's story. "I think about this a lot. Why is this happening to me? Why did I repeat the story? I've repeated my mum's story. I've turned out like my mother."

Yasmin expressed concern that her son was repeating her own fate. She certainly did not want him to grow up in institutional care, suffer as she had, and think ill of her, and she especially did not want him to be seen as illegitimate.

> Of course I want him. I carried him for nine months. I don't want him to be raised like I was. I don't want him to grow up thinking, "Your mother is immoral and bad." No, I'll tell him when he reaches a certain age so he can understand me and what happened to me. But for him to be raised the way I was? In a care home with abuse and insults? And for him to be of unknown lineage? No. I don't want the cycle to be repeated with him too. I want to raise him.

When reflecting on her predicament and position, she would go back in time to search for the source of her situation. Yasmin was angry with her parents. She believed that while she had been in institutional care, her parents had gotten on with their lives and only recently remembered her. "They married [different people] and moved on with their lives and had [other] children. Now they remember me?"

Yasmin was also angry at the system and questioned how she and others had been cast out and given no opportunity to obtain information about their birth parents. That information could foster reunification rather than losing all contact with their birth families. She asked, "Why didn't they tell me? If they had all that information, why didn't they say? What were they waiting for?" She said knowing about their families could help her and others assess their chances of perhaps living with kin, and especially for girls, doing so could help them fend off exploitation.

Although at times she expressed ambiguity and doubt about keeping her child, she also experienced new feelings, of anger, resentment, and pain at being separated from her son: "I never felt that way until I became a mother. . . . My life is over, a body without a soul. My future is lost. A piece of me was taken away. Who do I live for?"

When I asked what Yasmin saw herself telling me in five years' time, she said she would like to be able to share stories about her life with her son. Yasmin was as vulnerable, emotionally lost, and bewildered as she had been at the end of the first interview.

## Conclusion

Gender and social taboos led to Yasmin's admission to the institutional care system, and these circumstances make her one of the most disadvantaged children—a girl born to an unmarried mother who is rejected by her family and her society. Although eighteen years in group homes gave her some comfort, in that they provided her with places to live where her basic needs were met, they did nothing to alleviate her social disadvantage or help her manage it in society at large, particularly since she is regarded as the living product of a cultural transgression. The social strain and vulnerability that this introduces only add to the other challenges faced by these young people, and young women in particular, when they leave care. She exited the system without any support or network to help her in negotiating an independent life. She had to survive on her own but was unprepared for the trials and tribulations that she encountered as a woman without family in a collectivist society.

What could their years in institutional care have done to help Yasmin and other young people like her manage life as young adults? Cultural norms cannot be expected to change rapidly, but her story contains valuable lessons for practice and policy. Preparation for independence could have given her information about the difficulties of living alone and taught her simple skills to manage the difficult questions she would undoubtedly be asked. She would have benefited from a mentor or advocate to whom she could have turned for advice or support when managing difficult decisions and a safe haven to give her space when things went wrong. Even with this support, the stigma associated with her situation would have remained and operated as a force producing her economic and social marginalization and contributing to a generational cycle of further stigmatization. Nonetheless, a better system of care, and leaving it, could be one factor in improving the lives of these girls and women and breaking that cycle.

The predicament of these young people does not necessarily result in creating new generations of children of sin. However, as Yasmin's case illustrates, those who age out of the system are absolutely at higher risk of the abuse and sexual exploitation that lead to repeating their parents' stories. This risk increases stigma, reinforcing beliefs that such women are indeed bad seeds who produce more bad seeds, apparently justifying the construction that legitimizes the Jordanian normative social order. It is the system and society that are failing these young people by creating circumstances that produce bad-girl behavior despite their own personal goals as they embark on independent adult lives.

## Notes

1. Goffman writes that "society establishes the means of categorizing persons and the complement of attributes felt to be ordinary and natural for members of each of these categories"; 1963, 11. Stigma can be attached to those who are "disqualified from full social acceptance"; 1963, 9. Many such people are defined as having abnormal attributes that can be deeply discrediting, that is to say, stigmatizing. Despite the diversity within the Jordanian population, patriarchy in Jordan in its most general sense has clear parameters and expectations of society. These expectations stem from deeply rooted notions of honor and what is considered to be moral behavior—chastity and lawfulness. Young people with a history of institutional care, and especially those abandoned by or removed from their mothers, are associated directly with immorality. They are stigmatized for this, or as Goffman states, they are "deeply discredited" and therefore do not qualify for full social acceptance; 1963, 9.

2. Each year, between seventeen and twenty women reportedly are murdered in Jordan in the name of honor; Husseini 2009.

3. Student residence halls in Jordan are different from those in the West. Most are privately owned rather than belonging to universities; therefore, exceptions can be made for nonstudents. Most of the young women in these establishments come from areas within Jordan that are too distant for the students to commute on a daily basis, or they are young women from neighboring countries who have come to Jordan in pursuit of higher education.

4. It is unclear how this arrangement could have been of benefit to the couple, particularly the wife. Considering the legal risks in potentially being accused of child trafficking for falsely registering a child in one's name, and how the story unfolded with the husband, it may be safe to assume that the couple was suspicious and were taking advantage of Yasmin's vulnerability and desperate situation.

# References

Cinthio, Hanna, and Marcus Ericsson. 2006. *Beneath the Surface of Honour: A Study on the Interplay of Islam and Tribal Patriarchy in Relation to Crimes of Honour in Jordan.* Lund, Sweden: Lund University.

Gearing, R. E., M. J. MacKenzie, C. S. Schwalbe, K. B. Brewer, and R. W. Ibrahim. 2013. "Prevalence of Mental Health and Behavioral Problems among Adolescents in Institutional Care in Jordan." *Psychiatric Services* 64, no. 2:164–200.

Goffman, Erving. 1963. *Stigma: Notes on the Management of Spoiled Identity.* Englewood Cliffs, NJ: Prentice Hall.

Husseini, Rana. 2009. *Murder in the Name of Honor.* Oxford, England: One World.

Ibrahim, Rawan W. Z. 2010. "Making the Transition from Residential Care to Adulthood: The Experience of Jordanian Care Leavers." PhD diss., University of East Anglia, England.

Ibrahim, Rawan W., and David Howe. 2011. "The Experience of Jordanian Care Leavers Making the Transition from Residential Care to Adulthood: The Influence of a Patriarchal and Collectivist Culture." *Children and Youth Services Review* 33, no. 12: 2469–2474.

Joseph, Suad. 1996. "Patriarchy and Development in the Arab World." *Gender and Development* 4, no. 2:14–19.

Kawar, Mary. 2000. *Gender, Employment, and the Life Course: The Case of Working Daughters in Amman, Jordan.* Amman: Community Centers Association and Konrad Adenauer Stiftung.

Kulwicki, Anahid D. 2002. "The Practice of Honor Crimes: A Glimpse of Domestic Violence in the Arab World." *Issues in Mental Health Nursing* 23, no. 1:77–87.

Olmsted, Jennifer C. 2005. "Gender, Aging, and the Evolving Arab Patriarchal Contract." *Feminist Economics* 11, no. 2:53–78.

Rashad, Hoda, Magued Osman, and Farzaneh Roudi-Fahimi. 2005. *Marriage in the Arab World.* Washington, DC: Population Reference Bureau.

Stein, Mike. 2008. "Transitions from Care to Adulthood: Messages from Research for Policy and Practice." *Young People's Transitions from Care to Adulthood: International Research and Practice,* edited by Mike Stein and Emily R. Munro, 289–306. London: Jessica Kingsley.

United Nations International Children's Emergency Fund (UNICEF) and K. Allayan. 2002. *Evaluation of Rehabilitation Centres for Juveniles and Care Centres in Jordan.* Amman: UNICEF.

# The Making of Bad Palestinian Mothers during the Second Intifada

ADANIA SHIBLI

SIX

Examining media coverage of the Second Intifada reveals how Palestinian women came to be portrayed as bad mothers and even blamed for the killing of children by the Israeli military. The killing of children is not particular to this period, 2000–2005, or to the context of Palestine/Israel. Nor is holding their mothers accountable for their deaths. Blaming mothers for not being able to prevent external harm from reaching their children is a common practice and stems from certain social perceptions of motherhood. For instance, in their study of murdered children in the United States, Meyer and colleagues argue that gender role expectations lead to higher standards for women with regard to the care and protection of children, to the extent that they are blamed for the deaths of their children when they have nothing to do with the deaths (2001, 164). Mother blaming and the "bad mother" label in general have varied widely in content, cause, and consequence in different contexts and historical periods, but they often serve to shift attention away from a specific act, such as the killing of a child, to a person, the mother. Ladd-Taylor and Umansky (1998) trace the practice of mother blaming in the United States over the past century, noting its rise at times of social crisis. In these cases, mother blaming serves as an outlet for expressing anxieties related to change and an excuse for intervening in the social and cultural practices of nondominant communities. The Israeli claims against supposedly bad Palestinian mothers differ from these practices in the extremity of the accusations, that the women are sending their children to die in the fight against Israel. In this case, the state of Israel succeeded in constructing a narrative blaming mothers for the deaths of their children that was then widely circulated through Israeli and Western media outlets.

Choosing to focus on Palestinian mothers in fall 2000 stems from my personal experience as a producer and a translator for various television networks during the Second Intifada. This work allowed me to witness the process of turning Palestinian mothers into bad mothers who were culprits in the killing of their children. I offer here a detailed testimony of the process as it unfolded in a specific moment, tracing how a media narrative moved from scrambling to respond to a specific incident to ultimately arriving at this most powerful of strategies.

In an examination of the coverage of such incidents by various local and international media networks (Israeli, British, Swedish, and Palestinian), the killing of twelve-year-old Muhammad al-Durrah stands as a significant example. The general discourse on the victimization of Palestinian children by the Israeli army changed after his killing, coinciding with the emergence of an Israeli official narrative that claimed that Palestinians mothers were sending their children to death. I rely here on critical discourse analysis (CDA), a method often used in analyzing media texts, to highlight power strategies and techniques that may have been involved in the process.[1]

## The Killing of Muhammad al-Durrah

On September 28, 2000, accompanied by approximately two hundred Israeli policemen, Ariel Sharon, then leader of the Likud Party, "toured" al-Aqsa mosque in Jerusalem. The visit came as a provocation to Palestinian worshippers, who reacted with spontaneous demonstrations the day of the tour and the following day after the Friday prayer. During these demonstrations, seven Palestinians were killed and many injured by the Israeli forces. These killings, in turn, triggered widespread demonstrations all over Palestine, marking a new Palestinian uprising, which came to be known as al-Aqsa Intifada, or the Second Intifada. The main reason, though, behind this intifada was Palestinian frustration with the slow flow of negotiations with the Israeli government to end its military occupation of the Gaza Strip and the West Bank.

During the first month of these widespread, daily Palestinian demonstrations—which media outlets, national and international, covered continuously—Israeli gunfire killed an average of ten Palestinians and injured many more each day. Most of the people killed or injured were young, between sixteen and twenty-six years old, and several were children (Palestinian Central Bureau of Statistics 2001a,b,c). One event in particular that drew Palestinians out to the streets in the early weeks of the Second Intifada was the killing of a Palestinian child, Muhammad al-Durrah, which unlike other deaths was caught on camera.

On September 30, 2000, the second day of demonstrations, a France2 (F2) television crew filmed a father, Jamal al-Durrah, and his twelve-year-old son, Muhammad, close to Nitzarim junction in Gaza as they sought shelter from gunfire. The filming, which lasted for more than an hour and a half, caught the shooting that eventually killed the son and left the father suffering multiple injuries, mostly in his hand as he waved toward what he thought to be the source of the gunfire. An ambulance driver who was trying to save the two was shot dead.

The filming, though not the killing itself—many Palestinian children had been killed before by the Israeli army—was unprecedented. It caused a new discourse on the killing of Palestinian children to emerge, assisted by the media. A short, edited segment of this footage was broadcast by international television networks, affecting not only the Palestinian public but viewers around the world. Many politicians and officials reacted publicly to it, among them Bill Clinton, the US president at the time, who two days later said, referring to the footage, "I kept wondering if there was something the father could do to shield the child. . . . It was heartbreaking to see a child caught up in such crossfire." His remarks aired on October 2, 2000, on the Israeli Broadcasting Association (IBA) news program *Mabat* and other media. I offer a close reading of media coverage of the aftermath of the killing and that of later killings of children.

## From Denial of Responsibility to Soldier Victims

One of the main Israeli media outlets one might observe for shifts in the Israeli official narrative surrounding the F2 footage is the state broadcasting network IBA, which relies heavily on official sources. On September 30, 2000, the day Muhammad al-Durrah was killed while F2 was filming the boy and his father, the main evening news program of the IBA, *Mabat*, mentions the incident briefly. After announcing that "the Palestinians claim eleven people were killed" over footage of confrontations between Palestinian demonstrators and the Israeli army, the report continues with a high-ranking army officer saying, "The child who was killed did not die from the gunfire of Israeli soldiers." The footage of the boy's killing is not broadcast, and no information about the identity of the child in question is provided. Coverage then turns to other domestic news.

The brevity of the reference to the Muhammad al-Durrah incident and the lack of any F2 footage being aired shows IBA's attempt to ignore the killing. The broadcast did mention it briefly to address viewers who may have seen some of the F2 footage on another network. The IBA did so by including testimony from a high-ranking Israeli official who, acting as a trusted source, denied Israeli military responsibility.

This style of coverage points to a common strategy used by media outlets and known in CDA as "facework," that is, tactics normally used to maintain and negotiate an image in all communicative interactions. The main objective of facework is to manage and reproduce elite power and group dominance in the media by presenting the "self" positively. Within this strategy, negative aspects of the self are mitigated or excused (van Dijk et al. 1997). Moreover, it introduces mechanisms to prevent acknowledgment of one's responsibility for a problem (van Dijk 1993, 99). By including only the views of an Israeli army official who denied Israeli army involvement in the killing, the IBA mitigated an action the Israeli soldiers were widely perceived to have committed. Finally, by excluding the F2 footage from its broadcast, the IBA avoided showing images that would cast a damaging light on the Israeli army actions and having that footage reach a larger audience.

The next day, October 1, 2000, toward the end of the *Mabat* newscast and before a special edition on the Sydney Olympic games, a news report on the death of Muhammad al-Durrah was broadcast. It opens with the F2 footage, accompanied by a reporter's voice-over stating that television networks worldwide haven't stopped repeating this difficult image. The voice-over continues, "His name is Mahmoud [*sic*] al-Durrah, and they call him a new martyr. He came to join a Palestinian violent demonstration yesterday. Later, his father came to fetch him so he would not be injured." Then images follow from Muhammad al-Durrah's funeral and of his mother saying she could not believe it, that just yesterday he was in her lap. An Israeli army official appears after the mother, saying he feels sorry for the death of the child but that the Israeli army was not responsible for his death. The reporter repeats the same claim, saying that the Israeli army did not kill the child and adds that the army is checking the filming angles as well as the shooting direction to learn how the boy was killed. Finally, the reporter adds that kids twelve and thirteen years old are usually throwing stones at soldiers, and he ends with noting that eight children have been killed so far.

Though finally showing a report with the footage of the killing of Muhammad al-Durrah, the IBA placed this report toward the end of the broadcast, granting it less exposure. The reasons for including the footage in the newscast are presented at the beginning of the report itself: it had become impossible not to air it after television networks around the world had been showing it repeatedly for nearly two days. The strategy of reporting on news reporting offered a way to handle the footage and justify presenting it. In other words, the IBA shared it with its viewers not because it was newsworthy that a child was killed but because it was impossible to hide it any longer. This news style explicitly distanced viewers from relating to the boy's death itself, especially with expressions such as "they call him a new martyr," to insert an "other" (the Palestinians) between viewers and victim and mitigate any feelings of sympathy toward him.

The report goes on to clarify the images by introducing hypothetical reasons for the killing of al-Durrah, yet without relating them to any specific source. This is evident in statements such as "He came to join the demonstrators" and "The father came to fetch his son." The authoritative ring of these statements presents the event as clear, simple, and comprehensible. They also support a narrative that leads to the conclusion that the boy came to his death with his own feet, thus diverting viewers' attention away from the act of killing and any Israeli involvement in it.

Furthermore, when the Israeli army official categorically denied any relation between the Israeli army and the killing, then stated that the angles of the filming would be checked, he established the army as a reliable and impartial party rather than as a participant in killing al-Durrah. In fact, the only unreliable element that emerges from the report is the footage itself, which the presumably reliable official promises to check, deploying a language of neutral technology, that of filming angles. Viewers' attention is thereby diverted from the human implications of the incident to technical matters.

However, if after all this, some viewers continued to think the Israeli army was involved in the killing, an accusatory finger was directed toward the Palestinian children themselves, who "are usually throwing stones at soldiers" and hence not to be viewed as innocent after all. The final sentence of the report ("Eight children have been killed so far") is used to support that as well as to further diminish the significance of al-Durrah's death, suggesting that his was just one of the many unfortunate by-products of the conflict.

On October 2, 2000, the same report from the day before is shown without any alterations, also toward the end of the *Mabat* newscast. However, in the middle of the program, in a piece about how Israel's image in the world is sinking, the anchor mentions the incident and that Muhammad al-Durrah (his name is pronounced correctly this time) was probably killed by Israeli gunfire. An Israeli major-general questions how no soldier saw the boy, given that soldiers were positioned at five observation points. The anchor reports that even the president of the United States has referred to the incident publicly, after which Clinton's full speech is broadcast.

This edition of *Mabat*, unlike the previous two, includes a statement by an Israeli official confessing the army's probable responsibility for the killing while still framing the event as strange and incomprehensible, saying that if it was true that a soldier killed the boy, there must have been extenuating circumstances. The army official could not conceive of how the killing could have occurred. This view is manifest in the question "How could the soldiers not see him?" to imply that if they had seen him they would not have shot him. The rhetorical strategy of framing the death as unexceptional, as one of eight children killed, was abandoned here. Nevertheless, by then repeating the report from the day before, the confession of the army's responsibility in the killing was abandoned. In brief, now inconsistency and confusion emerged from the IBA's coverage of the killing.

On October 4, 2000, an IBA news program titled *Documedia*, which deals with media issues, includes a feature story about the al-Durrah incident. The story begins with what seems like archival images of Palestinians standing next to a wall and hiding behind barriers while throwing stones. The narrator says, "Palestinians are looking for excitement, hiding behind walls and fences. Otherwise, what would a father and his son be doing, hiding behind that block? Surely they did not come by accident to a war zone." The narrator's voice continues over images of Muhammad al-Durrah and his father crouching against the wall, with the father raising his hand: "The child is in panic and the father is crying, raising his finger in the direction of the soldiers." There is a cut to the end of the sequence, where the child is dead and his father injured, as the narrator concludes, "And that was the end of the story."

The feature story is followed by another about the father of an Israeli soldier who was badly beaten by Palestinians two years before near an Israeli military camp in the Ramallah area. Footage of that beating is shown, filmed by journalists present during the incident who recorded what was happening.

After the report, the father of the Israeli soldier appears as a guest on the program. He blames the journalists who watched his son getting beaten without interfering. The discussion thereafter revolves around the media's presence in life-threatening situations and whether it is ethical to film such incidents.

Here, the IBA resorted to a new attempt to deal with the al-Durrah incident while still relying on a facework strategy; it resuscitated a two-year-old story in order to contextualize the narrative of the Palestinian child victim within a larger narrative of Israeli victimhood. The comparison between the two incidents shows that "they" have committed bad things against "us." A father of one of "our" victims is brought to stand before viewers in counterpoint to the father of one of "their" victims. The juxtaposition suggests a parity and connection between two events from different circumstances, periods, and locations: child victim versus soldier, beating versus shooting death, the present versus two years ago, Gaza versus the West Bank. Moreover, the prime accusations are leveled at journalists. Their professional ethics are brought into question in an effort to shake trust in the ethics of filming violence. In sum, after the killing by the Israeli army is somehow acknowledged, the attempt to undermine the validity of the image continues in a new direction.

On October 5, 2000, a news story, once again aired at the end of the *Mabat* newscast, states that the child who was filmed in the famous image that shocked the world most probably died from Israeli army fire. In an interview with the father while he is still in the hospital, he says his son had said to him just before he died, "Maybe an ambulance will arrive. I'll wait and bear the pain until then." The father's sequence ends with his call upon everybody to stop the fighting and a statement on the senselessness of war.

In a move that builds on the parity established between Palestinian and Israeli victims in the *Documedia* story from the previous day, the IBA in this report resorts to the father's plea as a way to apportion blame for the violence. His call for an end to the fighting by everyone points indirectly to the Palestinians' responsibility for the recent events and not only to the Israeli army.

As the review of the day-by-day coverage reveals, one can find in the IBA's coverage of Muhammad al-Durrah's killing a constantly shifting take on the incident as an expression of the evolving narrative of the Israeli government around the issue of killing children. The coverage moves from a process of denial on the first day to offering various justifications and explanations for what might be behind the incident and the footage. Indeed, in his analysis of the coverage of the Second Intifada, Daniel Dor argues that Israeli media were unable to cover daily events of the intifada in a professional manner because of their heavy reliance on information from the Israeli government and high-ranking military officials (2001, 69).[2]

Israeli media outlets are not the only ones prone to forming their discourse based on the Israeli official perspective, as the BBC's coverage of Muhammad al-Durrah's death reveals. On September 30, 2000, the day he was killed, the BBC report starts with an extreme long shot of Palestinian demonstrators, and in the background the narrator says, "Their own police could not stop them." He adds, "Palestinian police itself had joined them fighting the Israelis." A medium shot follows of Israeli soldiers standing there calmly, then the image of Muhammad al-Durrah hiding behind his father. The narrator continues, "This man and his son Rami [sic] were trapped. The father tried to shield his son, but they both were shot and the boy died." The sequence consists of the father and the son hiding, then dust flying around them, obscuring what is happening. Then the correspondent appears standing next to some Israeli soldiers saying, "As we can see, Palestinians had approached Israeli soldiers, and the soldiers are responding with rubber bullets." In the entire report only once, and for very briefly, an Israeli soldier is shown actually shooting.

The way the Palestinians are filmed, shown mostly from a distance using extreme long shots, presents them as a mob with no clear personal features. They are also viewed from both the reporter's and camera's perspective as the attackers, while the Israeli soldiers are only reacting in defense and retaliation. The reporter achieves this perspective not only by stating that Palestinians approached Israeli soldiers and the soldiers responded with rubber bullets but also by locating herself physically next to the soldiers. Together, this leads to a reversal of responsibility for the action such that Israeli soldiers are the ones who are besieged by the Palestinians instead of a depiction of them as an occupying force operating within Palestinian territory. Eventually, this geographical and discursive dislocation suggests that the presence of Israeli soldiers is natural, while the Palestinians who resist their presence are the offenders, shown throwing stones or shooting. The soldiers are mostly calm, and when they shoot, they do so precisely and professionally. Within this context, the filming of Muhammad al-Durrah is then presented, without any reference to who had fired at the father and his son. The reporter suggests an equal probability of the boy having been killed by Israeli or Palestinian fire, leaving it to the viewers to decide. The reporter even refers to the boy by the wrong name—Rami instead of Muhammad.

n a follow-up report the day after the incident, pictures from Muhammad al-Durrah's funeral are shown. The narrator refers to the funeral as "fueling the furies of the people," while the boy is again referred to by the same wrong name. No further information on him is offered. The second main reference to him in the report is that "tragically, a child became a symbol of a protest." Women are shown at the funeral chanting, and the narrator translates their chants as calls for revenge. Next, the boy's father is shown saying that it was Israeli soldiers who shot at him and his son. The reporter states that Israel is denying responsibility for the incident and claiming that the boy died in an exchange of fire. Immediately afterward appear pictures of Palestinian fighters in Nablus shooting, and the reporter remarks, "Israelis became trapped themselves today in Joseph's Tomb." This segment clearly defines Israeli soldiers as victims, but in describing the al-Durrah case, the BBC report makes no clear references describing Israelis as aggressors or Palestinians as victims.

## The State Steps In

Initially, in the coverage by the IBA and the BBC, more attention was directed toward Muhammad al-Durrah's father than to his mother, who is shown only in one report and briefly. However, that would change within two weeks as a more cohesive Israeli narrative began to emerge. That narrative followed as the Israeli government took further public relations steps—such as appointing a team of spokespersons—to explain the government stance and respond to future incidents of the army's use of violence against Palestinian children. Among other duties, the team would be responsible for clarifying and even justifying Israeli military actions by spreading the claim that Palestinians were using their children as human shields, and, in particular, by blaming mothers for sending children to their deaths.[3]

The public relations team was formed under the supervision of Nahman Shai, the newly appointed official spokesman of the Israeli prime minister and best-known figure within the realm of promoting state public relations. He had served as Israeli army spokesman during the 1991 Gulf War (Dor 2001, 260). An article published by the English-language daily *Jerusalem Post* on October 20, 2000, summarizes this state of affairs:

> What changed the government's attitude, according to Nahman Shai, was the footage broadcast around the world of 12-year-old Muhammad al-Durrah being killed in the crossfire in Gaza as his father tried to protect him. That public relations nightmare ruined the good reputation Ehud Barak had been building up for months, and necessitated the appointment of Shai and a team of spokesmen.

In addition to appointing the team, the Israeli government sent Shimon Peres, then regional development minister, on an official visit to Europe on October 11, 2000, to explain Israel's position.[4] Peres was eminently suited for such a mission since he was seen in the West as a man of peace, especially after receiving the Nobel Peace Prize in 1994. Coinciding with the appointment of the team and Peres's visit to Europe, claims began to circulate that Palestinians were sending their children to death for propaganda reasons, that they were using their children as human shields, and that Palestinian mothers were encouraging their children to go out and die. These claims would circulate in the media whenever Israeli officials referred to a case in which a Palestinian child was killed by Israeli army gunfire. The argument is summarized by Captain Natan Golan, the Israeli Army official spokesman, who is quoted in the *St. Petersburg Times* on October 18, 2000, as saying,

> It's tragic to have a child fall in this violence, but there's no reason for the IDF [Israeli Defense Forces] to fire one shot if there's no violence. . . . All we're trying to say is "stop this incessant incitement to violence." We are dealing with a situation in which kids are cynically being used by being put on the front lines where they may be killed, maimed or injured. . . . If a young boy falls, it gives the Palestinians a lot of propaganda points.

Subsequent to the reiteration of similar claims by various Israeli officials, including Shai and Peres, other well-known and established critics affiliated with the center-left, like Shalom Yerushalmi, Dani Margalit, and Enat Gov, started replicating such allegations against the Palestinians as well. As a result the accusations gained further credibility and reached non-Israeli, mostly Western media.

## Western Media and the Emergence of the Bad Palestinian Mother

Just days after claims were spread that Palestinians used their children as human shields, the death of Palestinian children again became a central issue for Western media, this time with their mothers as the main focus. A number of networks began to address these claims either by shifting their focus and discourse or by directly investigating their validity. I examine here two reports, one by the BBC and the second by the national Swedish network Sveriges Television (SVT). As will be clear, the SVT report would have a major political effect on perceptions of Palestinians in the West.

The October 10, 2000, BBC report starts with the picture of a child in a surgery room, surrounded by doctors who, the reporter says, are "struggling to save the life of a Palestinian child who is claimed to be shot by Israeli army." The reporter then states that Palestinians are throwing stones and Israelis are responding with fire; the accompanying images now are extreme long shots of Palestinian demonstrators and medium shots and close-ups of Israeli soldiers. The filming is done mostly from behind the soldiers. Against this background, next appears in the foreground the reporter, who announces, "Israeli soldiers are on high alert," while Israeli soldiers are standing still. Then follows an interview with an Israeli official who explains that Israeli soldiers are not the ones who start the shooting. Immediately after this sequence come images of Palestinian fighters carrying guns as the reporter remarks, "They have lots of gear." The reporter adds, "Another Palestinian man was killed. He was claimed by Palestinians to be kidnapped and shot by Israeli settlers." Then the dead man's wife is presented as she stands next to her husband's grave, surrounded by her children. She says she will tell her son about what happened to his father and how he was killed so he can take revenge. The report moves afterward to the house of an Israeli settler's family to show an Israeli mother who is also surrounded by her children. The reporter says, "These children, too, are grieving the loss of their father." The mother says that the Israeli settlers would live with the Arabs, but the Arabs don't want to live with them. The report ends with the reporter standing next to a cave in which the body of the dead Israeli settler was found. The reporter gives the full name of the deceased settler, Hillel Lieberman, and says that he was kidnapped and killed by Palestinians from a nearby village.

On the whole, the reporter's language reverses the victim/victimizer roles of the news story by putting blame, responsibility, and guilt on the Palestinians while the settlers appear as peace seekers. This is supported when the Palestinian fighters are described as having "lots of gear," while Israeli soldiers are constructed as more reasonable and rational, retaliating rather than offending. One notices another strategy at work here: if an Israeli argument is not proven to be untrue, then it is considered to be true. This can be seen when Palestinians are assumed to be the offenders as long as they do not prove otherwise and more generally when most of what Israeli officials say about Palestinians is accepted as true as long as Palestinians do not supply evidence that such claims are false. This strategy is at work in claims that Israelis did not start the shooting and settlers want peace but Palestinians do not.

A clear disparity in where people are shown affects perceptions of what they say. The Israeli settler mother is interviewed at home in a calm setting. The Palestinian mother, in contrast, is shown next to the grave of her husband, where she is distressed and talking angrily and vengefully, thus establishing her as someone promoting violence and supporting the view that Palestinians are inherently violent and pass vengeance on to future generations. The reporter takes the woman's words as proof of her complicity in pushing her son to act violently rather than as an expression of the loss and anger people have in such a circumstances.[5] Finally, the report ignores any material that may divert attention to the violence of Israeli settlers against Palestinians that is suspected to have caused the killing of the Palestinian man. Instead, it uses the incident to show Palestinians' potential for violence, suggesting that they are definitely and inherently violent, in contrast to the peaceful and rational settlers.

The report a week later by the Swedish network SVT goes a step further by directly pondering the culpability of Palestinian mothers in the deaths of their children. The October 17, 2000, report starts with a close-up of the face of the corpse of a child who is being carried by Palestinian men. The reporter announces in a voice-over, "Bethlehem is burying thirteen-year-old Mu'ayyad Jawarish. Thousands of mourners are once more burying a boy killed by Israeli bullets." Then follow images of armed Palestinian fighters. The reporter continues, "These are armed phalanges who are showing off their weapons in a march, and among them are angry young men who are ready to die for Palestine." The sentence accompanies an image of Palestinian men shouting in Arabic, followed by an image of Palestinian women walking. "In the back are the women, mothers of these boys who condemn the Sharm al-Sheikh summit and shout to their sons, 'Don't be afraid! Your stones are like Kalashnikovs.'" Over a close-up of a woman marching silently, the reporter says, "In the very back walks Um Ahmad with her son Ahmad, who is thirteen years old. Ahmad also throws stones at Israeli soldiers, but today he is burying his best friend, Mu'ayyad Jawarish. We are following them on their way to give their condolences to Jawarish's mother in her house." The report cuts to Um Ahmad giving her condolences to the family of the deceased. The reporter continues, "But Um Ahmad is not sad that her neighbor lost her son." Um Ahmad says, "It is a very difficult feeling, but we have to sacrifice. The son of my neighbors is like my son; he is my son as he is the son of the whole nation. It is a very difficult feeling for every Palestinian mother to lose her son, but we also feel happy to give our sons as a sacrifice for the sake of our nation, for Palestine."

Next follows a clip of a few children and women walking together while the reporter explains, "For me it is just impossible to understand this, as it must be for Swedish mothers. And when we ask this very crucial question, 'How can she as a mother accept that?,' this happens." Um Ahmad is shown reacting to a sudden burst of shooting with a very worried expression on her face. The reporter continues over an image of Israeli tanks, "In Sharm al-Sheikh they have a ceasefire agreement, but here, outside Bethlehem, the shooting continues and the Israeli army is opening fire on Palestinians on a road used by Jewish settlers and where several Israeli soldiers were wounded in a fire exchange." Then the report returns to Ahmad walking and the reporter saying, "Protected by the wall, Ahmad is explaining the will to sacrifice, while his mother appeals to Swedish mothers to understand her." Um Ahmad is shown saying, "It is very difficult, but mothers will sacrifice their sons if they live our lives under our conditions. It is a little bit difficult, but we have to. Everybody has to participate, mothers, children, and old people. Everybody has to participate in this intifada and in the fight against Israel." Against a background of children throwing stones, the reporter resumes, "Ahmad, who just lost his best friend, does not hesitate to go out again." Then Ahmad is seen explaining his view, "We have to protect our country. Jerusalem is ours, and we cannot live without it." His mother then says, "The mother is always afraid. She's always afraid for her son. Yes, there is fear. It is a bit difficult, but I expect my son to go out and get injured and that the news about him getting killed might come; we are used to this. Palestinian people have gotten used to this. They have been living in constant sorrow and pain. We have never been happy. We have not encountered happiness."

It is immediately evident that the SVT report is focusing on questions beyond the event being covered, the killing of a thirteen-year-old child, Mu'ayyad Jawarish. Rather, the boy's death is instrumentalized to address a specific question: "Do Palestinian mothers encourage their children to die?" Such a strategy is known in CDA as "begging the question." The report constructs a specific narrative supported by a select set of images to convey a preconceived idea that may or may not correspond to the events that occurred. Suddenly, in support of the focus on Palestinian mothers, viewers see women taking part in funerals when previously mostly men have appeared in footage of Palestinian funerals. The slogans being recited are now uttered by mothers and directed to their sons. They are not seen as simply women, and appear to confirm an assumption that is voiced by the reporter without any evidence to support it.

Moreover, certain actors are presented as if they are involved in the incident when they actually have no central role in it; in this case, the neighbor of Jawarish, rather than Jawarish's mother, father, or other family member, is the focus in the report. At the same time, the report fails to indicate any questioning of a claim that originated with the Israeli authorities—namely, that Palestinian mothers are sending their children out to die. As a matter of fact, no one from the Israeli army, which is actually responsible for the killing of Jawarish, is included in the report. Rather, the report diverts viewers' attention from Israelis to Palestinians. Nowhere does the SVT report question the validity of the tactics used to quell the intifada and confront people throwing stones. What is more, the expected question to be debated in this case—"How can anyone kill a child?"—has instead become "How can one accept the killing of one's own child?" In answering that question, guilt is placed on Palestinian mothers for accepting the deaths of their children, rather than on the Israeli army for killing them. So, in developing its argument, SVT relies on presuppositions and unquestioned claims that act as subtle forms of implication; one proposition is assumed to be true for another proposition to be meaningful, while both may be irrelevant. And eventually, since the Israeli claim is not proven to be untrue, it is implicitly presented as true. The preconception of the report that Palestinian mothers are encouraging their children to die also results in the abandonment of common reporting practice, such as including information about how the incident occurred. In this case, Mu'ayyad Jawarish was shot by an Israeli sniper while walking home from school in his hometown of Bethlehem. However, this information is elided since it would show the irrelevance in this case of asking whether Palestinian mothers willingly send their sons to death.

It did not take long for the effects of the Israeli claims against Palestinian mothers to be widely adopted. Palestinian mothers finally emerged as bad mothers.

## The Political Consequences of Blaming Palestinian Mothers

By the end of October 2000, less than a month after the start of the Second Intifada, the Israeli claims started to be repeated by Queen Silvia of Sweden during a meeting of the World Childhood Foundation at the United Nations, at which she publicly criticized Palestinian parents for abusing their children in their fight against Israel. Reiterating the claim about bad Palestinian mothers, Israeli media took up Queen Silvia's comments and started to discuss the issue more freely and confidently. An October 27, 2000, article in the *Jerusalem Post* entitled "Child Sacrifice Is Palestinian Paganism" states, "After first buying into the Palestinian propaganda, the forces of morality in the world are beginning to confront this horrible reality. Sweden's Queen Silvia was among the first voices of conscience outside of Israel to raise this issue. In a meeting of the World Childhood Foundation that took place at the UN, she strongly criticized Palestinian parents for abusing their children."

Such open statements now replaced the confusion that characterized the reporting of the killing of children during the first week of the intifada. On the other hand, Palestinians would lose not only their children but also the right to protest their deaths, for according to the prevalent narrative, they had only themselves to blame.

Israeli officials succeeded in circulating the claim that Palestinian mothers were sending children to their deaths by avoiding images of the field, where the reality of occupation bristled with guns, armored jeeps, and tanks, and by deploying rhetorical strategies of debate, logical flow of language, and well-structured and carefully planned arguments in press conferences, official meetings, and media centers. They dropped any attempts at denying that Israeli gunfire was killing children, as such suggestions were bound to fail from the start. Instead, by assuaging guilt and suppressing international criticism, they normalized the killing and made it acceptable. They did so by using a discourse of familial love to position Israel as a civilized, democratic society like the Western nations it was addressing.

Media investigations into the validity of the Israeli claim that Palestinian mothers are sending their kids out to die, and the manner in which the investigations were carried out, fundamentally dehumanized Palestinian mothers in the eyes of viewers, turning them into bad mothers. Drawing on images of Palestinian mothers and excerpts of their views on sacrifice, Western media provided evidence of the claims originating from Israeli government sources.

How can one, though, understand these images if not through the framing provided by Israeli spokespeople and Western media? A word that holds a central position in these reports and is often used by the mothers is *shahāda* (martyrdom). Ahmed Baker, a Palestinian family counselor, explains that "to become a *shahīd* [a martyr] is very honorable. From a psychological perspective, [it is] to reconcile the possibility of death" (in Pitcher 1998, 18). Because Palestinians have been suffering under occupation for decades, their discourse has revolved around coping with repeated incidents of losing loved ones, be it a son, a brother, or a friend. They therefore share, exchange, and circulate the notion of *shahāda* that was established through a long process dependent on contextual metaphors and logic and familiar to Palestinian society. *Shahāda* was established as the highest and most honorable value a human being can reach. When one has nothing else to offer, voluntarily sacrificing one's life for something larger is a means of transmitting the sacredness of that sacrifice to oneself and one's loved ones (Shariati 1986, 236). In other words, framing the untimely death of a child or an adult as an act of *shahāda* is a means of organizing grief and maintaining a sense of self-worth under the conditions of violence and control that characterize the occupation.

Western journalists misrepresent the cultural value of sacrifice within Palestinian society when they present it as a cause for the deaths of Palestinian children. They victimize Palestinians once again by suggesting that a culture of bad motherhood is responsible for the deaths of Palestinian children. Despite journalists' claims to objectivity, by analyzing their discourse we find an alliance between culture, social beliefs, language, and power. Images of women tearing their dresses, singing, or ululating that seem to suggest that they are happy about the deaths of their children were taken out of context and, because they were misunderstood, were misrepresented and condemned.

Although no one can be entirely rational when answering questions about the death of one's children or other loved ones, Palestinian mothers have tried to respond to the Israeli claims, Western media, and Queen Silvia in a more organized and professional manner, such as via press conferences and demonstrations. On November 2, 2000, the liberal feminist organization Women's Affairs Technical Committee organized a press conference in Ramallah that hosted three Palestinian mothers whose children were killed by Israeli military, to reply to the Israeli and Western claims. As one mother put it, such reports turn Palestinians into creatures that lack even the basic animal instinct to love and protect their children. Reacting directly to Western accusations, the mothers argued that they did not want their children to die and did not tell their children to go out and die, but their children resisted and accepted martyrdom because of the misery and humiliation they experienced on a daily basis. The presence of Western journalists in these demonstrations and conferences was quite marginal; most reporters who covered the events were from the Arab media. One journalist from *The Guardian* attended the women's press conference, as did Israeli journalist Amira Haas from *Haaretz*. In short, Western media made no effort to investigate or challenge the Israeli claims regarding bad Palestinian mothers.

## Conclusion

Palestinians, in the end, were constructed as essentially different from Westerners: careless and unloving and prioritizing their commitment to violent struggle over the welfare or indeed the survival of their children. Paradoxically, through its discourse, the Israeli government succeeded in opening what appeared on its face to be a rational debate about what would otherwise have been unthinkable: the killing of children. The construction of Palestinian mothers as bad was fundamental to the dehumanization of Palestinians that allowed such a rationalization of violence to occur.

Meanwhile, the killing of Palestinian children itself would continue, manifesting as an ordinary thing. Death need not hide or mask itself any longer, and the Israeli government and officials need not deny it, as they would no longer be the ones who had to answer questions about how it happened and why. Rather, the Palestinians themselves, and especially Palestinian mothers, are expected to do so.

The Israeli government continues to kill children while alleging that Palestinians use their children as human shields. In the July 2014 massive Israeli military assault on Gaza, approximately a third of the more than two thousand Palestinians who were killed were children (Booth 2014). Such numbers can now be openly justified by Israeli politicians. On the eve of launching the attacks on Gaza, Ayelet Shaked, at the time an Israeli Knesset member and later appointed Israel's justice minister, posted on her Facebook page the following:

> This is an article by the late Uri Elitzur [a former adviser to Prime Minister Benjamin Netanyahu], which was written 12 years ago, but remained unpublished. It is as relevant today as it was at the time: "Behind every terrorist stand dozens of men and women, without whom he could not engage in terrorism. . . . They are all enemy combatants, and their blood shall be on all their heads. Now this also includes the mothers of the martyrs, who send them to hell with flowers and kisses. They should follow their sons, nothing would be more just. They should go, as should the physical homes in which they raised the snakes. . . .
>
> There is nothing more just, and probably nothing more efficient. Every suicide attacker should know that he takes with him also his parents and his house and some of the neighbors. Every brave Um-Jihad who sends her son to hell should know she's going with him, along with the house and everything inside it."[6]

Now, calls to punish these bad Palestinian mothers are repeated publicly by Israeli lawmakers, forming a political discourse that is in line with state violence.

## Notes

1. For more on CDA, see Fairclough and Wodak 1997.

2. Similar relations between the media and the military were created in the second US war in Iraq, in part through the practice of embedded reporting.

3. An earlier example of blaming parents for putting their children in harm's way is found in the discourse of South African officials in the period of apartheid. In late

1984, protests by South African people turned into a national uprising against apartheid, and thousands of them were killed, injured, and imprisoned; all along, South African officials claimed the government was engaged in a "reform" process that would give blacks some autonomy under total white control. Senior South African police officers complained at the time that their efforts to deal with the uprising were "hampered by the rioters' tactics, including the use of . . . children as human shields"; Parks 1985.

4. "Peres Travels Tomorrow to Paris and Will Try to Explain Israeli Stand" (in Hebrew), *Yediot Ahranot* (Ynet), October 10, 2000.

5. In contrast, an IBA report from October 24, 2000, on an Israeli child who lives in Gilo settlement, expresses his desire for revenge by calling on the Israeli army to stop Palestinian fighters from shooting at his area. In this case, a psychoanalyst refers to the boy's speech as a natural expression of anger that is rather healthy.

6. Translated in Abunimah 2015. Abunimah updated his original post of July 7, 2014, with a note that Shaked's Facebook post was deleted when she became justice minister. Also see Tharoor 2015.

## References

Abunimah, Ali. 2015. "Israeli Lawmaker's Call for Genocide of Palestinians Gets Thousands of Facebook Likes." *Electronic Intifada*, updated May 8. https://electronic intifada.net/blogs/ali-abunimah/israeli-lawmakers-call-genocide-palestinians -gets-thousands-facebook-likes.

Booth, William. 2014. "The U.N. Says 7 in 10 Palestinians Killed in Gaza Were Civilians. Israel Disagrees." *Washington Post*, August 29. https://www.washingtonpost.com.

Dor, Daniel. 2001. *Newspapers under the Influence*. Tel Aviv: Babel.

Fairclough, Norman, and Ruth Wodak. 1997. "Critical Discourse Analysis." In *Discourse as Social Interaction*, edited by Teun A. van Dijk, 258–285. London: Sage.

Ladd-Taylor, Molly, and Lauri Umansky. 1998. Introduction to *"Bad" Mothers: The Politics of Blame in Twentieth Century America*, edited by Molly Ladd-Taylor and Lauri Umansky, 1–30. New York: New York University Press.

Meyer, Cheryl, Michelle Oberman, Kelly White, and Michelle Rone. 2001. *Mothers Who Kill Their Children: Understanding the Acts of Moms from Susan Smith to the "Prom Mom."* New York: New York University Press.

Palestinian Central Bureau of Statistics. 2001a. Atfal Filastin: qadaya wa-ihsa'at. Ramallah. http://www.pcbs.gov.ps/Downloads/book670.pdf.

———. 2001b. *Atfaluna wa-l-intifada*. Ramallah. http://www.pcbs.gov.ps/Downloads /book694.pdf.

———. 2001c. *Kitab al-quds al-ihsa'i al-sanawi raqam 3*. Ramallah. http://www.pcbs .gov.ps/Downloads/book709.pdf.

Parks, M. 1985. "S. Africa Unrest Seen, out of Control Violence Called Worst in Decade; Police Appear Powerless." *Los Angeles Times*, June 3. Retrieved from ProQuest.com.

Pitcher, Linda. 1998. "The Divine Impatience: Ritual, Narrative, and Symbolization in the Practice of Martyrdom in Palestine." *Medical Anthropology Quarterly* 12, no. 1:8–30.

Shariati, Ali. 1986. "A Discussion of Shahid." In *Jihad and Shahadat Struggle and Martyrdom in Islam*, edited by Mehdi Abadi and Gary Legenhausen, 230–243. Houston, TX: Institute for Research and Islamic Studies.

Tharoor, Ishaan. 2015. "Israel's New Justice Minister Considers All Palestinians to Be 'the Enemy.'" *Washington Post*, May 7, 2015. https://www.washingtonpost.com/.

van Dijk, Teun A. 1993. *Elite Discourse and Racism*. New York: Sage.

van Dijk, Teun A., Stella Ting-Toomey, Geneva Smitherman, and Denise Troutman. 1997. "Discourse, Ethnicity, Culture, and Racism." In *Discourse as Social Interaction*, edited by Teun A. van Dijk, 144–180. London: Sage.

## "They Are Not Like Your Daughters or Mine"

Spectacles of Bad Women from the Arab Spring

AMAL AMIREH

M ost discussions of women and the Arab Spring that began in 2011 revolve around two sometimes competing but often overlapping narratives.[1] First is a celebratory one that points out the important role Arab women played in these upheavals as organizers and participants, how their participation cut across lines of class and generation, and how this involvement undermined social taboos and cleared a space for a new generation of Arab women activists. This narrative, which goes as far as to declare the protests the "Arab Spring for women," is part of a larger tendency that has dominated Middle East women's studies in the past two decades—a tendency to counter Orientalist stereotypes of Arab and Muslim women as passive victims by emphasizing women's agency and political participation (Cole and Cole 2011). It is a testimony to the success of this narrative that it has spread beyond scholars of the Middle East. In an article about the Arab Spring, American journalist Naomi Wolf is effusive about the "awakened women" whose fight for freedom could not be stopped (Wolf 2011).[2] Tawakkul Karaman, the Yemeni political activist who received the Nobel Peace Prize in 2011 and was dubbed "the mother of the revolution," is the official heroine of this story. The Kurdish women fighters defending Kobani against the Islamic State whose pictures were circulating in the press and on social media emerged as the most visible icons of this narrative in 2014.

The other narrative is a cautionary one that emerged after the Arab

Spring completed its first year. This is a skeptical narrative; it points out that despite women's participation in these revolutions, they are not empowered by their participation, and they in fact risk losing some of the hard-won rights they snatched from the toppled autocrats. There is a fear that the women of the Arab Spring will repeat the disappointing stories of Algerian, Iranian, and Palestinian women, just to name three prominent revolutions in which women played important roles but were nevertheless sidelined and disenfranchised (Ebadi 2012).

Both the celebratory and cautionary narratives have merit and are not mutually exclusionary. Indeed, Arab women have participated in the recent revolutions in their countries as they always did in the past. However, it does not follow that women's political participation automatically and immediately leads to changes in women's status and power in these societies. Even when women secure gains (education, right to vote, right to hold political office), gender and sexuality are much too complex to change overnight, whether in the Arab world or elsewhere.

They are less likely to change if revolutionaries insist that gender and sexuality are not central to the revolutionary process. Some observers contend that the Arab Spring was not about gender equality (Cole and Cole 2011; Pratt 2013). In response to some annoying if predictable Western media headlines that asked, "Where are the women of the Arab Spring?" some activists in the euphoria of the uprisings insisted that these revolutions were not about gender and sexuality per se. Therefore, such questions had a distracting agenda that sought to cast doubt on the achievements of these significant social movements. While one might reluctantly concede that gender and sexuality were not initially concerns of the Arab Spring, in the sense that there were no slogans specifically related to gender and sexuality raised at the beginning of the Tunisian, Egyptian, and Libyan uprisings, this degendering and desexualizing of the Arab revolutions is hard to maintain for revolutions that were from day one centered on the body.

For it was the burned body of Muhammad al-Buʿazizi in Tunisia and the battered body of Khalid Saʿid in Egypt that were said to instigate the uprisings in these two countries.[3] These bodies in pain mobilized people to put their own bodies on the line by demonstrating against the regimes of Zin al-ʿAbidin bin ʿAli of Tunisia and Husni Mubarak of Egypt. Al-Buʿazizi and Saʿid became, and continue to be, icons of the Tunisian and Egyptian revolutions, respectively. Their maleness, however, is relevant to their canonization. It is neither a coincidence nor a neutral fact, just as the "public space"—left vacant by postcoloniality and reclaimed by the Arab Spring (Dabashi 2012, 206)—is not genderless, either. It was and continues to be a masculine space.[4]

During the Arab Spring, women's bodies erupted onto this masculine space and disrupted it. Highlighting these disruptive moments, the reactions to them, and the ways they were deployed by different actors will help shed light on women's complex positions vis-à-vis nationalism and revolution and will problematize the two dominant narratives I have outlined. The eruptions are embodied by several women: the Tunisian Fayda Hamdi, a city employee accused of slapping al-Bu'azizi and sending him into suicidal despair;[5] the Libyan Iman al-Obeidi, who accused Qadhdhafi's men of gang-raping her; and the Egyptians Samira Ibrahim, who sued the Egyptian army for subjecting her to "virginity tests," Aliaa Elmahdy, who posted a naked photograph of herself on her blog, and finally the nameless woman who was beaten and disrobed by the Egyptian army and came to be known as "the blue bra woman," "Fatat al-Taḥrīr," or "Sitt al-Banāt."[6] The bodies of these women became sites where revolutionaries and counterrevolutionaries contested their claims regarding the nation's identity and future but also where state and communal patriarchies consolidated themselves.

I do not wish to talk about these bodies as sites and texts only but also as flesh and blood, something both feminist theorists of the body and postcolonial feminists have been ignoring (Davis 2007). By fleshing out the bodies of these women, I insist on the centrality of their gendered embodiment to their experience of the Arab Spring. It is the interaction between the discursive body and the flesh-and-blood body that forms the crux of my analysis. Focusing on individual women is one way to put the flesh-and-blood body back in the text and to counter the national and revolutionary impulse to symbolize and therefore abstract women, an abstraction that allows women to be present but renders them invisible.[7] These women became public spectacles on the national and international stages. The spectacular publicity that guaranteed the iconic status of al-Bu'azizi and Sa'id was the undoing of Fayda Hamdi, Iman al-Obeidi, and Sitt al-Banāt.[8] By becoming spectacles or by making spectacles of themselves, these women stepped into the limelight out of turn. They transgressed boundaries, and for that they were deemed unruly, to be speaking out of turn, in the wrong place. While I will consider them as contested sites and battlegrounds for competing discourses, my aim is not to reduce them to that but to keep them in sight as real women. These women's bodies resist becoming texts: any narrative retelling their stories and thus turning their material bodies into signifying ones is contradictory, full of silences and gaps, and incomplete. Their erupting material bodies, not their symbolized, abstracted, metonymized ones, form the sexual unconscious of the Arab revolutions. I will focus on two of these women: Fayda Hamdi and Iman al-Obeidi.[9]

## Tunisia: "The Slap That Was Heard around the World"

The official story of the beginning of the Arab Spring is by now well known. Muhammad al-Buʿazizi, a vegetable seller in the Tunisian town of Sidi Bouzid, publicly set himself on fire to protest unemployment, harassment by the police, and the lack of concern among government officials. In recounting al-Buʿazizi's tragic story, Tunisian, international, and social media explained that although al-Buʿazizi was unemployed for a while and forced to take a job beneath his qualifications,[10] what finally pushed him over the edge was being slapped in public by a woman police officer, Fayda Hamdi. That slap was unbearable to him. According to his brother, Salim al-Buʿazizi, the confiscation of his goods did not affect his brother; it was the slap by a woman that drove him to kill himself because, the brother explains, "it is known that in the tribe of al-Hammamt, any man hit by a woman we make him wear a dress."[11] According to this narrative, Muhammad al-Buʿazizi chose to set himself on fire because he did not want to wear a dress.

This story found traction with the public. Hamdi was vilified as a symbol of the abuses of the Bin ʿAli regime. Her picture wearing her official uniform circulated in the media and online, becoming evidence of her embodiment of an oppressive political system. She was a fitting symbol since much of the popular anger against the Bin ʿAli regime centered on his wife, Layla Tarabulsi. As a former hairdresser who rose to power with her husband and abused her position to favor her family members economically and politically, she received much of the ire of the public and emerged as a representative of the corruption of the regime, becoming the Marie Antoinette of Tunisia. A supposedly scandalous YouTube video circulated soon after the uprising to argue that she was the one behind Bin ʿAli's rule, since the video shows her telling her husband what to say.[12] Bin ʿAli is seen as the weak, emasculated husband who is manipulated by his domineering wife.

The emasculation of the head of state pointed to other emasculations in the body politic—emasculations for which working women like Hamdi were held responsible. The reactions to Hamdi's alleged confrontation of al-Buʿazizi reveal much gendered resentment. Early reports said she was single at thirty-five; later reports gave her age as forty-five.[13] This particular detail caught readers' attention and was used to demonize her. According to several commentators, she slapped him because she is ʿānis, that is, a spinster who hates men. Al-Buʿazizi should have found her a husband, perhaps rented one for her. She would have kissed his feet. One outraged commentator exclaimed, "Spinster at 35??? This is what happens when you ask for women's equality. She lost her femininity and istarjalat [became masculine] like Layla Tarabulsi and many of the women in Tunisia. She will die an unhappy spinster because no man will marry her." Another maintained that employed spinsters in particular are violent toward men. Several asserted that the slap was a result of the de-masculinization of Tunisian men because of the laws that favor women.[14] The anger on the street and online was palpable: people wanted her tortured, cut into pieces, burned alive.

As al-Buʿazizi emerged as the hero of the Tunisian revolution, Hamdi was seen as its villain. While Bin ʿAli was still in power, and as a measure to absorb the anger on the street, Hamdi was ordered arrested along with the two men who were working with her that morning. The men were soon released, but Hamdi was kept in jail with no charges and no trial for four months, a national pariah whom no lawyer agreed to defend. She was supported by her family, who defended her and tried to clear her name and free her by getting her version of what happened out. According to their story, she never slapped al-Buʿazizi because she realized that it would be unacceptable for her, a woman, to hit an Arab man. Her father insisted, "Our women never do such a thing. And my daughter has good manners and respects everybody." Moreover, she was a dutiful citizen who was merely carrying out her job by executing the local ordinances that regulated where street vendors could operate. She felt she was scapegoated by the Bin ʿAli regime (Day 2011). She was not a policewoman but a civil employee, and she did not carry a gun or a baton. She was among the first women to become public inspectors, a position of which she was proud. It was al-Buʿazizi who insulted her and violated her body; while resisting the confiscation of his goods, he hurt her hand, pulled her hair, and even grabbed her breasts, as well as assaulting her verbally by cursing God ("Kaffar alayya rabbī") and using lewd words that, her father said, "violate modesty and cannot be repeated" (in Bin ʿAtiyyat Allah 2011). According to one report, al-Buʿazizi told Hamdi as she was about to confiscate his scale, "You can weigh your breasts" (in al-Risunis 2011). His aggression was the reason she asked the two men to help (Bin Mahmud 2011).

With the support of her family, who at one point held a sit-in at the police station asking for either her release or a trial, and after she herself staged a hunger strike, Hamdi was eventually tried. A female lawyer, Basma al-Nasri, volunteered to defend her. The trial was centered on the infamous slap. Five witnesses testified that she had not slapped al-Buʿazizi, thus corroborating her version of the story. She was found not guilty and released, to the joy of her family and a small group of supporters who cheered the decision. News of her release was reported in the local, Arab, and international press.

Despite the legal vindication of Hamdi, she continued to be stigmatized as the woman who slapped Muhammad al-Buʿazizi. His family insisted on this version of the story even as they declared that they had dropped the charges. This insistence points to an important fact: the slap is constitutive of the myth of al-Buʿazizi and not incidental to it. If in the Tunisian town of Sidi Bouzid, al-Buʿazizi's self-immolation is to be seen as an act of courage and defiance against humiliation and oppression, then Hamdi's emasculating slap is essential. As some incredulous commentators asked upon the release of Hamdi, "If there was no slap, then why did he die?" When the well-known Egyptian journalist Waʾil al-Abrashi interviewed Hamdi in her house after her release, he too insisted on the slap despite the court decision and Hamdi's statements throughout the interview. "Your story is always going to be the introduction to the Arab revolutions," he tells her. His parting words leave no doubt as to what he means: standing face to face with Hamdi, he awkwardly thanks the hand that slapped al-Buʿazizi because it started the revolutions.[15] Thus after a long interview supposedly seeking the truth, al-Abrashi cannot let go of the fictional slap, even if now he has to thank the hand that started it all. *Interesting…* Hamdi, the flesh-and-blood woman standing in front of him, disappears. Only her hand is visible to him. This synechdoche of the woman is necessary to the mythmaking of the Arab Spring. It is as if without Hamdi's fictional slap, the Arab Spring was in danger of disappearing.

Al-Abrashi is not alone in seeing the woman he wants to see and not the one standing in front of him. Zainab Salbi, founder of Women for Women International, does the same. In an article in the *Huffington Post*, she reports on an interview she conducted with Hamdi as part of a documentary exploring the roles Arab women played in the Arab Spring (Salbi and Reticker 2013). So it is natural for her, she tells the reader, to seek to meet "the woman who contributed to the one event that led to the Tunisian revolution: Fadia [*sic*] Hamdi, the infamous city inspector whose confrontation with Tunisian street vendor Mohamed Bouazizi led to his self-immolation." At no point in her essay does Salbi mention the nature of the confrontation, referring to it only as an "explosive moment." The fact that the explosive moment was largely fictional is relegated to a hyperlink to a Reuters report headlined "Slap That Was Heard across Arab World 'Didn't Happen.'" Also, absent from the text itself is the fact that al-Buʻazizi had confrontations with two other city officials, whose names no one remembers, after his initial encounter with Hamdi.

*[handwritten margin note: mobilization for a movement...]*

Seeking to build Hamdi as a contributor to the Arab Spring, Salbi draws a portrait of a "powerful woman," "the strong figure in the family" who speaks with a "commanding voice" and is "aware of her historic role" as a product of all that is good and bad with the Bin ʻAli regime. She is "fiercely proud" of being among the first women inspectors in the streets of Sidi Bouzid. She is not reluctant to express her strong views; she dismisses a question about her "modern headscarf" "with the lightness most Arab women do when asked about the hijab," and she condemns politicians who want to legalize polygamy and child marriage and who blame working women for men's unemployment. Salbi fills her essay with colorful details and is eager to impart the sense of reporting on the ground and of having access to her subject, such as Hamdi's mother having facial tattoos and henna-orange hair and Hamdi's brother rocking his newborn child (Salbi and Reticker 2013). But curiously absent is any detail or discussion of Hamdi's imprisonment, hunger strike, trial, and release, all of which could be used to show Hamdi's vulnerability as well as her resilience and strength. Relegated to a hyperlink, that information is pushed outside the text. It is further undermined by being balanced by another hyperlink to a story, this one in *The National*, that repeats the myth of the slap (Thorne 2011). This omission is again necessary to maintain the feminist myth of the piece that Hamdi "contributed to a historical change in the Arab world" and that she continues to "*symbolize* Arab sentiment" (Salbi and Reticker 2013, my emphasis).

The mythical aspect of the story is perpetuated by the Arabic Wikipedia page about al-Buʻazizi. In that account, Hamdi not only slaps him but also hits him with a baton and curses his father. The article states that "she then went on to slap him in front of fifty witnesses. At that moment al-Bu'azizi felt humiliated [felt sorry for himself, *'azzat 'alayhi nafsuh*] and burst into tears of shame. He then yelled at the woman police officer, 'Why do you do this to me? I'm a simple person who wants to work.'"[16] It seems that no matter what Hamdi says or does to clear her name, she is not being heard. A recent headline in the *Telegraph* that supposedly quotes Hamdi blares the headline "I Started the Arab Spring. Now Death Is Everywhere and Extremism Is Blooming." Hamdi is quoted as saying, "When I look at the region and my country, I regret it all. Death everywhere and extremism blooming, and killing beautiful souls" (Addala and Spencer 2015). The article is accompanied by a close-up of Hamdi's sad face as further proof of her guilt. And guilt is all that is to be taken from this article. Arab media report Hamdi's words as a confession of guilt, a declaration of how sorry she is for what she did. Her face, tears, and even wrinkles are expressions of the agony of the guilty (al-Mahashir 2016; al-Sharif 2015).[17]

But in opposition to this mythologizing stands Hamdi's transformed body, now contained and domesticated. She returned to work, but instead of the pioneering job of walking the streets of Sidi Bouzid, she now has a desk job. The "snappy pilot-like cap of her police uniform" (actually an inspector's uniform) is replaced with a headscarf (Salbi and Reticker 2013). Hamdi eschews a political narrative about the freedom to wear the hijab that the revolution brought about. Instead, she explains that since her ordeal, her hair has been falling out. Her hand is also trembling. In a 2016 article in *Al-Shuruq*, Hamdi offers these markings on her body, her injuries, as material evidence of her innocence and to support her unspectacular version of the story. "He is a victim and I am a victim," she says, refusing to apologize (in Lakhal 2016). She insists that the slap is a myth manufactured by the media and that she wants to clear her name so she is not known by history—a history that is going to be taught—as the woman who slapped al-Bu'azizi and caused his death.

Hamdi's words and embodied self are eclipsed by her hand—not the trembling, traumatized one, but the mythical hand that allegedly started the Arab Spring and changed the course of history. She is a painful reminder that between the narrative celebrating the women of the Arab uprisings and the one lamenting their losses is a woman's injured body, a speaking body that is both transgressive and invisible. Seeing that body is revolutionary.

## Libya: When the Raped Body Speaks

On March 26, 2011, at the height of the rebellion against the rule of Mu'mar al-Qadhdhafi and shortly after NATO's military involvement, a woman entered the Rixos al-Nasr hotel in Tripoli, where the regime cordoned off foreign journalists, and told a dramatic story that was caught on video (Miller 2011). She recounted how she was kidnapped and repeatedly raped by men connected to the Qadhdhafi regime. Showing bruises on her body, blood on her inner thigh, and rope burns on her hands and feet as evidence to back up her words, she claimed that she was tied up and urinated and defecated on. Her story is told in bits and pieces, interrupted by the hotel employees and regime minders who try to stop her speaking and prevent the journalists from getting close to her. One of them brandishes a knife, another has a gun, and a woman screams at al-Obeidi that she is a traitor. In the most dramatic moment in the video, a waitress throws a dark coat over al-Obeidi's head. The distraught woman is whisked outside and shoved into a car that speeds away, leaving the journalists, who were pushed and punched, wondering if they would see her again.

That woman was Iman al-Obeidi, a twenty-six-year-old lawyer from Benghazi. The violence of those who sought to silence her was dramatic because it seemed to reenact the violence that al-Obeidi was alleging. As she was hustled out of the hotel, al-Obeidi screamed out, "See their brutality?" She thus underscored what is hard to miss—that this violence caught on tape and broadcast around the world lends credibility to the allegations of off-camera violence.[18] Had al-Obeidi launched her allegations calmly during a TV interview or at a press conference, the effect would have been very different. The high drama of the scene—al-Obeidi's screams, her disheveled hair, and the bruises on her face and legs—would certainly have gotten her some attention. But all this coupled with the violent reaction of the Qadhdhafi men and women in the hotel, her being pushed and shoved as reporters watched, the jostling and beating of journalists, the breaking of their cameras, and the car speeding away with al-Obeidi—all this lent her accusations a credibility that made her story top local and international news. Instantly, Iman al-Obeidi became a global icon testifying to the brutality of the Qadhdhafi regime and to the bravery of those opposing it.

In the weeks that followed, al-Obeidi did give calmer interviews to international media outlets like NPR and CNN. In these interviews she offered more details of her story, some of which were graphic. In an

April 12 NPR interview, which she gave in Arabic, listeners were warned in advance about the material they were going to hear (Garcia-Navarro 2011). The reporter, Lulu Garcia-Navarro, tells listeners that some of the things that al-Obeidi said were done to her are "so foul they can't be aired." The interview was conducted in Arabic in al-Obeidi's house by two women, Garcia-Navarro and an interpreter. In a teary voice that filters through the voice-over of the interpreter, al-Obeidi describes how several drunken men poured alcohol into her eyes and raped her. When she pushed them off her, the ringleader, whom she recognized as the son of a government minister, scratched her legs on the outside and inside. At this point in the interview, al-Obeidi "pulls down her shorts to show the fading marks."

In addition to presenting her body as evidence of the violence done to her, she verbally relates details of the rape: "During the rape they would close my mouth and stop me from breathing. They would put something over my head to suffocate me, and then they would rape me. My entire neck was blue because they were strangling me." As she continued to resist, the men tied her hands and legs. After much pleading, she was untied by another imprisoned woman. Al-Obeidi says, "I was naked the entire time. All I had was a see-through tablecloth around me, but I didn't care. I just wanted to get out of there." This is when al-Obeidi's rape and captivity narrative becomes a story of escape. After jumping out of a window and grabbing a metal bar, she charged screaming hysterically at the two African guards at the electric gate. Shocked at the unexpected sight of a wild-haired, naked, bleeding woman, the guards opened the gate for her and she escaped. The NPR reporter authenticates her narrative by stating that al-Obeidi "was physically examined and witnesses corroborated her story."

In later interviews, al-Obeidi would repeat these details and add more graphic ones. In a phone interview with CNN anchor Anderson Cooper in April 2011, a teary al-Obeidi reiterated the parts about being tied up and having alcohol poured in her eyes, adding that she was bitten and not allowed to eat, drink, or go to the bathroom. The most shocking moment in the interview occurs when she tells how she was sodomized with a Kalashnikov. As if to make sure that he heard correctly, a shocked Cooper asks, "They raped you with a gun?" She added that her rapists taunted her with "Let the men of the east [the rebels' stronghold at that time] know that they can't help you." At the end of the interview, al-Obeidi expresses her gratitude for the international support she had been receiving (in Cooper 2011).

Two days later, al-Obeidi spoke to Nic Robertson of CNN in an interview facilitated by Saʿdi al-Qadhdhafi, Muʿmar al-Qadhdhafi's third son. During this interview, which was in Arabic, al-Obeidi appears wearing a long, black abaya with some trim and a black head cover that shows some of her hair. She shows Robertson the marks on her arms and the bruises on her wrists and tells him that she has bruises all over her body. While al-Obeidi offered these marks earlier as evidence of the guilt of her rapists, she seems to offer them now as evidence of her innocence. Aware that people were blaming her for exposing her injuries in public, she defends herself by saying, "I was depressed," but then goes on to recount the details of what was done to her: "I was brutally tortured. They entered weapons in my body. They poured alcohol in my eyes. They prohibited me from traveling and beat me at the border. After the lies they were telling about me, I want to come out and defend myself. I want the whole world to know what's happening in Libya. Women felt for me. I'm an ordinary woman: Muslim, conservative, educated, from a good family." But a defensive al-Obeidi still demanded justice. She pleaded with her parents to pursue her case so she could join them in Benghazi; she thanked people around the world and CNN for following her case and checking with her every day; she demanded Saʿdi al-Qadhdhafi's help in clearing her name; and she defiantly declared that she wanted to sue Libyan state TV for libel (in Robertson 2011).

Al-Obeidi had good reason to be defensive. The moment she was whisked away by the regime's men from the hotel where she made her first accusations, the state apparatus began an orchestrated campaign to discredit her. The main instrument of defamation was the Libyan state satellite TV network Jamahiriya 2, through talk-show host Hala al-Musrati, attempting to destroy al-Obeidi's credibility. On March 30, 2011, al-Musrati declared on the *Libya on This Day* program that any woman who publicly says she was raped is automatically a liar: "Because we are Arabs, Bedouins, Libyans, we don't talk about rape." She reminds a national audience that a woman who claims rape may be killed by her family: "These are our morals, we Libyans. Free Libyans." She addresses al-Obeidi directly as a traitor, saying, "People like you lost Libya." Al-Musrati says she considers al-Obeidi worse than a whore because "the whore can be patriotic." She chastises al-Obeidi for "stripping naked" on non-Libyan news channels but refusing to appear on Libyan television. She concludes her session of character assassination by promising footage of al-Obeidi, unaware of being recorded, speaking candidly to her sister and a prison guard and telling the truth. The footage was promised for the next day (al-Musrati

2011a). In the following days, the promised footage did not materialize, but al-Musrati continued to defame al-Obeidi by calling her "a drunk" and "a whore," with a whole file about her, including damning pictures and videos. She predicted that al-Obeidi's honorable tribe would eventually disown her once they found out the truth about her (al-Musrati 2011b).

The "whore" label was used at all stages of al-Obeidi's defamation. During a press conference, when CNN's Nic Robertson asked about al-Obeidi, government spokesman Moussa Ibrahim replied, "Please, we are a conservative society. Let us not expose this woman" (in CNN 2011). Ibrahim earlier had acknowledged that al-Obeidi seemed to have been raped, but he added that this was "her line of work" (prostitution) and that the government had a file about her activities. He asserted that she was politically motivated since this was a criminal act that she was turning into a political act. And as if to seal the case against her, he said, "It's not like the whole Libyan army raped her" (in Garcia-Navarro 2011).

The Internet was used extensively for al-Obeidi's character assassination. A video was posted online that was ironically titled in Arabic "The Victim Iman al-Obeidi," showing a woman scantily dressed and dancing provocatively. It was meant to expose the real Iman al-Obeidi as immoral by focusing on her licentious body.[19] In discrediting the video, it was pointed out that the real Iman al-Obeidi had nine fingers and scars on her midriff, while the dancer did not (in Memmott 2011). Al-Obeidi's injured body was literally used as evidence to authenticate her identity, just like a thumbprint.

The government's attempt at depoliticizing al-Obeidi was an attempt to prevent the opposition from using her as a weapon against them. But it seemed to have the opposite effect. She immediately became the poster woman of the anti-Qadhdhafi revolution. One headline in a Libyan newspaper screamed, "She Is the Muslim, the Mother, the Soldier, the Protester, the Journalist, the Volunteer, the Citizen" (in Dabashi 2012, 185–186). Demonstrations in support of her were staged in the eastern part of Libya, at which some women carried signs with a caricature of Hala al-Musrati as a prostitute. Al-Obeidi's family supported her. Her mother gave an interview to Al Jazeera while wrapped in the Libyan rebel flag and carrying a picture of Iman. Iman al-Obeidi's mother insisted that her daughter was telling the truth and that the barrier of fear and taboo had been broken. She also revealed that she had received a call pressuring her to influence her daughter to change her story (McNaught 2011). In another interview, a female cousin declared her support.[20] But perhaps the most dramatic expression of support came from al-Obeidi's tribe in the form of a marriage proposal. While still in custody, al-Obeidi was married to a man who proposed to her through her family as a way to redeem her and declare her "honorable" despite the rape. The wedding celebration, from which the bride was absent, was reported as evidence of the support al-Obeidi was receiving from her tribe and family. The report made no mention of whether al-Obeidi accepted the marriage proposal and agreed to the wedding, as if that were an irrelevant detail. When al-Obeidi was asked later by Anderson Cooper about her groom, she said she appreciated the support, considering that hers is a conservative Muslim society and a woman who is raped is taboo (Cooper 2011). At no other point did she mention the husband in interviews, and she eventually got a divorce.

Al-Obeidi's honeymoon with the rebels eventually soured. Fearing for her life, she insisted on leaving Libya for Tunisia and then traveled to Qatar, where initially she was put up in a hotel and given some shopping money by the emir of Qatar. But after voicing criticism in May 2011 that she was not getting enough support from the rebels,[21] her privileges were soon revoked. The rebel leader Muhammad Shammam asked the Qatari government to send her back to Libya. She was physically assaulted and forcefully deported—an act Amnesty International condemned as a violation of international laws concerning refugees (2011). Her husband, Faraj al-Manbi, at one point spoke in her defense and accused the rebels of hostility toward her because she did not want to be used for their cause. He blamed them for not offering her any medical or psychological care (Mahmud 2011). In explaining the reason she was deported from Qatar, Ashraf al-Thulthi, the Libyan media spokesman in Washington, DC, explained that by insisting on repeating the "disgusting details" of her rape, al-Obeidi went against traditions and morals and alienated many people. He described her as someone who because of the trauma she had experienced, for which she received no help, had lost her "psychological balance" and was "caught in the crossroad between East and West" (Muhammad 2011). In short, she was asked to be silent, but she would not oblige and retaliated by criticizing some of the leaders of the Libyan opposition for wanting to use her and for not being fully supportive.

From that moment on, al-Obeidi managed to do what a dictator, a revolution, and a civil war had failed to achieve: she unified the country. Proponents and opponents of the regime united in vilifying her for damaging the reputation of Libyans by talking about rape. Following a Libyan online news article on April 15, 2012, one commenter declared, "We Libyans can kill and burn each other but will never rape" (*Al-Watan al-Libiyya* 2012). Therefore, she must be a liar. Her attackers from both sides insistently asked questions such as "How can she be honorable and expose herself like that?" and "It's not like she's the first woman to ever get raped!" and "She thinks herself a superstar!" Scandalous videos proliferated online parodying al-Obeidi's rape or claiming to show her in compromising positions.[22] What is evident in such reactions is the belief that a raped woman should be either silent or dead. It is incriminating enough that al-Obeidi survived the rape,[23] but what is worse is that she insisted on talking about it, something that was incomprehensible to her countrymen except as proof of guilt.[24] This reception of al-Obeidi echoes the reception Bangladeshi women raped during the war with Pakistan in 1971 had in their country. In that case, despite the government's efforts to rehabilitate the raped women by calling them "war heroines" and launching "marry-off campaigns," the women were rejected by the nation and retreated from public life into silence (Mookherjee 2006).

Insisting that her life in Libya was in danger, al-Obeidi finally succeeded in leaving her country a second time. She spent fifty-two days in a refugee processing center in Romania before getting political asylum in the United States in July 2011 with help from then secretary of state Hillary Clinton, who reportedly took special interest in her case (*Huffington Post* 2011). The decisions to leave her country and accept American sponsorship contributed to her guilt. Once she left Libya, she gave a few interviews about adjusting to her new life in Colorado but then seemed to disappear from public life.

After several years of silence, al-Obeidi reemerged in the news in 2015, but not as the subject of a feel-good story about the Arab woman rescued by a benevolent America from the brutality of her society nor as a hardworking refugee struggling to make a dignified life for herself in her new country. Rather, she again became a spectacle of unruly femininity, of badness. News articles accompanied by her mug shot describe al-Obeidi (who now goes by Eman Ali) as unemployed, destitute, and probably an alcoholic, suffering from serious mental health issues that manifest in substance abuse and aggression (Basu 2015). Since her arrival in the United States, she had been arrested six times for drunkenness and assault. After a jury found her guilty of attacking and injuring a woman in a bar, al-Obeidi was sentenced to six years in jail. While in jail, she attacked a fellow inmate and faced further criminal charges. Boulder District Judge Andrew Macdonald, while saying he believed that her previous trauma was at the root of her aggression and was concerned, told her at the sentencing, "You present a level of danger that needs to be addressed" (in Byars 2015). Not surprisingly, al-Obeidi's arrests and public transgressions in the United States are reported in the Arab media as conclusive evidence of her deviance and guilt. She no longer speaks of her rape.

Both Fayda Hamdi and Iman al-Obeidi have failed as icons of the Arab Spring. They do not fit the sanctioned scripts available to them—as silent victims or as outspoken women of courage. They neither attest to the success of the Arab Spring in mobilizing women nor signify its failure to do so. Their very existence, their material bodies, undermine them as metaphors and symbols. Hamdi's words and bodily injuries continue to be drowned by the myth spun about her ambiguous role, that she caused Muhammad al-Buʿazizi's death and was the spark of the uprising in Tunisia. Al-Obeidi briefly became a national symbol who was useful for mobilizing people against the Qadhdhafi regime, but she lost that status quickly by insisting on recounting the "disgusting details" of her rape. Like Hamdi, she was speaking up as a flesh-and-blood woman with real injuries. In doing so they were stepping into the glare of cameras out of turn and out of bounds, which made them not revolutionary icons of liberation but dangerous spectacles of unruly femininity.

## Notes

The quote I use as the title for this chapter, "They are not like your daughters or mine," is attributed to General ʿAbd al-Fattah al-Sisi of Egypt when he was the head of military intelligence, before he became president in 2014. He reportedly said it in response to accusations that the army subjected women protestors to virginity tests; Borkan 2011. Translations are mine unless otherwise indicated.

1. There has not been a consensus about what to call these upheavals; "Arab Spring," "Arab revolutions," and "Arab uprisings" are three of the contested labels. Throughout this essay I will use them interchangeably to reflect the contestation, ambiguity, and incompleteness of these movements. I am also employing the terms people used to describe what they were involved in.

2. Hamid Dabashi (2012) dismisses women academics and mostly quotes American journalist Naomi Wolf. It is ironic that in his praise of Arab women's agency he turns to Wolf as an authority on them and disregards their own voices.

3. Muhammad al-Buʿazizi was the Tunisian vegetable vendor who set himself on fire to protest ill treatment by state officials. Khalid Saʿid was the Egyptian young man who was beaten to death by police. His death inspired a social media protest campaign that then spread to the wider public.

4. The question that best represented the demarcation of public spaces as masculine was "Eh elli waddāhā henāk?" (What took her there, or why was she there?). The question was often asked by those who sought to deligitimize women's presence in the public square and justify any violence they may have encountered "there."

5. Media reports use the name Fadia, but Hamdi has been trying to correct that by saying her name is Fayda; al-Saʿidani 2011.

6. *Fatat al-Taḥrīr* means "the girl of Tahrir," a reference to Tahrir Square, where the Egyptian uprising was staged and where she was beaten up. *Sitt al-banāt* means "the best of the girls" or "the lady of ladies."

7. The literature is extensive on the national and revolutionary abstraction and symbolization of women, with the woman becoming a metaphor for nation. See, for example, Baron 2007; Kanaaneh 2002; Mookherjee 2008.

8. The deaths of al-Buʿazizi and Saʿid fixed their meaning, a necessary condition for their formation as icons. The women did not die, and therefore their meaning was not fixed.

9. One of the gaps in the narrative I offer results from not having direct access to these two women. I have neither met them nor interviewed them and have relied mainly on news reports about them.

10. Initial reports mention that al-Buʿazizi had a master's degree. Moroccan novelist Taher Ben Jelloun (2011) wrote a fictional account of al-Buʿazizi in which the protagonist has a bachelor's degree in history. Al-Buʿazizi's family later corrected those accounts and said he was a high school dropout; Al Jazeera 2015.

11. See Arabic Wikipedia, "Fadia Hamdi," https://ar.wikipedia.org/. An interview with Buʿazizi's brother is posted in Arabic at Al Bayda' Press 2011. Following an Al Jazeera article online, a commenter pithily expresses the importance of the slap: "When a man slaps a woman, she cries in her house. When a woman slaps a man, regimes and governments fall"; comment, Al Jazeera 2011.

12. "Fadihat Bin ʿAli wa-Layla al Tarabulsi" [The scandal of Ben Ali and Layla al Traboulsi], video, 4:43, posted to YouTube by "egyarab," June 15, 2011, https://www.you tube.com/watch?v=h9zJGdRKzls.

13. The Arabic Wikipedia page on Fayda (Fa'ida) Hamdi mentions in the first line that "she is still single"; https://ar.wikipedia.org/wiki/, accessed December 28, 2015.

14. Comments at *Al-Arabiya* 2011 and Lakhal 2012.

15. "Al-Haqiqa: Waʾil al Abrashi" [The truth: Waʾil al-Abrashi], Dream TV, July 6, 2011, posted to YouTube, https://www.youtube.com/watch?v=73uV4g5KaVc.

16. Arabic Wikipedia, https://ar.wikipedia.org/wiki/. I realize that Wikipedia is not an authoritative source, but I believe it is significant that such an entry exists and is not being challenged. The source given on Wikipedia for this information is an article titled "As-sharara allati ashʿalat diyar al ʿarab" [The spark that set Arab lands on fire], on Al Jazeera, March 27, 2011, http://aljazeera.net. As of December 2016 this account had not been challenged on Wikipedia.

17. For other news reports that continue to vilify Hamdi and read regret and guilt into her words and appearance, see El-Fagr 2015; Al-ʿAql 2015; ʿAbd al-Hamid 2015.

18. An online commenter said, "The truth of her story doesn't even matter when you see how the Gaddafi agents acted towards her, the international media, and freedom"; Channel 4 News 2011.

19. "Al-dahiyya Iman al-ʿUbaydi," video, 4:33, posted to YouTube by "Shabāb Libya," April 9, 2011, http://www.youtube.com/watch?v=KkOs3yu1RLQ.

20. "Update—Eman AlObeidi's Cousin Speaks Out," video, 7:01, posted to YouTube by "analibyana," March 28, 2011, https://www.youtube.com/watch?v=xJwYgNKFiNY.

21. On May 21, 2011, al-Obeidi posted a criticism of Shammam on YouTube in a self-recorded video (1:12), at https://www.youtube.com/watch?v=bnIUdiUpqck.

22. One such video, "The Rape of Iman al-Obeidi: Sound and Picture" (in Arabic), shows a woman, her face blurred, screaming, with Iman's voice-over from the hotel footage, as the woman is dragged on the ground, her abaya riding up and exposing her thighs; then she takes off her underwear and pushes her clothes farther up to expose herself. At the end, the maker of the video posted, "Iman and the Groom of Delight"; video, 1:07, uploaded to YouTube by "Nato rebels," July 12, 2011, http://www.youtube .com/watch?v=5cOXWxyav40&bpctr=1386089584.

23. A video used her survival against her, showing her walking around in Qatar as evidence of her guilt; "For Truth," video, 4:41, uploaded to YouTube by "For Truth," June 13, 2011, https://www.youtube.com/watch?v=AwLKWrQmnss.

24. I am in agreement here with Germaine Greer's assessment that al-Obeidi's "mistake was to survive. Because she did not die for other people's crimes, the offenses against her are now described as 'alleged.' Her credibility is shot"; Greer 2013.

## References

ʿAbd al-Hamid, Ramla. 2015. "Laytani lam Afʿal" [I wish I hadn't]. Al-Wasat, December 22. http://www.alwasatnews.com/news/1059493.html.

Addala, Radhouane, and Richard Spencer. 2015. "I Started the Arab Spring. Now Death Is Everywhere and Extremism Is Booming." The Telegraph (London), December 17. http://www.telegraph.co.uk/.

Amara, Tarek. 2011. "Slap that Was Heard across Arab World 'Didn't Happen.'" Reuters, April 19. http://www.reuters.com/article/us-arabs-unrest-idUSTRE73I6S020110 419.

Amnesty International. 2011. "Qatar Deportation of Eman al-Obeidi Violates International Law." News, June 3. http://www.amnestyusa.org/news/news-item/qatar -deportation-of-eman-al-obeidi-violates-international-law.

ʿAql, ʿAql-al. 2015. "Safiʿat al-Buʿazizi hazina nadima" [The woman who slapped al-Buʿazizi is sad, regretful]. Al-Hayat, December 22. http://www.alhayat.com/Opin ion/Akel-Il-Akel/12939480/%D8%B5%D8%A7.

Al-Arabiya. 2011. "Fadia Hamdi: Shurtiyya safʿat Buʿazizi fa-infajarat thawrat Tunis" [Fadia Hamdi: A policewoman who slapped al-Buʿazizi and the Tunisian revolution exploded]. January 19. http://www.alarabiya.net/articles/2011/01/19/134081 .html.

Baron, Beth. 2007. *Egypt as a Woman: Nationalism, Gender, and Politics*. Berkeley: University of California Press.

Basu, Moni. 2015. "Libyan Symbol of Freedom Now Facing Years behind Bars." CNN, July 23. http://www.cnn.com/2015/07/30/us/libya-rape-victim-sentencing.

Al Bayda' Press. 2011. "Qissat al-shurtiyya Fadia allati ja'alat Muhammad al-Bu'azizi yahriq nafsuh qahran" [The story of the policewoman Fadia who drove Muhammad al-Bu'azizi to burn himself]. January 21. http://www.albidapress.net/press/news_view_11596.html.

Ben Jelloun, Taher. 2011. *Par le feu*. Parish: Gallimard.

Bin 'Atiyyat Allah, Layla. 2011. "Sahibat Saf'at al-Bu'azizi tahawwalat min ramz al-zulm ila mulhimat al-thawrat" [The woman who slapped al-Bu'azizi turns from a symbol of oppression to the inspiration of revolutions]. *Al-Arabiya*, April 18. http://www.alarabiya.net/articles/2011/04/18/145897.html.

Bin Mahmud, Madiha. 2011. "Al-Bu'azizi: Jadid al tabuhat fi Tunis" [Al-Bu'azizi: The new taboo in Tunis]. *Babnet*, April 4. http://www.babnet.net/rttdetail-34132.asp.

Borkan, Betty. 2011. "Military Intelligence Head Says Virginity Tests Conducted out of Self-Defense: Amnesty." *Daily News Egypt*, June 26. http://www.dailynewsegypt.com/2011/06/26/head-of-military-intelligence-confirms-virginity-tests-conducted-out-of-self-defense/.

Byars, Mitchell. 2015. "Libyan Refugee Iman al-Obeidi Sentenced to Six Years in Prison." *Daily Camera* (Boulder, CO), September 2. http://www.dailycamera.com/news/boulder/ci_28742306/libyan-refugee-iman-al-obeidi-sentenced-six-years.

Channel 4 News. 2011. "Libya Crisis/Eman al Obeidi." March 26. Video, 3:11. Posted to YouTube by "Bruno Beloff," March 26, 2011. http://www.youtube.com/watch?v=WvfLJtdxkhc.

CNN. 2011. "Latest on Eman al-Obeidi." Video, 3:39. Posted to YouTube by "lapoesiadetusonrisa2," March 27, 2011. https://www.youtube.com/watch?v=JgAcFIgzOtk.

Cole, Juan, and Shahine Cole. 2011. "An Arab Spring for Women." *The Nation*, April 26. http://www.thenation.com/article/arab-spring-women.

Cooper, Anderson. 2011. "Alleged Libyan Rape Victim Speaks Out." CNN, April 5. Video, 14:35. Posted to YouTube by "Scarcemedia," April 5, 2011. https://www.youtube.com/watch?v=Tisai_ZKvpo&feature=youtu.be.

Dabashi, Hamid. 2012. *The Arab Spring: The End of Postcolonialism*. London: Zed Books.

Davis, Kathy. 2007. "Reclaiming Women's Bodies: Colonialist Trope or Critical Epistemology?" *Sociological Review* 55, no. 1:50–64.

Day, Elizabeth. 2011. "Fedia Hamdi Slap Which Sparked a Revolution 'Didn't Happen.'" *The Guardian*, April 23. http://www.guardian.co.uk/world/2011/apr/23/fedia-hamdi-slap-revolution-tunisia.

Ebadi, Shirin. 2012. "A Warning for Women of the Arab Spring." Commentary, *Wall Street Journal*, March 14. http://online.wsj.com/articles/SB10001424052970203370604577265840773370720.

El-Fagr. 2015. "Al-Mar'a al-Mutasabbiba fi indila' 'thawrat al-rabi' al-'arabi' tufajjir mufaja'a khatira" [The woman responsible for igniting the revolutions of the Arab

Spring bursts out with a new surprise]. December 18. http://www.elfagr.org /1964635.

Garcia-Navarro, Lulu. 2011. "Libyan Woman Tells Her Story of Rape, Uncensored." *Morning Edition*, NPR, April 12. http://www.npr.org/2011/04/12/135326966/libyan -woman-tells-her-story-of-rape-uncensored.

Greer, Germaine. 2013. "Guilt Poisons Women." CNN, March 12. http://www.cnn .com/2013/03/12/opinion/greer-women-and-guilt.

*Huffington Post.* 2011. "Iman al-Obeidi, Alleged Libyan Rape Victim Arrives in U.S — Report." WorldPost, July 29. Updated September 28. http://www.huffingtonpost .com/2011/07/29/iman-al-obeidi-us-_n_913148.html.

Al Jazeera. 2011. "'A'ilat al-Bu'azizi tasfah 'an safi'atuh" [The family of al-Bu'azizi forgives the woman who slapped him]. April 19. http://www.aljazeera.net/news /arabic/.

———. 2015. "Muhammad al-Bu'azizi . . . sharara atlakat al-rabi' al-'arabi" [a spark that ignited the Arab Spring]. Updated December 17. http://www.aljazeera.net/.

Kanaaneh, Rhoda Ann. 2002. *Birthing the Nation: Strategies of Palestinian Women in Israel.* Berkeley: University of California Press.

Lakhal, Farida. 2012. "Lam asfa' al-Bu'azizi" [I did not slap al-Bu'azizi]. *Al-Shuruq*, March 3. http://www.echoroukonline.com/ara/articles/123707.html.

Mahashir, Munira al-. 2016. "Fadia Hamdi." *Al-Yawm*, January 4. http://www.alyaum .com/article/4110884.

Mahmud, Khalid. 2011. "Ba'd tarhilaha min Qatar" [After her deportation from Qatar]. *Al-Sharq al-Awsat*, June 5. http://archive.aawsat.com/.

McNaught, Anita. 2011. "Eman al-Obeidi's Mother Speaks to Al Jazeera." Al Jazeera, March 28. Video, 2:40. Posted to YouTube by "apoesiadetusonrisa2," March 28, 2011. https://www.youtube.com/watch?v=ICH17sJNHg4.

Memmott, Mark. 2011. "Iman Al-Obeidi: 'I Want My Freedom.'" *The Two-Way*, NPR, April 12. http://www.npr.org/sections/thetwo-way/2011/04/12/135341289/iman -al-obeidi-i-want-my-freedom.

Miller, Jonathan. 2011. "Libya: A Woman's Desperate Cry for Help in Tripoli Hotel." Channel 4 News, March 26. https://www.youtube.com/watch?v=1iVH7wEwrJI.

Mookherjee, Nayanika. 2006. "'Remembering to Forget': Public Secrecy and Memory of Sexual Violence in the Bangladesh War of 1971." *Journal of the Royal Anthropological Institute* 12, no. 2:433–450.

———. 2008. "Gendered Embodiments: Mapping the Body-Politic of the Raped Woman and the Nation in Bangladesh." *Feminist Review* 88, no. 1:36–53.

Muhammad, Marwa. 2011. "Iman al-'Ubaydi yughadir Binghazi ila Malta" [Iman al-Obeidi departs Benghazi for Malta]. *Daoo*, June 5. http://www.daoo.org/news .php?action=show&id=33277.

Musrati, Hala al-. 2011a. "Gadhafi's Response to Victim Iman al-Obeidi." *Libya on This Day*, Jamahiriya (Tripoli), March 26. Video, 14:59. Posted to YouTube by "analibyana," March 26, 2011. https://www.youtube.com/watch?v=yVFeB4QN1xU.

———. 2011b. "Hala Musrati tarudd 'ala Iman al-'Ubaydi" [Hala Musrati responds to Iman al-Obeidi]. *Libya on This Day*, Jamahiriya, March 30. Video, 2:10. Posted to

YouTube by "Ynb0003," March 30, 2011. https://www.youtube.com/watch?v=YQ O5KmAiiGs.

Pratt, Nicola. 2013. "Egyptian Women: Between Revolution, Counter Revolution, Orientalism, and 'Authenticity.'" *Jadaliyya*, May 6. http://www.jadaliyya.com/pages /index/11559/egyptian-women_between-revolution-counter-revoluti%20.

Risunis, Sulayman, al-. 2011. "Al-Masaʾ taqdi ʿid al-fitr fi al-manzil al-jadid li-ʿaʾilat al-Buʿazizi bi-tunis" [Al-Masaʾ spends Eid in the new home of al-Buʿazizi's family in Tunis]. *Maghress*, September 4. http://www.maghress.com/almassae/139996.

Robertson, Nic. 2011. "Alleged Rape Victim Talked to CNN." CNN, April 7. http://www .cnn.com/videos/world/2011/04/07/robertson.rape.al.obeidy.short.cnn.

Saʿidani, Al-Munji al-. 2011. "Al-Shurtiyya allati ashʿalat ghadab al-tunisiyyin" [The police woman who angered the Tunisians]. *Al-Sharq al-Awsat*, April 29. http://arch ive.aawsat.com/details.asp?section=45&article=619324&issueno=11840#.WERowr tSmOI.

Salbi, Zainab, and Gini Reticker. 2013. "Fadia Tunis." *Huffington Post*, January 14. http://www.huffingtonpost.com/zainab-salbi/fadia-tunis-b_2448828.html.

Sharif, Lina al-. 2015. "Al-Marʾa al-mutasabbiba bi-indilaʿ al-thawrat al-ʿarabiyya: 'Laytani lam afʿal'" [The woman who caused the Arab revolutions: "I wish I hadn't done it"]. *Al-Shuruq*, December 18. http://www.shorouknews.com/news/view.aspx?c date=18122015&id=5df53c4c-32c0-424a-81ee-58c140d4cd1e.

Thorne, John. 2011. "Bouazizi's Courage Changed Nations." *The National*, December 17. http://www.thenational.ae/news/world/middle-east/bouazizis-courage-changed -nations/.

*Al-Watan al-Libiyya.* 2012. "Iman al-ʿUbaydi: Hawalu istighlali" [Iman al-Obeidi: They tried to exploit me]. April 15. http://alwatan-libya.com/more-21334-40.

Wolf, Naomi. 2011. "The Middle East Feminist Revolution." Al Jazeera, March 4. http:// www.aljazeera.com/indepth/opinion/2011/03/201134111445686926.html.

# "Fuck Your Morals"

## EIGHT

The Body Activism of Amina Sboui

ANNE MARIE E. BUTLER

Women have had nearly equal rights by law since the beginning of Tunisia as a modern nation-state.[1] However, this parity does not extend to many social systems in the country, where traditional gender roles and regulations remain difficult to disrupt. I will delineate how one young Tunisian activist, Amina Sboui,[2] has negotiated these contradictions through her self-portraiture. Sboui's images respond to conservatist developments in Tunisia around the Jasmine Revolution of 2010–2011,[3] as well as to what she has described as Internet images in which the bodies of women are violated and manipulated for the pleasure of the male gaze. When she came upon images from Femen, a Ukraine-based topless protest group, Sboui saw women using their own bodies in activism.[4] Her introduction to Femen and a subsequent conversation with Inna Shevchenko, one of the movement's founders and leaders, provided the impetus for Sboui to take action. With her first image, *Fuck Your Morals* (hereafter *Fuck*), Sboui purposefully transgressed one of the most important cultural proscriptions for Arab women, including Tunisians, by creating and disseminating a topless photograph of herself.

Born in 1994 in Tunisia and raised in a middle-class Muslim family, Sboui first uploaded *Fuck* to the Internet in February 2013 as a provocation against the oppressive social regulation of women and growing conservatism in Tunisia. She also intended to question the assumptions that she knew viewers of the image would make based on her toplessness. Although it was not her first radical action—she had been engaging in protests and demonstrations since her early teens[5]—the image received a level of reaction that she had not anticipated. While Sboui has released other images, I focus here on *Fuck* and two subsequent images by Sboui, *My Body Belongs to Me* (March 2013, hereafter *My Body*)[6] and *We Don't Need Your Di-mocracy* (August 2013, hereafter *We Don't*). In all three, Sboui dictates the terms under which her body will be viewed by inscribing slogans on her nude breasts and torso. The act of marking, indexed by the images, underscores Sboui's bodily authority and marries the slogans to her skin. Thus, she makes her body speak twice: once in terms of her assured and self-conscious portraiture and once in terms of her textual message. Through this dual communication Sboui's activism at once distances itself from the distorted feminism of groups such as Femen, with which she associated for a time, and from sexism in Tunisia. *Fuck* and *My Body* very much illustrate the first exploratory steps of Sboui's own negotiation of which feminist mode represents her best. They lack some continuity, although they respond to specific aggravations Sboui faced at the time she created them. Yet by the time *We Don't* was released, Sboui was demonstrating a dramatic shift in the level of confidence she portrays and in how she presents herself. The evolution seen in both presentation and audience engagement from *Fuck* to *We Don't* indicates Sboui's path toward her own tentative feminism—a mode of indigenous dissidence that draws on Western liberalist ideas of individual choice and is highly critical of patriarchal regulation of women's bodies in her home context, but that maintains an investment in local Tunisian conversations about gender and sexuality.

## Sboui's Femen Activism

In May 2013 Sboui was arrested and jailed after painting "FEMEN" on a cemetery wall in Kairouan, Tunisia. While in jail she began to reflect on Femen's organizational structure, funding sources, and tactics and came to realize that its operations did not align with her conceptions of activism. Although bare torsos are a type of transgression, with the removal of clothing Femen reveals its position of privilege. For Femen, nakedness serves as a gesture against social codes of white, bourgeois womanhood, but the critique Femen offers is therefore only always anchored to white, thin, able bodies. Anna Hutsol, another of the group's founding members, admitted to selecting specific types of women to belong to the organization based on race, able bodiedness, and physique, and Sboui confirmed that Femen holds casting calls like modeling agencies. In addition, Femen uses bare-breastedness to protest the supposed requirement of covering for Muslim women, and by criticizing Islam as a whole, it constructs itself against an other it has already created to fulfill its own needs.

After the release of her first image, Sboui's family removed her from public life and sequestered her on a farm.[7] In response, Femen called for an "International Topless Jihad Day," during which some protest participants enacted stereotypes of Muslim men by sporting towel head wraps, false beards, and penciled-on unibrows (Gordts 2013). The incident presented yet another reason for Sboui to break with Femen. Although she is secular, she has a basic respect for Islam. Unlike the Egyptian activist Aliaa Elmahdy, who left Egypt and continues to work with Femen, Sboui wants her feminism to be relevant to the Tunisian context. As a result, she cannot exclude the majority of people, including many friends and family members, who identify as Muslim to varying degrees.

While Sboui has cited Femen's disrespect for religious beliefs and lack of clarity regarding funding (Sboui 2014a), the biggest impetus for Sboui to leave Femen came when members of the group were called before a Tunisian court for engaging in a topless demonstration in Tunisia. Instead of supporting Sboui and the agenda they purport to follow, the women claimed to regret their actions and apologized for the demonstration. As a result, they were released from jail, while Sboui remained behind bars for three months. Sboui contends that the real challenge for committed activists is not the original act but the turbulence that follows it.[8] By reversing their opinions when challenged by a court, Femen members negated the potential effectiveness of their action. Sboui's disengagement from the group indicates an evolution of her own activism and understanding of feminist methods. She continues to use a specific aspect of Femen's protest, toplessness, yet no longer finds the group's platform useful for her purposes.

## Sboui's Body Incitements

Sboui uses the inherent politicism of her female body to make claims about her agency. These assertions disrupt expectations of male social and physical control over women's bodies. Elizabeth Grosz contends that "human subjects never simply *have* a body; rather, the body is always necessarily the object and subject of attitudes and judgments" (1994, 81; emphasis in original). If a body is always politically significant, then it is always signifying in itself. It is primarily through marking her nude torso with slogans that address gender-specific social oppressions that Sboui incites moralistic and misogynistic reactions; that is, she makes her body signify in a new way. The messages she writes and her toplessness work together to explode the social and cultural codification that still dictates how women may present their bodies.

The self-marking is a critical aspect of Sboui's dissidence. It was absolutely Sboui's intention to provoke reactions with her images,[9] and it is the presence of the text on her nude torso that incites controversy. Sboui indicates that she has tried to make herself her own subject by self-marking specific phrases that respond directly to her own precarity. If the body is constituted through marking by others, as in power relations that have control over the body by inscribing various positions onto it, then literal self-marking would be a form of reclaiming bodily control and therefore power.[10] Further, her body language indicates her attempts to assert her status as a subject. The same hands that wrote "Fuck your morals" underscore that message with their gesture. Sboui's full frontal pose and return of the viewer's gaze convey a directness that disrupts her construction as a passive sex object. It is Sboui's articulation of her authority to mark or display her own body that constitutes a claim to subjecthood, particularly through specific textual messages that use first- and second-person pronouns, thereby personalizing her statements.

In *Fuck*, Sboui stands against the white-tiled surface of a bathroom, wears no visible makeup, and her low-riding jeans sit below her hips. The words "Fuck" and "Your" frame her breasts, and "Morals" traverses her abdomen. She does not smile as she presents the middle finger of each hand to the camera, a gesture equally understood in Tunisia as in the West. She seems to smirk slightly and makes direct eye contact with the viewer, as if issuing a challenge. The quality of the image is amateur, but the "bathroom selfie" aesthetic fits with Sboui's casual appearance and the uneven lettering of the slogan, which she wrote on herself in gouache.[11]

At first, the use of English text in *Fuck* seems out of place because it is not directed solely to Franco-Arabic Tunisia, but Sboui used English because Femen uses mainly English to communicate its views and activities. Further, she wanted her message to be widely understood. It was thus the accessibility of the language that necessitated this choice. Writing in En-

**Figure 8.1.** Amina Sboui, *Fuck Your Morals*, 2013. Originally posted to Facebook but now widely available online. Reproduced with permission from Amina Sboui.

glish was undoubtedly a large part of what propelled her to international recognition. Had the text been in Arabic, her first image may not have seen the large circulation that it did.

She explains that she chose the phrase "Fuck Your Morals" because when she was a young girl, morals were presented as cultural requirements that were gender-specific. For example, she was taught to not be alone with a boy, to remain a virgin until marriage, and to not swear (2014b, 21–22). The image further responds to a growing conservative presence in Tunisia and recommendations regarding the moral behavior of Muslim women.[12] It is with the self-marked body that Sboui can demonstrate her authority by asserting that only she can make claims about her morality and sexuality. She describes morals as "social justice, personal morals, to act freely and conscientiously" (22). By marking her exposed breasts with the words "Fuck Your Morals," she directly rejects the connection between immorality and nudity. Sboui conceived of the image and promoted it in collaboration with Femen. Consequently, the composition of *Fuck Your Morals* very much aligns with Western liberalist ideals of individualism and choice. While Femen seems to present women with the choice to reveal their breasts in protest, the movement in fact coerces this ostensible choice through positioning itself as a liberationist endeavor.

*My Body Belongs to Me* was also produced in collaboration with Femen, but the text in this image can do the double work of according with the ideas of bodily autonomy and choice to which Femen subscribes while also stepping apart from Femen as a collective. The proclamation "My body belongs to me" can be read as distinct from Femen's co-optation of women's bodies in mass protest. Further, the Arabic text in the original version means that the message is not legible to most of Femen's members or audience. Text is written in four lines on her chest, two above her breasts and two below, on her abdomen. The script, which reads, "My body belongs to me, it is the honor of no one," is echoed by chalk markings above Sboui's head. Although cropped and therefore unseen in most of the circulated iterations of the image, the words "I am not a shame" are also written in Arabic in the original image.[13] In contrast to the English text of *Fuck*, the Arabic in *My Body* specifically counters personal attacks Sboui received after she posted her first picture. A critic of the *Fuck* image wrote, "You bring shame to your family. . . . Your body does not belong to you!" (in Sboui 2014b, 23). Statements like this indicate that the discord had more to do with controlling women's bodies than with nudity.

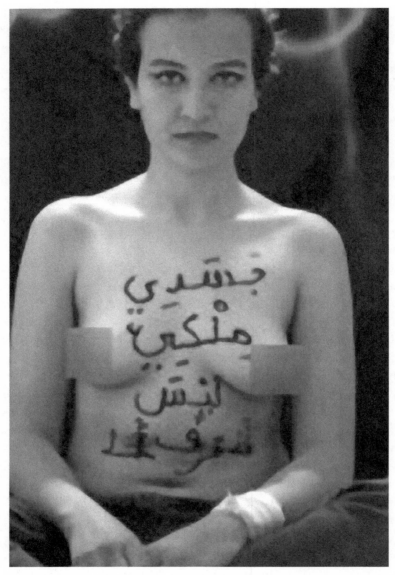

**Figure 8.2.** Amina Sboui, *My Body Belongs to Me*, 2013. Originally posted to Facebook but now widely available online. Reproduced with permission from Amina Sboui.

Sboui's first images have often been dismissed as pornographic. One explanation for this has been the taboo nature of public nudity for Arab women. Yet, had Sboui taken pornographic selfies and distributed them on the Internet, it is unlikely to have produced the same response; the images would have simply become several among trillions that inhabit cyberspace. Sboui made this point when discussing her first photograph: "I ask myself if the Tunisian people and Arabs in general are shocked by the photo or by its message. Because there are photos of topless Arab girls everywhere, on all the porno sites, and that, that does not pose a problem" (2014b, 29). It is not Sboui's naked breasts that threaten the social order but her self-representation.

In *My Body*, Sboui wears black jeans, dramatic black eyeliner, and bright red lipstick; her left wrist is bandaged with a white medical wrap. The bandage on her wrist appears to indicate self-harm, which raises the possibility of self-harm as the ultimate declaration of bodily sovereignty in response to trauma. Read thus, this visual clue bolsters her textual assertion and can be seen as a claim that she has survived the threats and verbal attacks since distribution of her first image. Her short, dark hair curls into the black background. Her face is soft, sweet even, yet her sexy presentation is a subversive part of her response. The question that must therefore be raised regarding *Fuck* and *My Body* is whether Sboui's topless strategy overshadows the textual message she wants to communicate. In other words, does she prove herself able, through her text and pose, to overcome the display of a sexually desirable body? While the male gaze is undiscriminating regarding the image maker's intent, Sboui disrupts this by putting her political message on her body: the text will be read if the body is viewed.

In a Facebook post from August 2013, Sboui states, "dimocracy because their dimocracy is not a democracy."[14] The image *We Don't Need Your Di-mocracy* was produced shortly after Sboui was released from jail in 2013, and her appearance changed from the earlier photos. Here, Sboui calls for the destruction of state hierarchy and power by marking her body with an anarchist symbol; a pink "A" in a circle appears twice on the front of her left shoulder just below her collarbone. She holds a Molotov cocktail as a symbol of revolution and destruction of the state. The English text "We don't need your dimocracy" is written on her chest and belly in black paint. The words "We don't" appear on her chest, centered above her breasts, with "We" on one line and "don't" directly below it. "Need," "your," and "dimocracy" appear on individual lines on her belly, below her breasts.

**Figure 8.3.** Amina Sboui, *We Don't Need Your Di-mocracy*, 2013. Originally posted to Facebook but now widely available online. Reproduced with permission from Amina Sboui.

Because "We" is on the same horizontal plane as the anarchist "A's" in another interpretation the text reads, "We [anarchists] don't need your dimocracy." The word "dimocracy" itself holds multiple interpretations. "Di" and "mocracy" are separated by Sboui's belly button, suggesting that the viewer should read them as separated. Further, when spoken aloud, the "di" in "dimocracy" is a homonym for "die," inviting an even more radical reading that alludes to the violence of revolution. To say that a democracy is actually a dimocracy not only subverts the English language but also highlights the hypocrisy of so-called democratic governments, such as that of former president Bin 'Ali, who had for decades manufactured the illusion of democracy while engaging in fraud and abuses of power. Something that it does not intentionally critique, however, is American and European interventions in the region. Although this might be one of the first connections a Western viewer might make, Sboui has denied any such intentions.

The emphasis on "di" as a prefix refers to two, twice, or double. In the postrevolution years when Sboui released her images, Tunisians were arguing about the direction their government should take. The concept of democracy was used to evoke a sense of progress. Yet for Sboui, people from the political right and left seemed to be equally united against her. No matter their opinions on the future of democracy in Tunisia, they could agree that, in Sboui's words, "this girl must disappear."[15] Sboui was frustrated that Tunisians were calling for democracy in their country while she was kept in jail on absurd charges. She was accused of encouraging civil war, using drugs, insulting a public agent, profanity, disobedience, forming a gang for the purpose of attacking people and property, committing a sexual act in public, possessing pepper spray, and defacing a cemetery. All but the last two charges were eventually dropped. Sboui was fined for the pepper spray and remains on conditional release for defacing a cemetery, although she had no news of any developments on this charge as of this writing more than two years later.[16] While the images she had produced up to that time were never officially brought to bear in her trial in May 2013, the excessive reach of the charges, and delays with the trial that kept her falsely imprisoned, point to the use of the arrest as a means to confine Sboui and her activism in order to send a message to other potential activists. Thus, Sboui is not wrong in her seemingly exaggerated claim that people wanted her to disappear. Her experiences in jail and with the Tunisian judicial system, combined with previous personal experiences of sexism in Tunisia, led Sboui to produce *We Don't*.

In this radical image, Sboui's attitude has changed markedly. A large tattoo is visible on each of her arms, and her hair is dyed a fiery orange. The appearance of the tattoos gives Sboui a tougher look, but they also function like the medical wrap in *My Body*. Kristine Stiles argues that tattoos can be visual markers of trauma. As with Romanian artists Lia and Dan Perjovschi's performance of bodily marking, Sboui's tattoos can be read as "[enunciating] the silence that is a rudiment of trauma and a source of the destruction of identity" (Stiles 1996, 45–46). Thus, in *We Don't*, Sboui is doubly self-marked, first by her tattoos and second by the writing on her body. Sboui started getting tattoos before she was arrested, but the appearance of the body art in *We Don't* and the medical wrap in *My Body* bolster the claim that Sboui passed through periods of distress but survived.

In addition to the pink "A's," another indicator of the image's anarchic message is the Molotov cocktail that Sboui uses to light her cigarette. Puffs of smoke drift away from her as she holds the slender cigarette in her pursed mouth. The color of the flaming cloth that protrudes from the neck of the clear glass bottle half-filled with orange liquid mimics the brassiness of her colored hair. Her stance is nonchalant, and her eyes are cast down at the cigarette she has just lit. The photograph is charged, however, with an intensity that leads the viewer to believe that in the next moment, Sboui might turn and throw the weapon. *We Don't Need Your Di-mocracy* has the most forceful visual language of the three images due to its connotations of violence, although in contrast with the other two, Sboui does not make eye contact with the viewer.

The lack of eye contact in *We Don't* is crucial to the purpose of this image. It is no longer necessary for Sboui to acknowledge the viewer in order to be clear that she owns her body. Here, she rejects the sexuality of *My Body* and conventional femininity as well. It is extraordinary that her "I don't give a fuck" nonchalance more than compensates for her disengagement with the viewer. In almost any other nude image of a woman, this would render her an object to be looked at rather than an active agent.

## Conclusion

Sboui no longer identifies herself as an anarchist or participates in anarchist groups. She discovered that anarchist systems run by men are not exempted from patriarchal structures and that, like Femen, anarchy does not serve her feminist-activist interests. While *We Don't* is not the culminating action from Sboui, it presents both a definitive shift away from Femen and a rejection of sexist domination. Positioning herself as independent of these ideologies, Sboui is able to emerge in her own strategic mode, which includes projects such as activism for undocumented workers in France and starting a new feminist magazine in Tunisia, *Farida*. The three images chart the faltering but eventually successful entrance of a new Tunisian feminism, one that espouses women's bodily autonomy and rejection of the specific aggressions of sexism and patriarchy and, finally, renounces Western liberalist interventions that re-create colonialist mindsets, such as misunderstanding the critical embeddedness of Islam in North African culture.

Amina Sboui does more than enact topless protest; she reclaims her body as a site of subjecthood through self-marking and specific text that forces the viewer to engage with the image beyond the superficiality of her bare breasts. With each self-portrait she demonstrates a step toward artistic maturity in terms of image quality and composition as well as content. The improvement in image quality arises from her use of professional photography equipment in the latter two. The change in attitude from the first to last, however, is more complex. In *My Body*, Sboui counters others' reactions to *Fuck* by portraying herself as defiant but still approachable. She sexualizes herself in an attempt to renew her claim over her own body regardless of its appearance or desirability. In *We Don't*, however, her entire demeanor changes. She is tough and angry, and she does not care what anyone has to say about her. She still makes claims regarding bodily sovereignty through marking but no longer returns the gaze of the viewer to express her own subjecthood. Nevertheless, she is able to achieve a strong measure of self-determination through her body language, specific markings such as tattoos and anarchist symbols, the message written in gouache, and the Molotov cocktail. In *We Don't*, she achieves a radical visual politic by combining nonchalant nudity with the threat of violence.

Sboui's relationship to the viewer through text and image content is specific and personal. She relies on her own singular body to signify her rejection of the imposed shame of Arab women regarding nakedness. As a result, her transgression is more culturally disruptive than Femen's protests and, further, less based on heteropatriarchal constructions of feminine normativity and sexuality. If the measure of success for Sboui was to disrupt, as she has claimed, then she has succeeded. But this is not her only goal. Perhaps with *Fuck*, the execution was not careful enough to sustain the message under the weight of the critiques that followed. The second and third images help to explicate the first, and when viewed as a group, the three show a quickly maturing activist.

## Notes

1. President Habib Burqiba instituted the Personal Status Code (Code de Statut Personnel, CSP) in 1956. The CSP provided women rights under the law that many other North African and Middle Eastern countries still do not have. The progressive agenda of Burqiba is primarily responsible for an attitude of bourgeois women in Tunisia regarding their status as total equals with men in social and political theaters. For a detailed history of the development of women's rights in modern Tunisia, see Charrad 2001.

2. Sboui is sometimes referred to in various media as Amina Tyler. This is only a nickname, however.

3. A series of uprisings culminated on January 14, 2011, forcing President Bin 'Ali from office. For a detailed analysis of prerevolution factors, see Clancy-Smith 2013.

4. Sboui 2014b, 16. For extensive critiques of Femen, see O'Keefe 2014 and Dornhof 2014, as well as many items in their respective bibliographies.

5. See, for example, Sboui's account of trying to protest the Israeli occupation of Gaza; 2014b, 64–66.

6. An uncensored version of this image was not available, as Sboui no longer had the original image.

7. Sboui describes her frustration regarding this time of isolation and control by her family but admits that her family was trying to protect her; 2014b, 31–32.

8. Amina Sboui in discussion with the author, June 19, 2015.

9. Ibid.

10. Foucault is summarized in Winter 2001, 175.

11. Sboui in discussion with the author, June 19, 2015.

12. Amina Sboui, Facebook Messenger communication, November 30, 2015.

13. Sboui in discussion with the author, June 19, 2015.

14. Amina Sboui, Facebook post, accessed May 20, 2014, no longer available.

15. Sboui in discussion with the author, June 19, 2015.

16. Ibid. See Human Rights Watch 2013.

## References

Charrad, Mounira M. 2001. *States and Women's Rights: The Making of Postcolonial Tunisia, Algeria, and Morocco*. Oakland: University of California Press, 2001.

Clancy-Smith, Julia. 2013. "From Sidi Bou Zid to Sidi Bou Said: A *Longue Durée* Approach to the Tunisian Revolutions." In *The Arab Spring: Change and Resistance in the Middle East*, edited by Mark L. Haas and David W. Lesch. 13–34. Boulder, CO: Westview Press, 2013.

Dornhof, Sarah. 2014. "Embodied Protest: Nakedness and the Partition of Gazes." In *Orientalism, Gender, and the Jews: Literary and Artistic Transformations of European*

*National Discourses*, edited by Ulrike Brunotte, Anna-Dorothea Ludewig, and Axel Stähler, 268–285. Berlin: de Gruyter.

Gordts, Eline. 2013. "International Topless Jihad Day: Femen Activists Stage Protests across Europe." *Huffington Post*, April 4. http://www.huffingtonpost.com/.

Grosz, Elizabeth. *Volatile Bodies*. Bloomington: Indiana University Press, 1994.

Human Rights Watch. 2013. "Tunisia: Grant Feminist Activist Pretrial Release." News release, July 17. http://www.hrw.org/news/2013/07/17/tunisia-grant-feminist-activist-pretrial-release.

O'Keefe, Theresa. 2014. "My Body Is My Manifesto! SlutWalk, Femen, and Feminist Protest." *Feminist Review* 107: 1–19.

Sboui, Amina. 2014a. "Amina Sboui: 'Mon corps de Tunisienne m'appartient.'" Interview by Patrick Simonin. *L'Invité*, TV5Monde, March 6. http://www.tv5monde.com/cms/chaine-francophone/Revoir-nos-emissions/L-invite/Episodes/p-27662-Amina-Sboui.htm.

———. 2014b. *Mon corps m'appartient*. Paris: Éditions Plon.

Stiles, Kristine. 1996. "Shaved Heads and Marked Bodies." In *Talking Gender: Public Images, Personal Journeys, and Political Critiques*, edited by Nancy Hewitt, Jean O'Barr, and Nancy Rosebaugh, 36–64. Chapel Hill: University of North Carolina Press, 1996.

Winter, Alexandra. 2001. "Writing and Skin." *Hectate* 27, no. 2:174–186.

# Syrian Bad Girl Samar Yazbek

## NINE

Refusing Burial

HANADI AL-SAMMAN

The unfolding Arab Spring brought about unprecedented women's participation in public squares, social media, and overall political presence. This activism created certain anxieties for supporters of the old regimes, who resorted to reviving traditional cultural myths, such as that of the pre-Islamic *jāhiliyya* practice of *wa'd* (that is, burying infant girls alive), to dub these women "bad girls." Interestingly, these women retaliated by owning their "bad-girlness" and incorporating this archetype as part of their revolutionary discourse.

In this vein, the Syrian writer Samar Yazbek epitomizes "bad-girlhood" when as an 'Alawite she participated in the revolution against that country's leader, Bashar al-Assad, a member of her own religious sect. *A Woman in the Crossfire: Diaries of the Syrian Revolution* (2012) is Yazbek's courageous response to the defamation propaganda that threatened to bury her alive, akin to the traditional victims of *wa'd*, for the treason of leaving the clan and embracing the enemy, the vilified other.[1] In her diaries Yazbek revives the context of the *wa'd* myth, traditionally seen as a safeguard against the infiltration of the enemy through the women who are taken as spoils in tribal raids in *jāhiliyya* times, and shifts its application from the women to the victimized citizens and country instead. In so doing, she manages to move the *wa'd* trauma from its personal realm, where it can be construed as an archaic practice affecting women in the past, to a vital contemporary issue afflicting the whole nation. In Yazbek's diaries, the *wa'd* trope is activated as a symbol denoting despotic practices of authoritarian regimes. The manner in which political dissidents are buried alive, in the regime's prisons, is akin to the *wa'd* ritual. This explains the prevalence of multiple revolutionary banners, particularly in the context of the Syrian revolution, contesting the burial of the country and its people under oppressive powers. By the same token, such a process revives the age-old connection between women as symbols of the nation, of its burial and resurrection (Baron 2005).

Yazbek is an 'Alawite writer from the coastal Syrian city of Jabla who in 2010 was recognized as one of the Beirut 39, a group of promising Arab writers under the age of forty. Her oeuvre encompasses novels, short stories, film scripts, television dramas, and revolutionary diaries. Though pushing the envelope of social critique and propriety through focusing on class inequity, oppressive military institutions, and same-sex female relationships in her previous novels, such as *Tiflat al-Sama'* (Heavenly girl, 2002), *Silsal* (Clay, 2005), and *Ra'ihat al-Qirfa* (2008, translated as *Cinnamon*, 2012), Yazbek did not anger the regime much until she explicitly critiqued its practices in her revolutionary diaries. Her 'Alawite sect seemed to offer her protection and freedom of subject matter up to the point of turning the examining lens inward in order to expose the regime's sectarian tactics. Her outspoken criticism of the brutality of the Assad regime against peaceful demonstrators during the revolution earned her its ire. After several detentions, she was forced to flee Syria before the end of 2011; she went to London and then Paris out of fear for her life and that of her daughter. Her daring work *Taqatu' niran* (2011), translated the next year as *A Woman in the Crossfire: Diaries of the Syrian Revolution* (2012), won her the prestigious Pen/Pinter prize as International Writer of Courage, the Swedish Tucholsky prize in 2012, and the Holland Oxfam/Pen award in 2013. The book has been translated into several European languages, and the Arabic original received much acclaim from Arab readers and critics alike since it is the first literary work to record the early stages of the Syrian revolution.

Yazbek is certainly not the first or the last Syrian woman to actively participate in the uprising since its inception on March 15, 2011. Notable participants range from Tall al-Muluhi (the nineteen-year-old blogger who has disappeared in the regime's prisons since then), Razan Ghazzawi (the blogger who documented stories of the revolution while in hiding inside Syria), Razan Zaitouneh (the human rights lawyer and activist who reported the regime's atrocities on her Syrian Human Rights Information link webpage and to CNN's Anderson Cooper using her real name in the early days of the uprising), and Suhair al-Atassi (co–vice president of the Syrian National Coalition). Yazbek is not even the only 'Alawite woman who publicly sided with the revolution. The actor Fadwa Sulayman, for example, participated in demonstrations on the ground in Homs and went on YouTube to defend the opposition. The Sunni national singer Assala Nasri defected to Egypt and recorded songs in support of the revolution. All of these public figures were stigmatized as traitors to the nation, their moral reputations attacked as they were branded with the bad girl image. Furthermore, countless unnamed Syrian women supported the uprising from behind the scenes and computer screens as bloggers, nurses to the wounded, and even warriors.

What makes Yazbek's dissent from the ranks of her sect more poignant, however, is that she is the only 'Alawite writer to record what she witnessed in the early days of the revolution in her diaries, thereby discrediting the regime's fabrications about the demonstrators as "infiltrators" and the "foreign, Salafi" origin of the uprising. To see the implication of her courageous act in siding with the revolution, one needs only to compare her stance to that of another prominent 'Alawite poet, Adonis (the pen name of 'Ali Ahmad Sa'id). Despite Adonis's pioneering work in the free verse poetic movement of the 1960s and his repeated insistence on the need to break the mold of dominant conceptions in Arab culture and poetics, he did not side with the Syrian revolution. He declared on Al-Arabiya satellite channel from his residence in Paris that he "could not take part in protests that emanate from the mosque," faulting the demonstrators for "not starting [their] protests in public squares" (in Antoon 2011). In an interview with the *Cairo Review of Global Affairs*, Adonis claims that "the Arab Spring in Syria lacked true revolutionary spirit. . . . The Syrian people didn't really participate in what happened. . . . They weren't big protests" (in Randal and MacLeod 2014). Yazbek's insistence on defying Adonis's and the regime's contentions that Islamists instigated the revolution is the reason she constitutes a threat to a sectarian regime that thrives on divide-and-conquer tactics.

Yazbek's transition from the regime's good daughter, the attractive, accomplished writer, to demonized bad-girlhood reflects the process of her iconization and demonization and simultaneously mirrors the anxieties she generates and endures as a result of her daring act. Her narrative explains why the demonstrators had to meet in mosques, redefines the concept of the Islamic hijab (veil) in a manner that implicates the regime, and finally documents women's participation in the revolution to assert their agency and prevent their erasure. The anxiety over erasure that she exhibits is directly tied to the historical trauma of *wa'd* and silencing of women's voices in political discourses. The expression of such anxieties in the national consciousness, however, bespeaks the survivability of these cultural myths in the turbulent political climate of the Arab uprisings. Before I turn my attention to the diaries, a word about the historical context of the *wa'd* practice is in order.

## Wa'd al-Banāt (Female Infanticide) in Pre-Islamic Arabia

The custom of *wa'd al-banāt* was first practiced in the pre-Islamic *jāhiliyya* era, when unwanted female infants were buried alive in the sand for a variety of reasons, chief among them fears of dishonor and of economic destitution. The warring, tribal lifestyle, with its austere, nomadic conditions, meant that tribes could only invest in raising boys, who would increase the tribe's army and, unlike girls, could never dishonor it by being captured as war spoils.[2] As war captives, females would be forced to be concubines and give birth to enemy offspring, thus bringing the foreign other home. Indeed, the perception of daughters as more prone to dishonoring and betraying the tribe than sons is rooted in the historical background of the first recorded *wa'd* incident in pre-Islamic Arabia. One account states that the first Arab father ever reported to practice female infanticide was Qays ibn 'Asim al-Tamimi from Tamim's tribe, whose adult daughter was taken as a war captive when the army of al-Nu'man bin al-Mundhir (King of al-Hira) raided their encampment. When a truce was declared among the warring parties, al-Nu'man gave the abducted women the right to choose between staying with their abductors or returning to their tribal homes. Qays ibn 'Asim's daughter chose to stay with her abductor rather than to return to her husband. It was at that point, the story goes, that Qays swore to bury in the sand any subsequent daughter born to him upon birth to avoid any such dishonor in the future.

The second account as to the origin of the *wa'd* practice is eerily similar; the tribe this time is reported to be that of Rabi'ah, with the daughter also preferring to stay with her abductor rather than returning to her father (Fadlallah 1978, 15–20). At the root of *wa'd* practice is the need to quell free will, which threatens and challenges authority. The discourse arising from *wa'd*, then, is inextricably linked to the politics of dissent and dishonor. The dishonor factor originates from the women's willingness to abandon their homelands, embrace mobility, and initiate a forbidden encounter (spiritual or sexual) with the other, thereby leading to an adulteration of the pure Arab lineage and to alliances struck with the foreign enemy. The concept of dishonor or shame represented in the Arabic original term *ʿār* interestingly has its linguistic roots in the words *ʿawra* (deficient, shameful, genitalia) and *ʿāra* (to bury a spring well). All three terms are linguistic derivatives of the Arabic trilateral verbal root *ʿawr*, which encompasses the meanings of deficiency, shame, and burial. The female infant symbolizes the essence of this trinity in the sense that her deficient femininity (*ʿawra*)[3] will bring about dishonor (*ʿār*) and is thus deserving of being buried (*ʿāra*) in the sands. This tribal fear of the female child's threat and potential danger to the stability of the patriarchal institution is manifested in the *waʾd* practice and in its survivability as a trope, particularly in Arab women's literary output (Al-Samman 2015).

Pre-Islamic Arabia was not the only society to practice female infanticide. For example, in ancient Greece and Rome, infanticide was legitimate until the fourth century AD (Giladi 1990, 185). Likewise, India and China are also reported to have engaged in such a practice and continue to do so today with the aid of contemporary medical technologies such as fetal ultra sound and selective chromosomal conception (Mungello 2008). Obviously *waʾd* was not practiced by all Arabian tribes; otherwise, the whole Arab line would have been obliterated.[4] Rather, only three tribes of northern Arabia were reported to practice it on a regular basis: bani Tamim, bani Kinda, and bani Rabiʿah. Among the Arabian tribes who practiced *waʾd*, the female infant was buried either immediately upon birth, at six years of age, or, in one account, even in late adolescence. Burial upon birth accounted for the majority of the cases, whereby a shallow grave was dug next to the laboring mother. If the infant was male, he was allowed to live. A female child, however, was immediately buried in the prepared grave. Fathers often instigated and perpetuated the practice, although reluctant mothers were also reported to do so for fear of abandonment by their husbands. Banning this horrific practice in the seventh century was one of Islam's greatest accomplishments, and newly converted, repentant fathers were reportedly haunted by the memory and voices of the daughters they buried in the sands in the time of *jāhiliyya*.

Indeed, it is precisely the voice of the *mawʾūda*, the daughters the fathers wanted to suffocate, that takes center stage in one of the primary Qurʾanic verses that condemn the *waʾd* practice among Islam's grave sins punishable in the hereafter. Although the *waʾd* practice is referred to in four other *suras* (6, 16, 17, 60), verses 8 and 9 of *Sūrat al-Takwīr* represent the only place in the Qurʾan where the word *waʾd* is used and the voice of the *mawʾūda* is revived.[5] They highlight the crucial moment of the *mawʾūda*'s resurrection and the return of her voice on Judgment Day, "when the female [infant], buried alive, is questioned for what crime she was killed" (wa-idhā al-mawʾūdatu suʾilat bi-ayyi dhanbin qutilat) (Sūrat al-Takwīr 81:8). The *mawʾūda*'s body stands as a trace, as evidence of the crime committed against her in secret collusion. On Judgment Day she will finally receive justice by presenting her buried body as proof of the insidious *waʾd* crime. Hence "the proofs will be drawn from the very means used for concealment"; body and voice join together in pointing the accusatory finger at the guilty fathers.[6]

*Al-mawʾūda*'s resurrection gives her this divine right to incriminate and condemn the fathers who buried their daughters in the sands. It is no wonder, then, that after realizing the error of their *jāhiliyya* ways, the fathers were haunted by this traumatic past. This history may explain why the motifs of body and voice are forever intertwined in Arab women's literature. Indeed, in the writings of some contemporary Arab women writers, such as Nawal El Saadawi, Hoda Barakat, Ghada al-Samman, Salwa al-Neimi, and Hanan al-Shaykh, this universal body/voice motif is merged with the *waʾd* trope in order to denote not only the burial of the female self but also that of Arab heritage, Arab cities, the nation, and the collective Arab self (al-Samman 2015).

## Surviving Multiple *Waʾd*

In her revolutionary diaries, Samar Yazbek assimilates the *mawʾūda*'s voice and persona, often pointing her accusatory finger not just at the patriarchy proper but at the inhumane, dictatorial regime and its systematic practice of killing its own people. The manner in which she engages with the three main components of the *waʾd* archetype—recognizing the threat of the other, identifying the culprit(s), and resurrecting the *mawʾūda*'s voice—is crucial to the success of her oppositional narrative. The book chronicles the first four months of the Syrian revolution, from March 15, 2011, to July 8, 2011, and records in painstaking detail the political chaos of the state and the status of the demonstrations in Darʿa (the birthplace of the revolution), Damascus, Homs, Hama, Baniyas, and Jabla, as well as other Syrian towns and villages. Yazbek's material comes from her own experience in demonstrations and security police offices as well as from direct testimonies of activists, political detainees, and martyrs' family members. In addition to gathering witnesses' testimonies, she maintained her involvement with the revolution's coordination committees on the ground and was vocal on her Facebook page in support of a free, democratic Syria. However, using her public persona as a prominent 'Alawite writer in this oppositional manner did not sit well with the authorities, and she was quickly summoned to meet a high-ranking security police officer. She was led blindfolded to his office, where he hurled insults like "Cunt" and slapped at her (Yazbek 2012, 82). His anger was compounded because, as an 'Alawite and a supporter of the revolution, Yazbek "betrayed the ties of blood and kinship" and brought about shame ('ār) to the 'Alawite clan (83). Their ensuing interaction is worth mentioning in this context, as it reactivates important components integral to the *wa'd* story.

> "We're worried about you," he said. "You're being duped by Salafi Islamists if you believe what they're saying."
>
> "I don't believe anyone," I said. "I went out into the streets time after time and I didn't see any Salafis. I saw how you kill ordinary people and arrest them and beat them."
>
> "No," he said, "those are Salafis."
>
> "They weren't Salafis," I told him. "You and I both know that."
>
> "If you keep on writing," he said, "I'll make you disappear from the face of the earth."
>
> "Go ahead," I said.
>
> "Not just you, but your daughter as well."
>
> In that moment, my heart stopped beating.
>
> Sitting down behind his desk, he said, "Put the knife down, you lunatic. We're honorable people. We don't harm our own blood. We're not like you traitors. You're a black mark upon all 'Alawites." (84)

Yazbek's stance in support of the revolution against Bashar al-Assad, a member of her own clan, brings to mind the fear of the feminine element in bringing the enemy home. In other words, in initiating an intimate, political encounter with the other, she dishonored the whole sect. If we recall the *wa'd* stories I referenced earlier, we find that the threat of enduring the 'ār of the daughter's betrayal is the main reason behind burying the daughter in the sand. Indeed, in the Arabic version of her book, the officer declares, "You're 'ār upon all 'Alawites" (Yazbek 2011, 104). The officer's threat that if Yazbek did not desist he would make her disappear from the face of the earth hints at the disappearance of thousands of political dissidents in Syria's modern history who were summarily arrested, never to be heard from again. Furthermore, his reference to the concepts of honor and blood betrays the tribal, sectarian nature of the Syrian regime. His desire to silence her voice by ordering her to shut down her Facebook account and never publish articles in support of the revolution in the journal *al-Quds al-Arabi* is akin to a symbolic *wa'd*, indeed.

Throughout the book, Yazbek narrates how the whole sect treated her as a traitor, how her own family and friends disowned her, how they turned her daughter against her, and how she was banished from her birthplace of Jabla, never daring to visit it again since the regime distributed pamphlets calling for her head there (2012, 35, 81). Yazbek's tactic in diffusing the regime's accusation of her so-called betrayal to turn the accusatory finger to Bashar al-Assad himself, calling him time and again the "murderous president," "a murderer," "a butcher" capable of committing massacres worse than Tamerlane, and a "cartoonish Frankenstein" (140, 193, 152, 164). She includes the chants of Dar'a women who held a banner stating, "Anyone who kills his own people is a traitor!"; in this way she redefines treason and points out, in a manner similar to the *maw'ūda*'s voice in the Qur'anic verse, who committed the crimes of killing and who the real culprit in the country's demonic demise was (153). In fact, a cartoon taken from the Facebook page Syrian Revolution against Bashar al-Assad in 2012 underscores the clownish yet bloodthirsty figure of Assad. Furthermore, it displays his being haunted by the souls of the deceased Syrian children who ceaselessly reiterate a variation of the female buried infant's Qur'anic question, asking Assad, "For what crime were we killed?" The shift from the singular feminine pronoun "she" in the Qur'anic verse to the collective pronoun "we" in the cartoon reflects an intensity of killing that engulfs the whole nation and a return to the *jāhiliyya*, an age of ignorance, in laws that are now synonymous with the Assad regime.

The questions that Yazbek raises throughout the diaries diffuse the regime's official narrative of Salafi infiltrators killing Syrians. She includes the testimony of an activist during the early days of the revolution who insisted that the youths organizing the demonstrations came from all the ethnic Syrian rainbow (Sunnis, Christians, 'Alawites, Kurds, and Druze); they were not religiously inclined, but they had to resort to launching the demonstrations from the mosques because those were the only places citizens were allowed to assemble in this martial law state (2012, 237). When we compare her stance with that of Adonis, the self-proclaimed revolu-

**Figure 9.1.** "For what crime were we killed?" Anonymous, posted to Facebook, 2012.

tionary who blamed demonstrators for gathering in mosques and insisted on giving Bashar al-Assad legitimacy by referring to him as "an elected president" in an open letter published in the Lebanese newspaper *al-Safir* in June 2011, we can appreciate Yazbek's relevance versus Adonis's "irrelevance" (Antoon 2011, Jaggi 2012).

At one point Yazbek wonders, "Where are all these murderers coming from?"; at another, "Who is killing the soldiers and the demonstrators?" (2012, 47). Her account of the strange physiognomy of some snipers, coupled with the unusual manner in which they groomed their beards, incriminates the regime in importing Iranian Revolutionary Guards and Hezbollah militias to help kill Syrians—a fact that became self-evident in the second year of the Syrian revolution, when both Iran and Hezbollah publicly admitted their military and logistic support of the Assad regime. Yazbek remarks, "I stared into his [the sniper's] eyes, which were like every other murderer's eyes that have appeared these days, eyes I have never seen before in Damascus. How could all those murderers be living among us? . . . The man's complexion was dark and his features hinted at a kind of foreignness we were all starting to wonder about" (54).

Yazbek's concern does not spring from xenophobia or a concern for ethnic purity; rather, she is intent on exposing the hypocrisy of the regime that accused the opposition of being led by "infiltrators and outside agitators" while simultaneously importing foreign fighters from Iran and Hezbollah. Clearly it is not the transgressive woman or the revolutionary activists who are bringing the foreign other to Syria, then; it is the duplicitous regime. Yazbek's owning of the term "infiltrators" turns the insult around to frame the word as an act of love, of caring for her fellow citizens. She asserts, "Now I am an infiltrator among my own family, an infiltrator in my own bed. Now I infiltrate everything and I am nothing. . . . I infiltrate the sorrow of every Syrian who passes before my eyes . . . trying to find one last document for salvation, claiming to be doing something adequate to my belief in the value of working for justice" (2012, 3). In her quest for justice she exposes the injustices committed by the regime's militias. For that reason, Yazbek's accounts do not spare the security police or the regime's gangs (known as *al-shabbīḥa*)[7] from incrimination. Almost all of her witnesses indicate that *al-shabbīḥa* were the ones shooting soldiers in the back of the head when the latter refused to shoot unarmed demonstrators, and that they were the ones who instigated *al-fitna al-ṭā'ifiyya*, a sectarian feud in Syrian villages of mixed ethnic demographics.

Another aspect of Yazbek's oppositional narrative is the way she challenges the regime's appropriation of Islam when it accused demonstrators of being Salafis, and the Islamic hijab as backward and anti–women's liberation. She starts by redefining the term "hijab," which in the regime's narrative takes on a sinister, derogatory connotation. In Yazbek's exposition, it is not the veil of the covered women that Syrian citizens should be wary of; rather, it is the security "veil" that acts as a wall preventing citizens from interacting with each other and from seeing the truth as it "grows and grows until it becomes an entire country" (46).

Her reclamation of the gendered Islamic veil trope ultimately leads to another activation of a pre-Islamic one, namely that of *wa'd*. In deploying this trope, Yazbek's intention is to point out that the culprits in committing the crime of *wa'd* in modern-day Syria are not the *jāhilī* idol worshippers of times past but instead the Assad regime, which endorsed the cult of the sole leader whose idol-like statues dominate and suffocate its people. In fact, the dismemberment of rebellious Syrian cities via several security checkpoints, cutting them off from electricity, water, food supplies, transportation, and access to the Internet and other communication methods, all while continuing the aerial bombardment of them, renders those cities dead. In besieged Darʿa, for example, Yazbek remarks that "the land is being surrounded, buried [*arḍun maw'ūda*]" (30) and that "Damascus was a ghost town" (31). In defiance of the regime's isolationist tactics, Yazbek increased her efforts to connect the activists through a network of coordination committees (187, 219). Moreover, she insists on documenting Syrian women's role in launching and supporting the uprising. Women of all walks of life, ethnicities, and religious affiliations were part of the struggle and active members of the Syrian Women in Support of the Uprising initiative, which specialized in delivering assistance to the wounded and to martyrs' families (150). Yet despite Yazbek's moderate success in mobilizing women's committees, the trauma of the buried cities weighed heavily on her soul, and she felt its effects on her own body as fear, anxiety, insomnia, vomiting, and madness. Increasingly, she experienced the dismemberment of Darʿa *al-mawʾūda*—buried in her own body as "a disintegrating corpse" (81). In this instance, the personal *waʾd* is conflated with the national one as the transgressive bad girl assimilates the persona of the *mawʾūda* to become the image of a resurrected, revolutionary dialectic.

## Resurrecting the *Mawʾūda*'s Body

In its efforts to contain her, the security police placed Yazbek under close surveillance. The repeated threatening phone calls and summons of the high-ranking officer were meant to intimidate her and break her spirit. In every visit she was taken to the torture chambers where political dissidents were tortured and humiliated. She was forced to see their wounded bodies oozing blood and pus as they hung lifeless from the ceilings of their cells. The piercing screams of the tortured detainees haunted her at night, giving her constant insomnia. She coped during those trips to the prison underworld by pretending that she was a fictive character and that the humiliation she was enduring was actually happening to someone else.

> I would pretend I was a character on paper, not made of flesh and blood, or that I was reading about a blindfolded woman forcibly taken to an unknown location, to be insulted and spat upon because she had the gall to write something true that displeased the tyrant. At this point in my fantasy I would feel strong and forget all about how weak my body was, about the vile smells and the impending unknown. (2012, 90–91)

This dissociative technique united her on a symbiotic level with the body of the *mawʾūda*, indeed, with the body of the buried nation and its people. The dissociation allowed Yazbek to leave the present moment and channel the pain of her compatriots in an affective way. Through this unification she was able to experience their traumatic history in her own body, a process that forever replays and assimilates what Maria Root, quoted in Laura Brown (1995, 107), has called "insidious trauma," which can be intergenerational as well. Brown asserts that mainstream trauma theory has started "to recognize that post-traumatic symptoms can be intergenerational," but more work is needed in order to admit that these symptoms "could spread laterally throughout an oppressed social group" (108). Yazbek's assimilation of this insidious trauma is complete when she attempts to write down the testimonies of the tortured detainees and her body trembles as it experiences the same pain endured by her compatriots. "My fingers started trembling," she reports, "a condition I know all too well. Rarely can I finish recording a testimony without winding up crying or shaking. Rarely can I write down the words coming from the mouths of the tortured without them washing over me as though it were happening for real. What sort of torture is this?" (2012, 120).

As the security police surveillance increased its grip on every aspect of her life such that she could not leave her house or communicate with others via the Internet or in person, Yazbek started to view her body as a buried corpse demanding its right to be heard. The corpse refused to be silenced and gained power through the transfer of trauma as Yazbek documented the stories of the tortured prisoners and the martyrs in her writing. She drew strength from their stories, and her narrative witnessing took on a poignant slant as she became the voice of the voiceless. People were literally deprived of the agency to tell their stories, like the singer Ibrahim al-Qashush, whose lifeless body was dumped in the Orontes River with his throat cut out. Her inclusion of the lyrics of his song in her text is a resurrection of his voice (216). In the same vein, the testimonies she documents on the regime's security agents stealing the martyrs' bodies and selling and buying their body parts incriminate the regime even further in atrocious crimes against humanity (125, 232). She was haunted daily by the corpses of the tortured, and her responsibility toward documenting the stories of the witnesses took on an added urgency when they became martyrs themselves in subsequent demonstrations.

Corpses dominate the scene in this morbid tale, and before long this revolutionary bad girl started to refer to herself as the living dead, *al-mayyita al-akthar huḍūran* (Yazbek 2011, 101); she was a "dead woman, yet still present somehow" (Yazbek 2012, 81). The voice and the body of the *maw'ūda* compete for presence, for reunification, for rebirth in her person. Yazbek remarks, "The paper woman in my fingertips told me, 'Bloodshed or humiliation, it's either one or the other.' I told her to shut up and just leave me alone for a little while, like a corpse calmly fighting against its own decomposition" (2012, 134). In "Mythical Bad Girls: The Corpse, the Crone, and the Snake," Rebecca Copeland highlights the importance of the disintegrating corpse of the Japanese goddess Izanami, who was silenced and confined to the underworld but managed to break away by generating thunder from every part of her decomposing body (2005, 20–21). Similarly, Yazbek celebrates the rebirth of her dead cells in the following passage:

> I understood how important it is for a human being to be capable of regenerating herself and bringing her dead cells back to life; this may seem like a line out of a book but it's a real feeling and not a metaphor I write down in words here. Truly, I was a dead woman, bones encased in dry skin, cells that need to be regenerated—something straight out of a science fiction movie. (2012, 104)

This resurrection will occur through writing the testimonies of the witnesses to the revolution. Only through this narrative witnessing can the body of the victims be resurrected and the *maw'ūda*'s voice, both the woman and the country, be heard from beneath the rubble again. In light of the descent of the country into a brutal civil war, the value of Yazbek's diaries springs from her faithful documentation of the early months of the Syrian uprising and in reminding us that

> this is the people's revolution of dignity. This is the uprising of a brutalized people who wish to liberate themselves from their humiliation. That's how the uprising in Syria broke out. I saw it among the people I first interviewed, before I was prevented from moving between the Syrian cities and before the security services and the *shabbīḥa* and the Ba'thists placed a bounty on my head wherever I went. (2012, 218)

The regime's intimidation forced Yazbek to flee Syria in 2011, but she was determined to be the voice of the revolution and its victims, and returned to write the next chapters of her war-torn country's story.

## Traversing Buried Cities

Yazbek chronicles her return to her homeland on three separate occasions between August 2012 and August 2013 in *Bawabat ard al-ʿadam*, in Arabic, and published in English as *The Crossing*, both in 2015. Typical of Arab diaspora women writers who carry the homeland's pain within in exile and whose shuttle journeys inevitably lead them back to the homeland (al-Samman 2015), Yazbek's homecoming was motivated by a profound need to reconnect with the spatial dimensions of her country and to understand the reasons behind the revolution's setbacks.

Yazbek visited three northern Syrian townships that were hotbeds of the Free Syrian Army's operations. In addition to interviewing war victims, opposition fighters, regime army defectors, and even leaders of the Islamist Nusra front, she created centers to help women of the destroyed areas make and sell their products through networks across the border and support traumatized children through learning and theatrical arts. With each trip, Yazbek had to smuggle herself across the border through multiple networks and thereby redraw the cartography of her homeland through divided factions and landscapes. *The Crossing* uncannily captures the dismemberment of the country, the horrific destruction to country and citizens alike, and the surreal absurdity of civil-war Syria.

With her every border crossing, the open wound of the orphaned revolution — betrayed by global and local powers alike — is exposed. Yazbek reflects on the altered landscape and on the resilience of the Syrian people who stayed in their homes despite the shelling and barrel-bombing by the regime. Her descriptions of these mangled buildings border on the surreal, exposing the grotesque when the fluidity of buried warm bodies are mixed with the cold steel of destroyed homes. This is a scene in Ma'arat al-Nu'man:

> All around, entire buildings had twisted to the ground. They hadn't been blasted apart in the usual way, rather the iron and concrete seemed to have melted into liquid right before my eyes, curving and bending. A four-storey building drooped so that its roof was touching the pavement, unfurling like a theatre curtain. And beneath it disappeared a mass of human bodies. Buildings leaned in to touch each other, they bowed down to sleep, amid the huge piles of rubble that filled the city. (Yazbek 2015, 74)

Despite the violent alteration of the city's topography, Yazbek depicts the resilience of the Syrian people who opened their homes to each other to create safe pathways around bombed areas and snipers' fire. Internal walls are demolished to allow safe passage for neighbors, while external walls are colored with the revolution's graffiti. Yazbek was awed by the determination of a mother who, despite the risk of a sniper, crossed the courtyard of her house to bring water and food to her children. In Saraqib, she interviewed an artist who painted the walls of liberated cities while doubling as the city's undertaker. The change in urban architecture simultaneously highlights the brutality of the regime, the resilience of the

Syrian people, and the intersections between the demolished city and the writing of its history. "'I bury the bodies,'" the artist tells Yazbek, "holding out the palms of his hands as he said 'bodies.' 'I can tell you the story of each and every one of them. But it would take a long time. I bury Saraqeb's [sic] martyrs and paint Saraqeb's walls. I'll never leave this place'" (in Yazbek 2015, 12). The focus is on the duty of those who witness the traumatic killing of innocent people to transmit their stories through the process of narrative witnessing.

As she walked through the demolished streets and talked to the victims, Yazbek assumed a dramatically different role than the typical flaneur. The flaneur as a figure first developed by Baudelaire and later disseminated in the works of Walter Benjamin and Michel de Certeau establishes walking as primarily a masculine urban act capable of retrieving the lost history of the city (Benjamin 1985; de Certeau 1984). By contrast, the female *flaneuse*, as depicted in Yazbek, is interested not in retrieving but in exposing the discontinuity of the architecture, the dismemberment of the city and its people. She does not depict images through her singular lens but rather captures the national body politic by recounting the collective viewpoints of Syrian people. Yazbek's detours do not follow typical street routes, but traverse through people's homes, making unusual yet necessary topographic and intimate connections. By interviewing all affected parties in the struggle, she establishes walking as a "space of uttering," to use Michel de Certeau's analogy. Certeau contends that "the parallelism between linguistic uttering and pedestrian uttering" reinforces the association between the "here/there," initiating an interaction between an "I" and "*another* relative to that 'I,' and thereby establish[es] a conjunctive and disjunctive articulation of places" (Certeau 2000, 107).

Indeed, Yazbek's depiction of the private gardens that turned into graveyards due to people's inability to access cemeteries poignantly displays the tension between the conjunctive and the disjunctive articulation of places. When gardens become graveyards, and graveyards, in turn, generate gardens, we encounter an odd spatial articulation that is both intimate and intimidating. She observes, "Cemeteries began to live among the people, another everyday part of life like the shops and the streets that wind between the houses. Massacre after massacre pitted the soil with craters filled with the bodies of Syrians" (Yazbek 2015, 90). One man tells her, "This cemetery is where we can breathe a sigh of relief. . . . We're expanding it and knocking down the wall, so that our boys can sleep in peace under the soil!" (91). The intense shelling notwithstanding, Syrians defied

**Figure 9.2.** "Only in Syria do dolls lose children." Ma'arat al-Nu'man massacre, January 12, 2016. Syrian Revolution Network.

the forced destruction of their urban landscape by charting a new revolutionary cartography to resist the discourse of death. After losing most of his family in a prolonged aerial bombardment, a firefighter found a doll instead of his four-year-old daughter. "This burns my heart," he tells Yazbek. "Here we are looking for her under these rocks and all I've found is this . . . . It's hers" (89).

Instead of letting her journalistic "I" dominate, Yazbek developed a relational encounter with the space and its people that underscores discontinuity, defiance, effective opposition, and survival. It is left to her to resurrect the body of the buried nation and its people, to revive the trace and the voices of the *maw'ūda* and all of the deceased in her haunting narrative.

*The Crossing*, like *A Woman in the Crossfire*, remains faithful to a belief in the just demands of the Syrian revolution and an investment in the bad girl, revolutionary image of its author. *The Crossing* focuses on the northern parts of Syria and covers a two-year span, while *A Woman* focuses on the south during the onset of the revolution. Yazbek's description of the *shabbīḥa* focused on Assad's militias in *A Woman*; in *The Crossing* the term also encompasses Islamic State foreign fighters. She is struck by the similarity of the hollow gaze that "sees nothing" and the muscular build of the agents of both forces: "They annihilate the place with equal nullity. An

Assad dictatorial vengeful nullity, and a religious suicidal nullity that sees rebirth in death. However, the former nullity is the mother of the second one" (2015, 108, my translation of the Arabic). Throughout *The Crossing*, Yazbek validates the rebels' assessment that the Islamic State is the foil for the Assad regime. Time and again she documents the Assad regime's plan to derail the revolution from its peaceful path into a militarized one by, for instance, arresting moderate activists and releasing fundamentalist Islamists from prison (2015, 238, Arabic edition). She notes that Assad and the Islamic State do not target each other but rather aim their fire at the Free Syrian Army. More important, she conveys the general consensus that the world community's failure to create a no-fly zone to prevent the Assad regime from bombing its own people has caused the influx of Islamic State fighters into Syria and the ensuing refugee crisis.

In her second and third trips to Syria, Yazbek notes the alarming changes in women's mobility, and signs of increasing religiosity manifested in strict hijab rules. She attributes this surge in religiosity to the regime's intentional shelling of minarets and sowing of the seeds of sectarian division, as well as the agendas brought by foreign fighters who joined IS and other Islamist brigades. In Saraqib, Yazbek observes the successful self-governance by civic activists. They manufactured their own electricity, rebuilt homes, ran hospitals and civic engagement projects, and even published a children's weekly, *Zaytun wa-zaytuna*, designed to build civic selfhood and to protect children from Islamic State ideology. "The men here," Yazbek states, "were taking part in a unique program of self-government in a civil society. They were clearly capable of such self-government, but there were those who didn't want their democratic revolution to succeed" (2015, 157, English edition). The activists were all too aware of this conspiracy, as a young journal editor tells her: "Everything you're seeing now is happening in order to transform the democratic revolution into a religious war. . . . These *takfiri* Muslims . . . they don't know what they're doing, but their leaders do" (158).[8] True to her bad girl image, Yazbek conducted an interview with a leader of the Nusra front without disclosing her 'Alawite identity. He informed her that his motivation for joining the group was the brutal slaughter of Sunni villagers, the rape of the women, and the execution of soldiers who refused to engage in these despicable acts. She was troubled by the revenge rhetoric that peppered his conversation. Yazbek left the interview with several questions: "Who were the people financing [the Islamic State]? Who were the people financing the Nusra Front? Who was assassinating the commanders of the

Free Army? Who was killing the journalists and pacifist activists? What was causing this abduction of the revolution, this transformation of it into a religious war?" (269).

Yazbek's accusatory finger was directed at Assad in *A Woman*, while in *The Crossing*, as evident in these questions, she accuses the whole world, which stood on the sidelines watching Syria spiral into the abyss, a world that concocted an Assad/IS duality as "a scarecrow" to justify its apathetic positioning toward the revolution. She remarks, "Voyeurs the world over are getting a kick from watching Syria's desperate fight for survival — a scene composed essentially of the heaped-up corpses of Syrian victims" (272). It is precisely these forgotten Syrian corpses that take center stage in her witnessing narrative. Yazbek's incrimination reveals the difference between the *flaneuse*, the female who regains the dismembered bodies' agency in her narrative, and the stance of the world as a flaneur, a male engaged in passive voyeurism who locks the body into an arresting paralysis. It is the celebration of this Syrian body in its overcoming of decades of fear, its courageous stance against tyranny, its subsequent dismemberment by regime fire, and its potential rise from the ashes after the dust settles that propel the narrative of Yazbek's diaries. By recounting these narratives, Yazbek heeds Liisa Malkki's call for "a radically 'historicizing humanism' that insists on acknowledging not only human suffering but also narrative authority, historical agency, and political memory" (Malkki 2009, 115). Along the way, the resilience of the Syrian people, particularly that of women, holds the promise of a new beginning. For example, a woman who insisted on weathering the shelling rather than becoming a refugee declares, "I live amidst war and bombardment because I want to teach the girls how to create a beautiful life. We want to marry, procreate, and build our lives. We refuse to surrender to death" (in Yazbek 2015, 200).[9]

In her afterword to the *Bad Girls of Japan* anthology, Miriam Silverberg reminds us that every "bad girl is a 'returnee' reincarnated from another bad girl" (2005, 195). Yazbek's reappropriation of the *maw'ūda*'s badness in exercising her free will and seeking forbidden encounters with unwanted others allows the writer to be incarnated in the archetype's image. Using the *maw'ūda*'s Qur'anic, divine right in naming those who have committed crimes against humanity, Yazbek identifies the criminals who have buried Syria and condemned its peaceful revolution to the spiraling hell of civil war. Her courageous actions in first documenting the early days of the revolution and later returning to Syria to reflect on the causes of the revolution's derailment landed her in the crossfire. Doing so caused her to be burned by enemy and ally fires alike,[10] but as she hastens to point out, "Fire scalds. Fire purifies. Fire either reduces you to ash or burnishes you. In the days to come I expect to live in ashes or else to see my shiny new mirror" (2012, 258). Yazbek's final words express hopes for the phoenix, for Syria's resurrection from the ashes to write glorious chapters of dignity and freedom for all of its citizens.

## Notes

Earlier versions of part of this chapter were published in Hanadi al-Samman, *Anxiety of Erasure: Trauma, Authorship, and the Diaspora in Arab Women's Writings* (Syracuse, NY: Syracuse University Press, 2015). I thank Syracuse University Press for granting the permission to reprint.

1. Yazbek's *Woman in the Crossfire* was originally published in Arabic as *Taqatuʿ niran: Min yawmiyyat al-intifada al-Suriyya* (2011). References are to the 2012 English translation unless stated otherwise.

2. Male children were considered assets since they could enhance the tribe's wealth by participating in raids, and enhance the tribe's prestige and number by fathering offspring, preferably more males. Children were considered extensions of their paternal family line and the property of the father, not the mother. A daughter could only produce offspring to enhance the prestige of her husband's tribe.

3. One hadith attributed to the prophet Muhammad states, "Woman is an *ʿawra*." On what constitutes *ʿawra* in a woman's body, the legist Ahmad ibn Hanbal (d. 241/855) declares, "Everything in women is an *ʿawra*"; Ibn Hanbal 1986, 29 ff.

4. Saʿsaʿa bin Najiyya bin ʿIqal, the grandfather of the famous Umayyad poet al-Farazdaq (641–730 AD), is reported to have saved 280 female babies from infanticide. After his conversion to Islam, Saʿsaʿa asked the Prophet whether God would reward him for these kind deeds in the hereafter. The Prophet's response was affirmative; Giladi 1990, 189, 200.

5. *Surat al-anʿam* 6:151; *Surat al-nahl* 16:58–59; *Surat al-israʾ* 17:31; *Surat al-Mumtahina* 60:12.

6. I cite the Qurʾan originally published in 1906 by the King Fahd printing house in Medina and edited by the IFTA (Presidency of Islamic Research); the 1989 edition cited is *The Holy Qurʾan: English Translation of the Meanings, and Commentary*, edited by Abdullah Yusuf Ali.

7. *Al-shabbīḥa* are hired gangs often recruited by the Assad regime to terrorize citizens. Their name is derived from the expensive black cars they drive (called *al-shabbaḥ*, "the ghost" in Syrian dialect) and is thus indicative of their ability to kill, to make ghosts (*tashbīḥ*) out of people by making them literally disappear.

8. *Takfīrī* is a derogatory term used by strict religious groups, such as the Islamic State, that proclaim that people who disagree with their interpretations of Islamic scripture are *kuffār*, heretics.

9. My translation from the Arabic. This passage does not appear in the English translation of the book.

10. In addition to the regime's demonization of her, Yazbek has, at times, been accused by some members of the opposition of not being vocal enough in her critique of the regime before the onset of the revolution in 2011; Yazbek 2012, 107.

## References

American University in Cairo (AUC). 2014. "Uprising Will Not Topple al-Assad Regime." *Cairo Review of Global Affairs*, May 14. http://www.aucegypt.edu/media/media-releases/syrian-poet-adonis-cairo-review-global-affairs-uprising-will-not-topple-al.

Antoon, Sinan. 2011. "Adunis, the Revolutionary Poet." Al Jazeera, July 11, 2011. http://www.aljazeera.com/indepth/opinion/2011/07/201179124452158992.html

Baron, Beth. 2005. *Egypt as a Woman: Nationalism, Gender, and Politics*. Berkeley: University of California Press.

Benjamin, Walter. 1985. "Central Park." *New German Critique* 34:32–58.

Brown, Laura. 1995. "Not outside the Range: One Feminist Perspective on Psychic Trauma." In *Trauma: Explorations in Memory*, edited by Cathy Caruth, 100–112. Baltimore: Johns Hopkins University Press.

Certeau, Michel de. 1984. *The Practice of Everyday Life*. Translation by Steven Rendall. Berkeley: University of California Press.

———. 2000. *The Certeau Reader*. Edited by Graham Ward. Malden, MA: Blackwell, 2000.

Copeland, Rebecca. 2005. "Mythical Bad Girls: The Corpse, the Crone, and the Snake." In *Bad Girls of Japan*, edited by Laura Miller and Jan Bardsley, 15–32. New York: Palgrave Macmillan.

Fadlallah, Mariam. 1978. *Al-mar'ah fī ẓil al-Islam* (Woman in the shadow of Islam). Beirut: Dār al-Zahrā', 1978.

Giladi, Avner. 1990. "Some Observations on Infanticide in Medieval Muslim Society." *International Journal of Middle East Studies* 22, no. 2:185–200.

Ibn Hanbal, Ahmad. 1986. *Ahkam al-Nisa'* (Rules on women). Edited by ʿAbd al-Qadir Ahmad ʿAta. Beirut: Dār al-kutub al-ʿilmiyya.

Jaggi, Maya. 2012. "Adonis: A Life in Writing." *The Guardian*, January 12. https://www.theguardian.com/culture/2012/jan/27/adonis-syrian-poet-life-in-writing.

Malkki, Liisa H. 2009. "Speechless Emissaries." In *Cultures of Fear: A Critical Reader*, edited by Uli Linke and Danielle Taana Smith, 101–116. New York: Pluto Press.

Mungello, D. E. 2008. *Drowning Girls in China: Female Infanticide in China Since 1650*. Lanham, MD: Rowman and Littlefield.

Pearlman, Wendy. 2016. "Narratives of Fear in Syria." *Perspectives on Politics* 14, no. 1:21–37.

Randal, Jonathan, and Scott MacLeod. 2014. "Age of Darkness." *Cairo Review of Global Affairs*, no. 13 (Spring). https://www.thecairoreview.com/q-a/age-of-darkness/.

Samman, Hanadi al-. 2015. *Anxiety of Erasure: Trauma, Authorship, and the Diaspora in Arab Women's Writings*. Syracuse, NY: Syracuse University Press.

Silverberg, Miriam. 2005. "Afterword: And Some Not So Bad." In *Bad Girls of Japan*, edited by Laura Miller and Jan Bardsley, 190–196. New York: Palgrave Macmillan.

Yazbek, Samar. 2011. *Taqatuʿ niran: Min yawmiyyat al-intifada al-Suriyya*. Beirut: Dār al-Adāb.

———. 2012. *A Woman in the Crossfire: Diaries of the Syrian Revolution*. Translation by Max Weiss. London: Haus, 2012.

———. 2013. "I Write with Blind Eyes and Forty Fingers." *Index on Censorship* 42, no. 4:130–133.

———. 2015. *The Crossing: My Journey to the Shattered Heart of Syria*. Translation by Nashwa Gowanlock and Ruth Ahmedzai Kemp. London: Rider. Originally published as *Bawabat ard al-ʿadam* (Beirut: Dār al-Adāb, 2015).

## Reel Bad Maghrebi Women

TEN

FLORENCE MARTIN AND PATRICIA CAILLÉ

The fiction films directed by Maghrebi women directors have long projected images of disobedient women engaged in seditious behaviors. Yet, over the past few years, not only has their production increased, but also they have filmed a more complex subversive female behavior that targets the foils of local archaic cultures or national histories as well as local, national, or even transnational political struggles. A "reel bad Maghrebi girl" is then both in front of the camera (a female protagonist) and behind the camera (a defiant filmmaker).

The notion of the reel bad girl is inflected culturally. To wit, women's standard film narratives of righteous women struggling to achieve self-fulfillment may appeal to European audiences; a narrative that does not conform to such a Western hegemonic format threatens the success and visibility of the film internationally. This is why an honest look at reel bad Maghrebi girls from pioneering works to today's cinema requires differentiating good bad girls — film protagonists who are good girls in the eyes of Western audiences — from really bad girls, those who resist Western standard binary oppositions or worldviews. We examine, in three case studies of recent films, a new type of female protagonist who redefines the terms of her own oppression and possible emancipation and inflects the director's storytelling techniques. Reel bad Maghrebi girls occupy the screen against the grain of the official (male) narrative and film, resisting the patriarchal *grand récit* that overshadows their habitats, which suddenly and brilliantly have come unveiled on Arab feminist screens.

## A Few Thoughts about Bad Girls at the Movies

In classic cinema that seems to reproduce a mainstream heterosexual order, the presence of bad girls on-screen interrogates the heterosexual norms associated with femininity and masculinity. Refusing the position that patriarchal tradition has assigned to women, bad girls tend to transgress the limits of sexual activity imposed by decency on good girls. Martha Wolfenstein and Nathan Leites, in *Movies: A Psychological Study* (1950), analyze these figures in American, British, and French postwar A films in order to understand the subconscious processes that characterized the audience's psyche. In their study they isolated several recurring characters, including the "good-bad girl," who appears suspicious but is found innocent of any wrongdoing in the end. This character simultaneously gratifies men's lower impulses and noble aspirations.[1] Linda Williams notes (1991) that the difference between the good girl and the bad girl is rooted in the viewer's negotiation of pleasure: the bad girl pays the price for her pleasure; the good girl receives it in spite of herself.[2] Bad girls are also "femmes," stigmatized for transgressing gender and sexual norms. Hence the only "positive reading of femme as a critical reading of femininity" emanates from a queer perspective from which it is possible to redraw alternative models of desire and gender (Harris and Crocker 2013, 3).

The analysis of classic films explores the subconscious leanings constructed by a cinema targeting mass audiences that consume national and transnational entertainment. From an academic standpoint, it is not feasible to theorize the "good-bad girl" in Maghrebi or Arab auteur films that have traditionally privileged social realism and aimed to enlighten international audiences in the same terms. The psychoanalytic model that underlies much of the theoretical construction of the gaze cannot account for the specific historical and cultural conditions of the film-viewing experience. Rather, the issue of viewing pleasure as it pertains to bad girls in Maghrebi cinema seems to trifurcate along lines of gender, class, and origin.

The films do not target vast audiences eager to be entertained but a more restricted group willing to be politically engaged (Gugler 2011; Lang 2014). The bad Arab girl is a screen activist, not a sexually alluring woman redeemed by her pristine soul. She may be a high-tech expert and bisexual woman (*Bedwin Hacker*, directed by Nadia El Fani, Tunisia, 2002), a daughter grappling with her identity (*A Door to the Sky*, directed by Farida Benlyazid, Morocco, 1988; *Les secrets*, directed by Raja Amari, Tunisia, 2010), a mother struggling with addiction (*Flower of Oblivion*, directed by Selma Baccar, Tunisia, 2006), or a class-conscious, single, heterosexual woman (*Sur la planche*, directed by Leila Kilani, Morocco, 2011). The bad Arab girl gives visual pleasure to her audience as an empowered character surviving social injustice from whatever social position she occupies, whether she is a daughter (Sabra in *The Trace*, directed by Néjia Ben Mabrouk, Tunisia, 1988; Alya in *Silences of the Palace*, directed by Moufida Tlatli, Tunisia, 1993), a daughter-in-law (Zakia in *Flower of Oblivion*, directed by Salma Baccar, Tunisia and Morocco, 2006), a mother (*Satin rouge*, directed by Raja Amari, Tunisia, 2006), a wife (Zeinab in *The Sleeping Child*, directed by Yasmine Kassari, Morocco, 2004), or a heterosexual, single woman (the title character in *Rachida*, directed by Yamina Bachir-Chouikh, Algeria, 2002).

Visual pleasure, classically considered the province of Western, heterosexual, male viewers, therefore takes on divergent routes once it is inscribed in a Maghrebi context and becomes the province of mostly women in the Maghreb. A recent survey by Caillé on the ways in which men and women from different generations watch films in Tunisia highlights the extent to which women show a taste for films featuring women protagonists with whom they can identify even though they never raise the issue of the filmmaker's gender as having a possible impact on the representation (Caillé 2017).

For now, the woman spectator can identify with a woman character on-screen who is defiantly freeing herself from injustice and oppression: Alya leaves the palace that has enslaved her mother; Rachida will go on teaching in spite of the obstacles thrown in her way. Women spectators thus experience vicariously the sweet pleasure of female victory against the odds of the traditional patriarchal social order that the viewer and character share. This form of pleasure—intensely political—is female in the context of the corpus we are examining here.

Although some good-bad Arab girls from the Maghreb and the Levant on-screen have pleased Western, heterosexual audiences imbued with feminist missionary views of the global South,[3] their more recent incarnations have troubled the waters, given the move toward an "Arab re-authenticity" (Naber 2006)[4] or a political discourse that contradicts Western hegemonic discourses on the "Arab Muslim world," as do Annemarie Jacir's *Salt of This Sea* (2008, Palestine) and *When I Saw You* (2012, Palestine).

However, the Maghrebi bad girls projected by women directors are located not on the Arab re-authenticity side, but rather in between constructs of Eastern and Western feminisms (Lazreg 1988). The notion of the bad girl as a Maghrebi character defies both regimes of truths. Let us now turn to the characteristics and history of the reel bad Maghrebi girls and the reception they elicit offscreen.

## A Line of Reel Bad Maghrebi Female Protagonists

Early women protagonists in Moroccan, Algerian, and Tunisian films appear highly educated, having embarked on quests for freedom and equality on their own terms. Hence, state-sponsored films by women directors, such as *The Nuba of Women on Mount Chenua* (Assia Djebar, Algeria, 1978), *Fatma 75* (Selma Baccar, Tunisia, 1976), and *A Door to the Sky* (Farida Benlyazid, Morocco, 1988), feature sophisticated women with a healthy degree of agency and power over their destinies. Only later did narratives of emancipation (roughly 1990–2005) come into place to lure large international audiences into cinema theaters. These later films offered a commercially successful and standardized version of good-bad girls in the eyes of international (Western) audiences.

Maghrebi women pioneers started their film careers in the wake of their male colleagues, after independence (1956 in Morocco and Tunisia, 1962 in Algeria). The cinematic narrative of the nation and its prowess was male, while women shot films praising the national, precolonial culture. Such was the case with *The Nuba of Women on Mount Chenua*, directed by Assia Djebar (Algeria, 1978), a docufiction film in which the story of *mujā-hidāt* (female freedom fighters) during the independence struggle is told in a highly inclusive way, with each woman interviewed speaking in turn on film at eye level, and through music, reconnecting with the rich Andalusian musical tradition of Algeria. In some ways the badness of women characters in Maghrebi women's films starts right there: the monolithic male national narrative displaced offscreen leaves room for women's plural narrative of the independence struggle against the French occupiers. Djebar's narrative deviates from the national male one in form and content. Using anamnesis as a narrative strategy, Djebar pieces together a collective history, not the hegemonic tale of male heroism, thus, Ann Donadey notes, "resisting the occlusions created by official history, . . .

recovering the traces of another, submerged history in order to create a counter-memory" (1999, 112).

To piece together this plurality of stories, the filmmaker sets up three temporal subjective tracks with three memory lanes: the recorded reminiscences of the women interviewed by Lila, the narrator (who never speaks directly) in the Cherchel region; the oral memory of Lila's evocation of her grandmother's tale of the 1871 Amazigh resistance to the French army on Mount Chenua; and the transmitted myth of the seventh wife of a benevolent local saint.[5] Hence women's memory spills out of the strict frame of the Algerian revolution to better point to a historically (and mythically) grounded resistance by women to invaders. Djebar establishes women's past silence as an act of resistance, by way of a flexible narrative structure that allows a fictitious character to interrupt the interviews of a documentary in progress in order to give full voice to the traditionally mute.[6] Once their silences are broken, the women's hidden histories are projected onto the screen. Although this first film by an Algerian female director had the support of the state, the director's refusal to conform to the male narrative of the dominant Front de Libération Nationale (FLN)[7] caused screening problems for her at the Journées Cinématographiques de Carthage (JCC, known in English as the Tunis Film Festival);[8] feminist Djebar had defiantly affirmed a female, collective narrative that had been erased through the construction of the official, male history.

This deviation from a prescribed cinematic path is repeated again and again in the other national cinemas of the region. Selma Baccar's *Fatma 75* (Tunisia, 1976), for instance, a documentary on the history of women in Tunisia that gives equal voice to women of all walks of life, was sponsored by Habib Bourguiba, who wished to garner praise for his *Code personnel* (Family code, 1956). But Baccar's film also pointed out the deficiencies of the legal apparatus. In Baccar's and Djebar's films, a fictitious female character simultaneously sutures and interrupts a documentary in progress. In each case, the Muslim tradition of *nushūz* (female disobedience in the intimate sphere, analyzed by Fatima Mernissi in her 1996 essay) became enlarged to embrace the filmmaker's public sphere. In each film, the female director diverged from the norms imposed by the male ruler, finding her way to tell a story she was supposed to keep offscreen, in a rebellious use of her camera. Such disobedience had repercussions. *Fatma 75* was banned until 2006 in Tunisia; *The Nuba* was decried by Algerian male critics at the JCC film festival in Tunis.

Some films project the image of what may appear to Western audiences to be a good-bad girl—a bad daughter, mother, or single woman—who dares to defy her local cultural norms while seemingly adopting norms from a Western model widely hailed as universal. And yet in these film narratives, Western patterns of woman's emancipation are complicated by socioeconomics or history/herstory of the end of colonialism. To wit, Sabra, in the starkly realist film *The Trace* (Néjia Ben Mabrouk, 1982), may seem like a good reel bad girl who keeps on studying in spite of her father's prohibition, but her story of emancipation also denounces the economic stratification of Tunisia and the difficulties of the poor; Alya, in the lushly photographed *Silences of the Palace* (Moufida Tlatli, Tunisia, 1993), was viewed by Western critics as a feminist character breaking free from the chains of patriarchy, yet the film also reflected the end of colonialism and access to independence.

## Reel Bad Maghrebi Girls Now

More recently, women filmmakers have moved away from the pitfalls of an edifying and moralizing social realism, in particular its implicit hier-archization of cultural values that positions the Orient as eternally lag-ging behind the West. According to Laurent Jullier (2002), "edification," one of the most widely shared criteria used by audiences in assessing films, evokes the gratification spectators may get from being taught some-thing while watching them; examples would be learning about the plight of Tunisian women toward the end of the colonial era in *Silences of the Palace*, the role of women freedom fighters during the Algerian war of lib-eration in *The Nuba*, and the long line of powerful political female figures in Tunisia in *Fatma 75*. This educational goal raises the issue of visual plea-sure for outside audiences peeking into the otherwise inaccessible inner world of Maghrebi women. Today's filmmakers have developed new forms of storytelling to rephrase complicated issues of power and domination. In their narratives, subjugation, in the form of sexual oppression or eco-nomic deprivation, is no longer the sole outcome of cultural traditions emanating from isolated, remote locations. It results from the combined effects of local and transnational forms of economic and cultural domi-nation. Among them, the hegemonic narrative forms imposed by the need for films to circulate internationally largely codify the terms of that domination.

The reception of *Satin rouge* (Raja Amari, 2002), the last Tunisian success at the French box office, marks a turning point in the international (or, more specifically, European) circulation of commercially successful Tunisian films coproduced with France. Like other successful films from the Maghreb, this film was considered to be essentially about the plight of Maghrebi women. French critics praised the boldness of the film (a virtuous and bored widow unexpectedly discovers and finds pleasure in belly dancing), in contrast to the unfavorable responses of Tunisian audiences at the time, thereby highlighting the ambiguity of the gaze and pleasure of Western audiences when confronted with such films. After *Satin rouge*, French audiences and critics became warier of crowd-pleasing narratives of women's emancipation, turning against the films themselves instead of questioning the position critics and audiences used to enjoy (Caillé 2007). Exploring the relationships of power that oppress women and men thus also means unraveling existing narrative forms that contain the codes of that domination. This is what women filmmakers have done in their new ways of imagining a bad girl's quest for freedom.

Three films offer interesting new models of reel bad girls in this vein. While *L'Amante du Rif* explores the ways a particular economy of desire may seal the demise of a protagonist, *Sur la planche* explores how and to whom the subaltern speaks in the era of global capitalism, thus posing the question, To whom does the Bad Girl speak? *Les secrets*, on the other hand, reveals the unspeakable in the narrative of the home and the nation.

## L'Amante du Rif, a Quest That Cannot Be Told Any Other Way

Narjiss Nejjar's third feature fiction film, *L'Amante du Rif* (2011, Morocco), is a loose adaptation of the eponymous 2004 novel by Noufissa Sbaï, the director's mother. This film weaves together a range of stories and their variations, drawing its central theme and metanarrative, one that is not in the novel, from a song in Georges Bizet's *Carmen* ("Love is the gypsy's child. It has never ever known a law. Love me not, and I love you. And if I love you, beware!").

The emblematic opening scene shows Aya (Nadia Kounda) sitting at a small, worn-out wooden table in a dark, empty cell in prison. Her handsome features are captured in a chiaroscuro as she hums the tune and sings the chorus. She looks at the camera as she tells her cousin Moune and us the story of her own downfall, yet another retelling of Carmen's timeless, tragic narrative that unfolds inexorably like the four acts of the opera. *L'Amante du Rif* constitutes a strikingly complex lacing of images and narratives that progressively imprison Aya in spite of her unwavering commitment to attain her freedom on her own terms.

The first act is a flashback to the multistoried, luminous, yellow-blue-and-white family home in Chefchaouen, a small town in northern Morocco. It focuses on Aya and Rabia (Ouidad Elma), two friends who spend their days getting a tan on the terrace baked by the sun. They long to feel the pangs of love while spying on a drug lord, the boss of Aya's brothers, whose power, black car, and large sunglasses fascinate them. Wearing sexy dresses, the young women run carefree around the village under the condemning eye of a silent and domineering figure, a neighbor dressed in a black niqab.

*L'Amante du Rif* is also the story of an unfinished film, the film that Aya's cousin Moune, whom we hear but never see on-screen, started shooting with a shaky handheld camera. Spectators experience the relationship between these two young women through Moune's images of the initially joyful play between one looking and the other being looked at. Moune lives in France and returns every year "to film people in Morocco," thus fueling Aya's desire to become an actress. Moune's project of filming an exotic locale and lifestyle from the invisible, hybrid perspective as an insider in her family and an outsider who lives in the West raises the issue of the power of desire in the enunciation of the film. Does Moune show and maybe provoke what she longs to see or believes the viewers would like to see, her images propelling the fiction? Her curiosity, which merges with the spectators', is challenged by the improvisations of her own actors. Ehad, Aya's brother, angrily asks Moune if she is trying to film a "postcard of Morocco."

After Moune disappears mysteriously and does not answer calls any more, Aya herself seems ambivalent, saying, "We missed you, Moune, but when you thought you were making us free, you were locking us up." The images that remain propel the narrative, and the tragedy unfolds. It is the desire for Moune to make a film and for Aya to star in it that briefly opens up the possibility of a life worth living, a desire nurtured by Bollywood musicals and Carlos Saura's adaptation of *Carmen* (1983), a VHS Moune had left as a present that Aya and Rabia watched with delight. Looking back, Aya insists that "in the film, he loved her." Rabia retorts, "But at the end he killed her."

Aya knows there is no possible happy end for young women in a village where "a woman's honor is her hymen." Thrown into the arms of the drug lord by Ehad (turned Judas in exchange for a plot of land), Aya, still longing to be loved, is robbed of her virginity. Hanging onto her passion, she fights back, while Rabia takes her chances. Does wanting to be loved and wanting to be part of the short-lived thrill of power and danger that may come with the prospect of participating in another adaptation of *Carmen* make Aya or Rabia a bad girl? Aya's mother (Nadia Niazi) relentlessly tries to obtain her release, and Aya ends up trapped between an irresistible and doomed longing that makes her feel alive and the prospect of an arranged marriage. Marriage is what Aya feels has left her mother "dead inside." She tells her, "To me, Hell is all that you suggest."

The bright colors progressively give way to the gray and dark environment of the prison where Aya, wrongly accused of assault and violence, rots away with a group of women who have chosen to live their passions, whatever the consequences. The prison paradoxically becomes the place where a lesbian couple can be free and the starting point for resisting the patriarchal order. Meanwhile, the family home, its colors washed out by the rain and its furniture sold off, stands as the symbol of the scattered and ruined family. *L'Amante du Rif* reinscribes the repression of desire and sexuality within a much larger, multilayered popular and tragic allegory that gives life to the characters while it condemns them to their own demise. The film closes with a voice-over of Aya asking Moune to come back to tell "them" all that Aya dreamed of and did not want to become. To whom does "them" refer? She probably refers to her mother, who stood by her and desperately tried to help her recover her honor, to the hypocrites Noufissa Sbaï condemns in her novel, to all those who have sought to force Aya into lives she had to refuse, thus raising the question of where the spectators actually stand in the story. Narjiss Nejjar's dedication, "You died on 23 January 2003, it was 35 degrees, you will not celebrate your 21st birthday," a text superimposed on the image of a car's windshield wiper on a rainy day, brings viewers back to the actual cost of a young woman's transgression, in sharp contrast with this retelling of the eternally defiant mythical Carmen. In *L'Amante du Rif*, the camera "frames" the character in all senses of the term; it captures Aya and tells her story with or without her. Her doomed struggle for freedom is endlessly reformulated in metanarratives that have shaped Aya's and the spectators' dreams.

## Sur la planche

An acclaimed documentary maker, Leila Kilani in her first fiction film, *Sur la planche* (2011), breaks with all Maghrebi women protagonist stereotypes in a drama/thriller-genre film. It explores questions of empowerment and agency and brings work, class relations, and globalization to the forefront. A high-angle shot frames and dwarfs lines of tiny, indistinguishable figures wrapped in spotless white overalls and hairnets, sitting in close rows of white plastic chairs along large rectangular tables, shelling heaps of shrimp. Detached from her community of origin, Badia is one in a large crowd of female migrants working in the many factories that rely on cheap, unskilled labor in Tangier. Her fairly rough facial features and sulky expression set her apart from any standard cinematic images of femininity or seduction. She defies the hypocritical respectability imposed by her landlady, who looks sternly on her frequent comings and goings. Keenly aware of the segregation that organizes the division of labor and her own exclusion, Badia stands out from the mass of her co-workers thanks in part to her capacity to lecture endlessly on the conditions of her own oppression and the strategies she deploys to improve her condition. She is a relentless fighter, but class struggle is not her thing. Instead, she embarks, with a friend in tow, on an exclusive struggle for upward mobility by all possible means.

What makes her an unusual character is the construction of her subjectivity. At the beginning, alone, bouncing against a wall in her white overalls and hairnet, Badia mumbles to herself, "Pride lies, and rightly so. Why? Better to be standing up, propped by one's own lie, than to be lying down, crushed by someone else's truth. I don't steal: I get my money back. I don't break in: I take back. I am not a trafficker: I trade. I am not a prostitute: I invite myself over."[9]

Badia's power lies in her ability to construct and narrate her own sense of self outside any specific value system or worldview. In the scams she cooks up, she replicates the same amorality as the invisible power that exploits her, which allows her to claim very early on, "I am ahead of truth, my truth."[10] But, as her friend notices later, "No one is listening."

The film is constructed as one long flashback leading to her arrest by the police. A handheld camera records the vertiginous energy Badia invests in ongoing, frenetic activity, her movements poignant as she becomes gradually entrapped. The shifts between the days under the bright neon lights in the factory and the nights out become the two faces of the same quest to give meaning to her life and improve it. This quest takes Badia back and forth across Tangiers, a city we no longer see or recognize, as it is reduced to a map we experience only through her constant trespassing of forbidden spaces. This increases the sense of her own confinement even though she manages to talk her way into the very secure "free zone" or invites herself into villas where she grabs all she can get. *Sur la planche* transforms the terms of the viewer's identification because the filmic choice forces audiences to adhere to Badia's hyperactivity, and lectures through a camera that remains so close that it prevents any overarching view, thus paradoxically increasing the sense of her vulnerability.

Her frantic activities include sex with strangers in broken-into villas, yet sex remains offscreen. Sexuality is detached from all considerations of liberation, happiness, pleasure, or self-fulfillment; it is just a way to get what she can get no other way. She struggles with her own body, its odor of shrimp or sex, fiercely scrubbing her skin with soap and wrapping up her clothes in airtight containers, a compulsion that hints at her desperate attempt to keep her body unspoiled by her present condition.

Reinscribing social determination in a genre film, *Sur la planche* constructs a fearless subaltern, endowed with a strong will and a strong voice, whose discourse constructs the terms of her own sense of herself while the noose of a socioeconomic order that denies her any rights gets tighter around her. Yet, in the end, the interiority and humanity of this mouthy reel bad girl remain out of reach.

## Les secrets/Buried Secrets

*Buried Secrets* (Raja Amari, 2010) is a disturbing film in its content, in its relentless deviation from the narrative norms it simultaneously shows and debunks, and in the way it constructs its protagonist, whose identity shifts to reveal a unique bad girl defying all expectations.

The story is structured like a fairy tale: once upon a time, there were three women living in the servants' quarters in the basement of a big house. The oldest is "the mother," who remains anonymous throughout the film; the second one, Radhia (Soundes Bel Hassen), is the "sister," and the youngest, Aïcha, "the daughter" (Hafsia Herzi), is the one whose point of view is given in most of the shots. When the villa owner's grandson Ali and his beautiful girlfriend, Selma (the princess), suddenly arrive with a group of young merrymakers to have a huge party upstairs (Cinderella's ball), Aïcha is mesmerized. Defying her family's strict interdiction to go upstairs, she roams through the house, steals a pair of red dancing shoes from Selma, and attends the ball. The Cinderella-like fantasy shows fissures straight away when Aïcha breaks the heel of one shoe, before turning into a potential horror story. Selma discovers the secret trio downstairs. The three women panic and kidnap her. The narrative turns to the relationships that unite and tear the trio of women confronted with Selma, as the four of them now cohabit downstairs.

Raja Amari, who became well known in Tunisia and Europe for her previous *Red Satin/Satin rouge/Al sitar al ahmar* (2002), stated that she planted elements of the fairy tale in *Buried Secrets* to anchor her narrative in Aïcha's inner world. Aïcha seems to be in a state of arrested development, a characterization rendered sonically by the film's haunting lullaby (also the meaning of its Arabic title, *Dowaha*). But then the fairy-tale structure, à la Vladimir Propp (1968), deviates from its prescribed path in several ways.

Selma, princess-like, faints upon being kidnapped and is put to bed. When she awakens, Aïcha, in the role of the waiting prince, smiles, and the two adults look on sternly. Selma's charming Prince Ali, meanwhile, gives up on the search for her a little too soon, is easily convinced that Selma has simply left him, promptly betrays her with another woman (princesses seem expendable upstairs), and leaves the palace altogether. Radhia and Aïcha have spied upon Ali and Selma making love in the first part of the film. Radhia clearly fancies Ali. Sex happens upstairs, not downstairs. Radhia goes upstairs to the bathroom to pleasure herself in secret.[11]

There is some nudity in the film, but the way Selma's naked body is filmed being washed, for instance, diverges from the standard Orientalizing hammam (also known as Turkish baths in the West) scenes of the Tunisian cinema of the 1990s (Boughedir 1990). She is seen from the back, sitting in the tub, being vigorously scrubbed clean by Radhia. The camera never lingers on parts of her body, except for the hair being energetically shampooed, and never fetishizes her body. The bath scene also features the first full dialogue between the two women, as the camera angle places Radhia and Selma at the same level even if Radhia plays her part as servant in the villa. Radhia scrubbing Selma's body produces meaning on several levels: a haptic reading of the scene—along the lines of Laura Marks's (2000) or Jennifer Baker's (2009) feminist reading of the sense of touch on-screen—contains no hint of eroticism in the projected harsh feeling of a loofah scouring the skin; a cultural viewing of the scene reminds the extradiegetic viewer of the community of women meeting at the hammam to wash together, not posing languidly as in an Orientalist painting. Finally, the tenor of the dialogue foreshadows the end; to Selma's question "Why don't you go out?" Radhia responds with a sibylline "You know where my father is. And the baby as well," which makes no sense to the viewer at this point. The scene astonishes the viewer through a carefully staged surprise by the director, who takes her viewers into uncharted territories.[12]

Several forces are at work here. The most blatant one, revealed at the end of the film, is the force of the family-held secret, handed down unconsciously from mother to daughter; the second one is the filmic medium itself, which hides and reveals; the third one is the political dimension of the film. The family secret is almost always about identity and sex. Tisseron notes that the family secret endures thanks to the silence surrounding, and the interdiction against knowing or, therefore, asking questions about, the painful, traumatic event that is unsaid from one generation to the next (2011, 8). The trauma, called "fracas" by Boris Cyrulnik (2012) because it can shatter the inner world of its victim, is unsaid by the first generation, unspeakable by the second, and unthinkable by the third (Tisseron 2011, 58–61). Yet the absence of words around the fracas is unreliable; pent-up emotions find other ways to express themselves.[13] Unbeknownst to the subject—because her silence around the secret has unconscious effects that escape her control—something "oozes" (suinte, writes Tisseron) on the outside that reveals the existence of an unmentionable fracas inside and ripples out from one generation to the next.

The trio looks like the female embodiment of the family secret that ties them together and pulls them apart. Their literally "obscene" existence (they live offstage, "below" the villa and society) allows them to keep silent to the outside world, while the secret of the origin (who is Aïcha's father?) oozes into their daily lives. Aïcha eventually uncovers the truth; the viewer and Aïcha understand that she is the incestuous daughter of Radhia and her father. When the fracas catches up with Aïcha, it triggers a hyperviolent reaction. To free herself from the family secret and from the obscene, she kills her sister/mother and her grandmother before she leaves the haunted villa. She then enters the world outside and walks to the center of Tunis, on Avenue Bourguiba.

The director films the bodies and the oozing of the secret in close-ups.

Recurring shots of the three women standing at a doorjamb spying on the couple upstairs repeatedly frame them as a three-headed entity. Radhia's face never smiles. Her mother's face only smiles when she admires herself in the privacy of the bathroom, alone. Aïcha is heard humming a lullaby, dreamily smiling to herself. Although the two older women seem strong and independent, neither can function without the other or without Aïcha. Hence, when the identity of each of the three women, welded by the secret surrounding the violating act of one man, becomes unglued, defying all norms of womanly emancipation, Aïcha liberates herself by killing the two patriarchal avatars and victims. Aïcha's violent rebellion seems strangely logical, for the mother and Radhia have internalized the shame of the incestuous rape and the guilt of their murder of the rapist. Yet they also exercise patriarchal power in a most disturbing scene in which they check Aïcha's virginity when she comes down from the ball.

The jarring juxtaposition of fairy-tale and realist elements gives the film a bitterly ironic distance through which the viewer receives highly composed images with an almost painterly quality. In the end, then, the story of Aïcha's self-emancipation is not an allegory of a woman's liberation by any standard, whether Western or not, but rather the starkly realistic projected narrative of an individual finally seeing through the lies of her foremothers and their fairy tales.

Furthermore, the visual narrative sets up a larger story, that of the national, political killing of the father. Filmed shortly before the Tunisian revolution took off and ousted dictator Ben Ali in January 2011, the ending of the film seems prophetic: Aïcha, having killed her prison guards, who had killed the father, is now free to walk on the central walkway in the middle of Bourguiba Avenue in downtown Tunis. The camera focuses on her ecstatic smile and bloodstained white dress and slowly zooms out to reveal her solitude. Yet, the farther the camera zooms out, the larger the influx of indifferent passersby invading the walkway, occupying the center of the now iconic avenue that would host crowds of revolutionaries during the ousting of Ben Ali. Here the visual narrative exceeds the edges of the filmic one as it foretells the story of a national liberation about to happen offscreen. One could also read this film in the wake of Tlatli's *Silences of the Palace* in its depiction of women's liberation away from a prison/palace, a wrenching liberation that stages the murder of the mother (the avatar of patriarchal power who remains as silent as a stone about the secret of filiation), this time at the hands of her daughter. Since Tlatli's landmark film, the violence of national and female liberation has clearly cranked up the volume a couple of notches.

These three films all project an image of a Maghrebi bad girl protagonist with a strong sense of self who clearly refuses the trajectories of emancipation that may make them look like good-bad girls in the eyes of audiences globally. And yet, it looks like there are no possible positive outcomes to their quests. Alya cannot wrestle free from all the narratives that have shaped her childhood dreams and those of her audience. There is no alternate narrative that can account for her desire. Badia cannot beat the system, as there is no third way for an exploited woman to make it to the top. Aïcha may be free from the bowels of the villa, but she has the limited freedom of an autistic child whose place in society is unclear in the last images of the film. Audiences are left with the chimera of their own identification with a character whose subjectivity remains inaccessible. Maghrebi bad girls model a fiercely individualistic behavior, outside all traditional social and cultural norms. The narrative of their coming into badness revisits and interrogates the power of classical structures (the opera that immolates a woman, the fairy tale) and gives them a voice of excess that saturates the soundtrack, or a humming voice that fails to soothe their malaise in the world.

In the end, then, in the wake of their foremothers who opened the screen for the dissident voices of disobedient women, the Maghrebi filmmakers of the millennium construct utterly dissident protagonists in the Maghreb and the world who have done away with the set of binary oppositions that underlie the circulation of films between the Maghreb and Europe. While the reel bad Maghrebi girl fights injustice tooth and nail, be it patriarchy or global capitalism, her narratives also operate as powerful reminders of the consequences of such bold transgressions.

## Notes

1. Taking Wolfenstein and Leites's model, Edgar Morin describes the good-bad girl played by Marilyn Monroe as a "very sensuous woman, whose appearance is that of a prostitute. . . . In the European imaginary, there is a powerful dissociation between two kinds of love: the pure virginal woman whom we worship without daring to touch her and the prostitute. The good-bad girl successfully bridges these two kinds of love. A very attractive and sensuous woman, she has a beautiful soul nonetheless"; Morin 2004, 9. Bad girls have been associated with the excess of sensations that the genre

films of popular cinema, like weepies, horror films, and pornography, generate in viewers; Williams 1991, 2–13.

2. Williams asserts, "Under a patriarchal double standard that has clearly separated the sexually passive 'good' girl from the sexually active 'bad' girl, masochistic role-playing offers a way out of this dichotomy by combining the good girl with the bad: the passive 'good girl' can prove to her witnesses (the super-ego who is her torturer) that she does not will the pleasure that she receives. Yet the sexually active 'bad' girl enjoys this pleasure and has knowingly arranged to endure the pain that earns it. The cultural law which decides that some girls are good and others are bad is not defeated but within its terms pleasure has been negotiated and 'paid for' with a pain that conditions it"; 1991, 8.

3. "The global South" is here a shortcut by no means intended to reify or homogenize a variety of cultures geopolitically located south of Europe.

4. This re-authenticity movement is seen, for instance, through the reveiling that has occurred throughout the Muslim world; Lazreg 2009. However, the good-bad protagonists rarely wear veils in films by Maghrebi women.

5. For a detailed reading of *The Nuba*, see Martin 2011, 48–62.

6. *The Nuba* can be viewed as an illustration of Marnia Lazreg's theorization (1994) on Algerian women's silence as a tool of resistance.

7. The Front de Libération Nationale (FLN, National Liberation Front) was the most powerful organized movement that led freedom fighters against the French, then took power in 1962, and has been at the helm of Algeria ever since.

8. The Journées Cinématographiques de Carthage is the Arab-African film festival that takes place in Tunis every other year. On the film festival, see Caillé and Martin, 2017.

9. My translations from French film subtitles. "L'orgueil ment et a bien raison de le faire. Pourquoi? Mieux vaut être debout tenu par son propre mensonge qu'allongé écrasé par la vérité des autres. Je vole pas: je me rembourse. Je cambriole pas: je récupère. Je trafique pas: je commerce. Je me prostitue pas: je m'invite. Je mens pas: je sais déjà ce que je serai."

10. "Je suis en avance sur la vérité: la mienne."

11. The bathroom is the place of all secrets for the women. This is where Mother is seen smoking with obvious delight and letting her hair loose to admire it in the mirror; this is where Aïcha shaves her legs, which she is not allowed to do.

12. In a 2009 interview Amari explains, "I like establishing a rapport with the viewer in which he can recognize himself and to which he can adhere, to then lead him onto uncharted territory, to take him where he does not want to go" (J'aime bien établir un rapport avec le spectateur où il peut se reconnaître et adhérer pour glisser peu à peu vers un terrain inconnu, de l'emmener là où il ne veut pas aller); Amari 2009.

13. Cyrulnik writes, "Il est difficile de se taire, mais il est possible de ne pas dire. Quand on ne s'exprime pas, l'émotion se manifeste encore plus forte sans les mots"; 2012, 8.

# References

Amari, Raja, dir. 2006. *Satin rouge*. Film. Tunisia.

———. 2009. "Emmener le spectateur là où il ne veut pas aller." Interview by Olivier Barlet. *Africultures*, November. http://www.africultures.com/php/index.php?nav=article&no=9015.

———, dir. 2010. *Buried Secrets*. Film. France and Tunisia.

Baccar, Selma, dir. 1976. *Fatma 75*. Tunisia.

Baker, Jennifer. 2009. *The Tactile Eye: Touch and the Cinematic Experience*. Berkeley: University of California Press.

Boughedir, Férid, dir. 1990. *Halfaouine, Boy of the Terraces*. Film. Tunisia.

Caillé, Patricia. 2007. "Figures du féminin et cinéma national tunisien (1990–2002)." In *La fiction éclatée: Etudes socio-culturelles*, edited by Jean-Pierre Bertin-Maghit and Geneviève Sellier. Paris: L'Harmattan.

———. 2017. "Pratiques de films, représentations et cultures de cinéma en Tunisie: Que nous raconte l'enquête?" In *Regarder des films en Afrique aujourd'hui: Représentations et pratiques du cinéma*, edited by Patricia Caillé and Claude Forest. Lille, France: Editions du Septentrion.

Caillé, Patricia, and Florence Martin. "Women Directors in the Maghreb." In *Arab Cinema*, edited by James Neill. Volendam, Netherlands: LM, 2017.

Cyrulnik, Boris. 2012. *Mourir de dire: La honte*. Paris: Odile Jacob.

Djebar, Assia, dir. 1978. *The Nuba of Women on Mount Chenua*. Film. Algeria.

Donadey, Ann. 1999. "Between Amnesia and Anamnesis: Re-Membering the Fractures of Colonial History." *Studies in Twentieth Century Literature* 23, no. 1:111–116.

Gugler, Josef, ed. 2011. *Film in the Middle East and North Africa: Creative Dissidence*. Austin: University of Texas Press.

Harris, Laura, and Elizabeth Crocker. 1997. *Femme: Feminists, Lesbians, and Bad Girls*. London: Routledge.

Jullier, Laurent. 2002. *Qu'est-ce qu'un bon film?* Paris: La Dispute.

Kilani, Leila, dir. 2011. *Sur la planche*. Film. Morocco, Germany.

Lang, Robert. 2014. *New Tunisian Cinema: Allegories of Resistance*. New York: Columbia University Press.

Lazreg, Marnia. 1988. "Feminism and Difference: The Perils of Writing as a Woman on Women in Algeria," *Feminist Studies* 14, no. 1 (Spring):81–107.

———. 1994. *The Eloquence of Silence: Algerian Women in Question*. New York: Routledge.

———. 2009. *Questioning the Veil: Open Letters to Muslim Women*. Princeton, NJ: Princeton University Press.

Marks, Laura. 2000. *The Skin of Film: Intercultural Cinema, Embodiment, and the Senses*. Durham, NC: Duke University Press.

Martin, Florence. 2011. *Screens and Veils: Maghrebi Women's Cinema*. Indianapolis: Indiana University Press.

Mernissi, Fatima. *Women's Rebellion and Islamic Memory*. London: Zed Books, 1996.

Morin, Edgar. 2005. "La culture de masse: Le choc des années 50 et 60." Transcript of a dialogue between Edgar Morin and Eric Macé. *Médiamorphoses*, no. 13 (May):7–19.

Naber, Nadine. 2006. "Arab American Femininities: Beyond Arab Virgin/American-(ized) Whore." *Feminist Studies* 32, no. 1:87–111.

Nejjar, Narjiss, dir. 2011. *L'Amante du Rif*. Film. Belgium, France, Morocco.

Propp, Vladímir. 1968. *Morphology of the Folk Tale*. 2nd ed. Austin: University of Texas Press.

Sbaï, Noufissa. *L'Amante du Rif*. Paris: Paris-Méditerranée, 2004.

Tisseron, Serge. 2011. *Les secrets de famille*. Paris: Presses Universitaires de France.

Tlatli, Moufida, dir. 1993. *Silences of the Palace*. Film. Tunisia.

Williams, Linda. 1991. "Film Bodies: Gender, Genre, Excess." *Film Quarterly* 4, no. 44: 2–13.

Wolfenstein, Martha, and Nathan Leites. 1950. *Movies: A Psychological Study*.

# New Bad Girls of Sudan

## ELEVEN

Women Singers in the Sudanese Diaspora

ANITA H. FÁBOS

Setona al-Magirus swept into the Sudan Culture and Information Center lecture hall in Cairo followed by her entourage. After a brief introduction by the center's director, she began to sing, accompanying herself on the *daloka*—a medium-size drum associated with women's performative culture in northern Sudan and, specifically, *aghānī al-banāt*, the songs sung by women that audiences associate with Sudanese wedding traditions. The large, almost entirely Sudanese audience, at that moment in the mid-1990s, expressed appreciation at hearing the familiar music associated with homeland rituals of marriage and gendered notions of traditional Sudanese culture by enthusiastically clapping and singing along.

But this performance was not simply a nostalgic act for a collection of immigrants yearning for the familiar. Nearly everyone in attendance that evening had left Sudan for Egypt under threatening circumstances created by the Islamist government that had taken over in a military coup in 1989. Some of these exiles, losers in the battle between democratic political change and fundamentalist military rule, had experienced severe violence at the hands of the regime and fled for their lives. Others had suffered harassment, threats, dismissal from employment, and other means—both bureaucratic and thuggish—to punish Sudanese men and women for their supposed transgressions. Such transgressions were defined differently for women and for men, often in accusations of immoral behavior as defined by Article 152 of the penal code, a significant tool in the Sudanese state's Islamic Civilization Project tool kit. Among the most severely treated by the regime were musicians, and women musicians in particular. Scores of musicians went into exile in protest and to continue their professional activities without restrictions or penalties. Setona Al-Magirus—the stage name of Fatima 'Ali Adam 'Uthman—was one of those who left their musical careers in Khartoum behind to join other Sudanese in a spreading diaspora.

I focus here on the participation of a subset of Sudanese women singers outside of Sudan in the ongoing Sudanese conversation about identity and change. Women diaspora singers are at odds with the state-sponsored reorganization of Sudan's gender system, thus transgressing the borders of the Sudanese homeland and the boundaries of gender norms. Regardless of their personal preferences or complex relations with Sudan as a claim on identity, Sudanese women who perform as Sudanese-identified artists become lightning rods for those benefiting from the status quo. As such, their professional role itself is transgressive, pegged by a social, political, and legal system and its chief guardians as improper.

I introduce three contemporary diaspora women singers—Setona, Rasha, and Alsarah—whose musical participation in the complex geography of the Sudanese diaspora bridges genres, cultures, and histories. While bad girls have notably been part of the Sudanese popular music scene since its inception in the pre-independence period, the Internet and interactive social media sites in particular present opportunities for a new group of Sudanese bad girls beyond the immediate reach of the Sudanese state to participate in national conversations. Though they may not see themselves as bad girls, their Sudanese origins, global visibility, and challenges to the ethnic, religious, class, and gender status quo position them as subversive in the face of state-sanctioned regulation of musical performance.

These new bad girl singers succeed a raft of celebrated women of an earlier era of Sudanese music who pushed to be included in Sudan's flourishing state-sponsored music industry and fought those who blocked women's paths to participate publicly as artists. Political conditions have meant an absence of new bad girls from the national music scene, a circumstance that has allowed the voices of diasporic singers a larger platform for their commentary and participation. The three singers have had very different exilic experiences, career paths, and relations with the Sudanese music scene—they are based in Madrid, Brooklyn, and Cairo—

but together provide a lens on a broader debate over a Sudanese imagined community spanning the nation and its diaspora.

"Bad-girlness" is a useful perspective from which to view contemporary politics in Sudan for a number of reasons. In her analysis of the genesis of the Islamist state in the 1980s, Hale (1996) demonstrates the hegemonic male positioning of women in both left-wing and Islamist revolutionary movements. In the post-independence social and political transformation of Sudan that lasted from the mid-1950s to the 1990s, Hale and other scholars of the Sudanese state (Ali 2004; Bernal 1997; Willemse 2007) note women's robust participation in Sudanese politics, the co-opting of this participation by powerful patriarchal interests, and a restructuring of women's public roles in the years following the Islamist takeover of the state in 1989. Women who departed from the cultural and social script laid out by the Islamist movement, for example, have been labeled "bad" on the grounds not only of religious morality, but also—building upon earlier tropes of femininity as incorporating propriety (Fábos 2010), gender complementarity (Boddy 1989), and whiteness (Fábos 2012)—of ethnic nationalism.

## Musicians and Morality: Transgressing the Social Order

The association of musical expression with transgression of social and gender rules is not new and certainly not limited to Sudan or other societies in the Arab world. "In many countries, and in different historical periods," asserts Karin van Nieuwkerk, "entertainers have been held in low esteem" (1995, 3). Explanations for the low status of music and dance include the opposition of some religions to worldly pleasures; the performative display of bodies, particularly female bodies, as immoral or sexualized; and the peripatetic nature of many entertainers serving the cyclical needs of settled communities for weddings and other celebrations (Berland 1983; van Nieuwkerk 1995). In societies where women's public roles are circumscribed, female performers—whose professions fall outside social norms for women's activities and who may display their bodies through their art—transgress the gender and social order and thus frequently incite repression.

In Sudan the variety of cultural practices, musical styles, and gender norms makes it impossible to generalize about the status of musicians, but I focus here on recorded popular music with high production values that is marketed globally and to a largely urban audience in northern Sudan. Ambivalence toward musical expression and women's voices is evident in the national discourse, as women's public role in musical culture has ebbed and flowed over the decades since independence. Since the early twentieth-century inception of Sudan as a national project, musicians have had an association with nationalist struggles and protests. From the 1960s through the 1980s, a small number of women singers took to the public stage. Peter Verney names three: "Demurely echoing the rise of the 1960s girl groups in the West, a few female duos rose to local popularity including Sunai Kordofani, Sunai el Nagam and Sunai el Samar" (1999, 676).

In the mid- to late 1980s, however, women performers were increasingly censured as a result of the rising tide of political and social conservatism that accompanied Sudan's emerging Islamist power brokers, the influence of Wahhabi Islam via returning migrant men, and the rekindling of the war with South Sudanese rebels. These and other economic and political pressures brought a military coup in 1989 and new forms of social control, including robust regulation of women's bodies, behaviors, and roles. Women and men singers and musicians experienced a backlash associated with the gendered policing of morality. In 2012, even as the beloved anticolonial icon Hawa al-Tagtaga was being honored by President Omar al-Bashir for her performance for Sudanese troops while wrapped in the national flag on the day of Sudan's independence nearly six decades earlier, "a group of Salafi clerics visited Insaf Medani, the Hawa incarnate crowned as the contemporary 'queen of the *daloka*,' at her home in Khartoum North, advising her to stop *ḥarām* singing and dedicate her talent to the recitation of *ḥalāl* hymns" (El Gizouli 2012). The bold performer Hanan Bulu-bulu (Sudan's Madonna), who scandalized and delighted Sudanese society in the 1980s, was banned from performing, beaten up, and insulted for her "half-Ethiopian" heritage—a euphemism for licentious behavior (Verney 1998).[1]

Musicians were among the first to be targeted by Sudan's Islamist regime after it seized power in a military coup in 1989; they were accused of promoting inappropriate comportment, such as mixed-gender dancing, and expressing political opposition through lyrics. Scores went into exile to protest and to continue their professions. In 1991 the singer and bandleader Yousef El-Mousely set up a recording studio in Cairo where musicians could produce music banned in Sudan, but Egypt's tough immigration policies led him and thousands of others in exile to move farther along migration routes to more stable situations in asylum-granting countries, such as the United States, Canada, and the United Kingdom.

## Regulating Women Musicians

The Sudanese state now regulates and polices the public behavior of women living in Sudan through the 1983 Penal Code and 1991 Criminal Act, both of which are part of a trend in some Muslim countries to re-Islamize previously secular legal systems by introducing Islamic criminal offenses and sanctions in their codified laws (Sidahmed 2001, 188). Women singers of popular music have struggled to overcome not only their association with slave-origin musicians but also Sudanese notions of gender impropriety, including performing in public spaces. As a result of ongoing government surveillance and raids on public and private performance spaces—for example, the 2009 arrest and punishment of Lubna Hussein and twelve others for the "indecency" of wearing trousers in a nightclub—women's public musical performance is very much sanitized and tamed. Even private weddings are subject to state policy requiring permission papers for wedding parties, an 11 p.m. cutoff time for the festivities, and the prohibition of mixed-gender dancing. Furthermore, broadcasts of Sudanese culture, like those on the state-regulated Blue Nile TV channel, constrain performers' depictions of the sensual bridal dance tradition to modest movements.

The Sudanese state's regulatory control of women's bodies in the realm of musical performance has its supporters in Sudan and the diaspora. The Internet has served as a site for monitoring, harassment, and abuse along gender and racial lines in accordance with the hierarchies of power maintained by Sudan's dominant Arab Muslim elite (Wureta and Fábos 2012). Despite attempts by guardians of the status quo to bully their fellow Sudanese, alternative visions of Sudanese identity have emerged, and creative new artists have flourished beyond the reach of the state. As the career trajectories of Rasha, Alsarah, and Setona illustrate, the widening of Sudanese cultural and gender discourse to include singers who identify as Sudanese but who do not live in Sudan has made it more difficult to police the behavior of women singers who transgress Sudanese cultural norms.

## Breaking Bad—Three Women Singers
## in the Sudanese Diaspora

Women and men continue to make music in a variety of private or underground settings in Sudan, but the risk of arrest or violence is great (Canada 2014).[2] Away from these direct threats, women singers like Rasha, Alsarah, and Setona have the freedom to sing what they choose and participate in the political debate over Sudan's future. The public personas of these women have made their accomplishments—whether celebrated or denigrated—visible within national borders and beyond.

In the early 1990s, growing militarization and Islamization prompted each singer to leave the country. Setona and Rasha both headed to Cairo, while the somewhat younger Alsarah was taken to Yemen by her parents. Setona found an audience for her folk-style music and henna art among a significant community of recent Sudanese exiles as well as older Sudanese immigrant communities in Egypt. Her musical and entrepreneurial abilities brought her to the attention of international music promoters, and she released her first "world music" album,[3] *Tarig Sudan* (The way of Sudan), in 1998. Rasha moved from Cairo to Spain in the mid-1990s and developed a musical style that incorporates Sudanese musical expression, Spanish and jazz influences, and her own acoustic arrangements. Her first album, *Sudaniyat*, was released in 1997 to international acclaim. Alsarah's family moved to the United States in the mid-1990s; Alsarah studied ethnomusicology, and in 2010, enriched by the vibrant musical scene in New York, she founded her own group, the Nubatones.

Broadly speaking, Setona specializes in what the music industry describes in a rather scattershot way as folk, international, world, African traditions, East African, and/or Sudanese, but her Sudanese audiences most appreciate *aghānī al-banāt*. Women performers of *aghānī al-banāt* in northern and central Sudan have a history of providing social commentary—sometimes quite saucy—on Sudanese gender, class, and other hierarchies (Malik 2010). These performers—*ghannānat*—have been largely excluded by the Sudanese popular music industry due to their gendered association with the work of former slaves. As a popular singer in Sudan, Setona appealed to Sudanese pride in and nostalgia for an authentic culture, but she did not have a significant recording career until after her move to Cairo. Before becoming known for their Sudanese music, Rasha and Alsarah worked with African and Middle Eastern roots music groups.

All three have received attention from world music promoters while continuing to appeal to audiences inside Sudan and in the Sudanese diaspora.[4]

These women's music cannot easily be classified as a single genre. All three sing mainly in Arabic and publicly acknowledge their origins and links to Sudan. They also rely on some elements of traditional Sudanese music, such as the pentatonic modal scale and rhythms common to the musical traditions of northern Sudan, and Sudanese instruments (bongos and the *darabukka*, a type of drum) and the oud. The northern Sudanese female folk tradition of *aghānī al-banāt* is a consistent musical and philosophical influence in all three women's work. While Setona exclusively sings *aghānī al-banāt*, Rasha and Alsarah are inspired by other musical influences as well—Rasha by the music of Spain, and Alsarah by a broad array of East African and other genres.

Representing different musical generations, the artistic output of Setona, Rasha, and Alsarah has helped to provide a point of reference for diaspora Sudanese coming to terms with mobile lives and fluid notions of belonging. All three are popular within and outside Sudan and thus play a bridging role through their recordings, live performances, and Internet presence. In terms of mapping the three singers' careers and genres against a Sudanese diaspora timeline, Setona had the longest presence in Sudan and only came to the attention of the international world music industry after many years as a well-established professional. Rasha, who also started her career in Sudan, nevertheless was quite young when she moved to Spain and developed a new approach to Sudanese musical expression as a singer-songwriter. Alsarah's career has taken shape entirely outside of Sudan, and she describes her music as belonging to the genre of East African retro pop. This rough map of the singers' border- and boundary-crossing decisions illustrates the interplay of Sudanese diaspora movements and musical expression and sets out the parameters within which their innovations, entrepreneurial practices, and identity stances have been judged by their Sudanese listeners inside and outside of Sudan as acceptable or transgressive.

## Giving Voice to Political Convictions

In Sudanese exile politics, opposition discourse shares many of the same racialized and gendered assumptions about the nation that the regime in power holds (Ali 2015). The music making of Setona, Rasha, and Alsarah, on the other hand, builds on a tradition of political and social engagement in Sudanese women's music to reflect an alternative and even transformative politics. The significance of this discourse is evident in the ways in which voices of the status quo engage it critically through social media.

Within Sudan, women musicians have long used song to share analyses of political, economic, and social events and processes. As a politically and socially marginalized group, women have historically been absent from public discourse, but women's private gatherings, including the elements of weddings that are typically segregated, have offered a critical space for expressing views not found in the mainstream. The genre of *aghānī al-banāt* in particular is associated with Sudanese women descended from slaves and hence has a particular racialized, gendered connotation (Malik 2010; Westende 2009). Malik explains, "Despite being labeled as 'loose' and 'bad' singing, *aghānī al-banāt* provided a discursive space through which the Sudanese women voiced their alternative narratives of social and gender relations. The songs offered both a framework of negotiating the existing relations as well as a dream of improvement" (2010, 3).

Apart from *aghānī al-banāt*, women singers of popular music in Sudan today primarily perform songs or poetry written by men (Fábos and Alsarah 2016). Sudanese media outlets now present *aghānī al-banāt* as a Sudanese folk tradition, but the lyrics are also written by men. The performers' clothing and dance movements are constrained, Malik finds, to "conform with what the government perceives as an 'ideal' image for the Sudanese woman performer in the media" (2010, 141). These co-opted and sanitized public performances are a world away from the *aghānī al-banāt* that Sudanese women continue to perform in private.

Beyond the constraints of the Sudanese state and the government-controlled media, women in the diaspora use the space of exile to publicly transgress the cultural and political barriers through their music. Alsarah has given voice to Sudanese women's experiences and cultural expression through her performances of traditional genres such as *aghānī al-banāt* and songs of return in a new transnational context, thereby making an important statement about the worth of women's music to a global public.[5] She also articulates a deep respect for people experiencing structural violence: "I sing about migration, voluntary and forced, I sing about people the world likes to ignore except when speaking of them in the past, and I sing about what it means to yearn for home. I also sing about survival and love and joy, which is how people continue despite policies that change the course of their existence" (in Hansen and Obling, 2013).

*Silt*, the debut album she recorded with the Nubatones in 2014, is built around Nubian "songs of return." In the 1960s nearly a million Nubian people on either side of the Egyptian-Sudanese border were forced to relocate when their ancestral land was flooded by the damming of the Nile River at Aswan. In Egypt and Sudan, Nubian identity has been subsumed into the broader national project; the Sudanese state has long suppressed the teaching of Nubian languages and in 2007 violently put down a demonstration by Nubian villagers protesting the planned damming of the Nile farther upstream (Asanzi 2015). Through her insistence on singing these songs of return, Alsarah not only taps into her own ethnic heritage and chides powerful states for repressing minorities but does so to a global audience.

Rasha, on the other hand, has been publicly committed to social issues and used her position as an internationally recognized musician to speak out for the rights of refugees, women, and Sudanese youth. Through benefit concerts, visits to refugee camps, and her own musical platforms, she has had an active humanitarian presence since the early 2000s. Rasha has also made a foray into pointed political critique about war and militarization in Sudan. Her 2001 album, *Let Me Be*, includes the single "Your Bloody Kingdom," which combines spoken-word Sudanese Arabic commentary about how Sudan has lost its way with an English chorus demanding "freedom to be myself." In a short biography in a festival program she explains, "I tried to give a message in that song, to talk about what's going on in Sudan, in my way. I'm not a political person at all, but at the same time, I couldn't just make love songs, like most of the Sudanese songs. So I was trying to talk about the situation in Sudan, all this war in the 20th century" (DEMWE 2008, 9).

Setona, Rasha, and Alsarah engage directly with Sudanese politics to different degrees. While Setona's political sensibilities are less apparent in her songs, Rasha and Alsarah are outspoken about countering abuses of power that they link to the military government. The lyrics of Alsarah's song "Vote," which incorporate rapping in English by the rapper Oddisee into her mostly Arabic-language song, extol the virtues of democracy and participation for all of Sudan's people ("get outside your house and stand / right next to your brother man / whether he from north or south / it's not about your color or religion") while offering a blistering criticism of the Islamist regime. Addressing the "long bearded and the faked prayer and lies," she says, "the country is waiting to be rescued." In *La Sudan Maʿalesh*, Rasha similarly offers hope for the future of Sudan and a return to the

Sudanese homeland for the yearning *ghurba* (diaspora). She addresses Sudan as the beloved whose sons will return from abroad, then goes on to lament the young people who have died in war and the misery their loss has caused their mothers. The sentiments expressed in both of these songs point to diaspora engagement with Sudanese politics and public critique that is beyond the reach of singers within Sudan.

The significance of Setona's, Rasha's, and Alsarah's diaspora participation in conversations about national politics and identity is evident in their contentious reception by Sudanese audiences, who use their performances to express anxieties surrounding race, gender, and national identity. In his profile of Setona (1998) Hassan notes Setona's appeal to a Western world music crowd based on stereotypical ideas of African-ness. YouTube comments on the singers' music videos from viewers residing in Sudan and the diaspora who identify as Muslim, Arabic-speaking Sudanese demonstrate a range of stances regarding Sudanese identity.[6] While two-thirds of the comments express approval, support, and appreciation for the songs and performers, the remainder range from disapproving to harsh and insulting.

Comments cluster around a few key themes—the singers' racial and ethnic heritage, their gendered appearance and comportment, and their "Sudanese-ness"—in essence, their perceived right to represent Sudan through music and words to the world. Comments about the singers' hair (calls for singers to control their hair or expressions of appreciation of "natural" hair) join the drumbeat of anxiety about whether African-ness is a part of Sudanese national identity. On Rasha's video performance of "La Sudan Ma'alesh," one commenter says, "Anyway, you don't even look like a Sudanese women [*sic*]. Whatever you say or whatever you do, a woman like you doesn't mean anything to us. I hope your background is not Sudanese and I hope that you never go back again to Sudan because you do not belong to us. We are not proud that a woman who looks like you to be Sudanese. We are very happy with our government. Fuck you."[7]

Similarly, comments on the singers' clothing, such as exhortations to wear a head covering, are sometimes linked to criticism of the performers for their inauthenticity, living in the West, and comporting themselves incorrectly according to Sudanese traditions of religiously inspired modesty. Doubts about the origins of the singers, and requests that they drop the claim that their music has anything to do with Sudanese traditions, are extensions of this trope.

## Conclusion

Salah Hassan has asserted that "acting as a female musician in the public has never lost its connotation of indecency in Sudanese society" (1998, 1). The new bad girl musicians of the Sudanese diaspora raise their voices in a context of shifting patterns of global migration, national integration policies and the dispersal of families, contemporary expressions of supposed Islamic authenticity and anti-Muslim sentiments in the West, and gender and generational tensions among refugee and migrant Sudanese. Performers like Alsarah, Rasha, and Setona use a world music stage to comment on gender and racial hierarchies, chide Sudanese power brokers about their transgressions, and encourage a more inclusive and just society. Their gendered transgressions are made more feasible from their positions outside of Sudan, since the Sudanese diaspora is not as readily regulated. The multisited diasporic discourse and the expansion of the public domain due to the Internet allow for the voices of Sudan's bad girl singers to be heard despite ongoing government regulation and patriarchal resistance to ideas of gender and racial equality inside Sudan.

## Notes

Thanks to the women singers whose voices have long enchanted me and whose perspectives I seek to honor, in particular Alsarah, Rasha, and Setona. Thanks to Elizabeth Bishop, Rula Qawas, Nadia Yaqub, Sondra Hale, Gada Kadoda, and John Therekan. Robert Rubinstein, Azra Hromadzik, Nadine Fernandez, and other colleagues at the Department of Anthropology at Syracuse University offered thoughtful and helpful suggestions. My appreciation to Padini Nirmal and her students in Feminist Theory at Clark University, and thanks for help with translation to Amira Abderahman Ahmed, Hiba Burale, and Salah Hassan. Any mistakes are entirely my own responsibility.

1. The pejorative term *habasha* for a woman of Ethiopian or Eritrean descent stems from a presumed connection between prostitution and migrants to Sudan from these countries.

2. The youth movement Girifna (We Are Fed Up) uses songs, poetry, and "flash mobilizations," among other strategies, to voice its opposition to the ruling National Congress Party and has seen its members subjected to security crackdowns.

3. Originally a marketing category for non-Western traditional music, "world music" encompasses many different styles, largely drawn from non-Western traditions but also fusion music that incorporates multiple traditions. There has been significant criticism of the catchall term "world music" even by those who work within the industry. The music journalist Anastasia Tsioulcas writes (2014), "It smacks of all

kinds of loaded issues, from cultural colonialism to questions about what's 'authentic' and what isn't (and who might get to police such inquiries), and forces an incredible array of styles that don't have anything in common under the label of 'exotic Other.'"

4. For more on the world music industry and its relation to Sudanese singers in the diaspora, see Fábos and Alsarah 2016.

5. The performance of "Habibi Safr Mini" by Alsarah and Nahid Abunama-Elgadi, followed by a description of the genre by Alsarah, can be watched on You Tube, posted by Porto Franco Records on July 19, 2012, at https://www.youtube.com/watch?v=dPOnonHh6a4. An arrangement of "Habibi Ta'al" performed by Alsarah and the Nubatones from their debut album, *Silt*, preceded by an explanation by Alsarah, can be watched on YouTube, posted by "The Root" on June 22, 2016, at https://www.youtube.com/watch?v=1OycgeosMqE&list=PLpjteAL-JeqKqQf4bxzJv1QNzfOR Gsavu&index=7.

6. I rely on usernames, photos, biosketches, and use of Sudanese colloquial Arabic to determine which commenters identify as such. I collected complete sets of uploaded performances for the three profiled singers, eliminated videos with fewer than five comments, and captured and coded the associated comments and interactions for each remaining song, for a total of fifteen videos and 648 comments. I used the qualitative data analysis software Atlas.ti to analyze the resulting text for recurring themes. For methodological dilemmas related to research with virtual communities, see Murphy et al. 2014. Despite these problems, such communities are key to understanding how diasporic communities stay in touch and make meaning of their predicament and shifting identities, and as such they cannot be ignored.

7. In my field notes. The article and comment, like several online materials about Rasha, have been removed.

## References

Ali, Nadia Mustafa. 2003. "Thorny Issues and Perilous Coalitions: Addressing Women's Human Rights in the Context of Conflict and the Struggle to Restore Democracy in Sudan (1989–2000)." *Al-Raida* 21, no. 103 (Fall):31–38.

———. 2015. *Gender, Race, and Sudan's Exile Politics: Do We All Belong to this Country?* Lanham, MD: Lexington Books.

Asanzi, Ange. 2015. "Fighting for Nubia's Rich Culture." *International Rivers*, November 9. https://www.internationalrivers.org/blogs/337-7.

Berland, Joseph. 1983. "Peripatetic Strategies in South Asia: Skills as Capital among Nomadic Artisans and Entertainers." *Nomadic Peoples* 13, no. 1 (July):17–34.

Bernal, Victoria. 1997. "Islam, Transnational Culture, and Modernity in Rural Sudan." In *Gendered Encounters: Challenging Cultural Boundaries and Social Hierarchies in Africa*, edited by Maria Grosz-Ngaté and Omari Kokole, 131–151. London: Routledge.

Boddy, Janice. 1989. *Wombs and Alien Spirits: Women, Men, and the Zar Cult in Northern Sudan*. Madison: University of Wisconsin Press.

Canada, Immigration and Refugee Board. 2014. *Sudan: The Girifna Movement*. December 19. Reprinted by UNHCR at http://www.refworld.org/docid/54f042cb4.html.

Dawn Elder Management and World Enterprises (DEMWE). 2008. Sudanese Music and Dance Festival program. Los Angeles: DEMWE.

El Gizouli, Magdi. 2012. "Sudan's Hawa: The *Banat* Come of Age." *Sudan Tribune*, December 19, 2012.

Fábos, Anita H. 2010. *"Brothers" or Others? Propriety and Gender for Muslim Arab Sudanese in Egypt*. Revised and expanded ed. Oxford, England: Berghahn Books.

———. 2012. "Resisting 'Blackness,' Embracing Rightness: How Muslim Arab Sudanese Women Negotiate Cultural Space in the Diaspora." *Ethnic and Racial Studies* 35, no. 2 (February):218–237.

Fábos, Anita H., and Alsarah. 2016. "Navigating Musical Identities, Knowledge Production, and 'Authenticity' in the Diaspora: A Conversation with Alsarah." In *Networks of Knowledge Production in Sudan: Identities, Mobilities, and Technology*, edited by Sondra Hale and Gada Kadoda, 179–195. Lanham, MD: Lexington Books.

Hale, Sondra. 1996. *Gender Politics in Sudan: Islamism, Socialism, and the State*. Boulder, CO: Westview Press.

Hansen, Andreas, and Karen Obling. 2013. "Alsarah, the New Star of Nubian Pop." *The Guardian*, September 24. https://www.theguardian.com/world/2013/sep/24/alsarah-sudan-music-nubian-pop.

Hassan, Salah M. 1999. "The Queen of Henna—Setona Tarig as-Sudan African Crossroads." *The Art of African Fashion*. Trenton, NJ: Africa World Press.

Janbey, Ghada al-Atrash. 2009. "The Deeper Meaning of the Arabic Word 'Ghurba.'" Blog post, May 15. http://ghadaalatrash.me/the-deeper-meaning-of-the-arabic-word-ghurba.

Malik, Saadia. 2010. "Exploring *aghānī al-banāt*: A Postcolonial, Ethnographic Approach to Sudanese Women's Songs, Culture, and Performance." PhD diss., Ohio University.

Murphy, Joe, Michael W. Link, Jennifer Hunter Childs, et al. 2014. "Social Media in Public Opinion Research Executive Summary of the Aapor Task Force on Emerging Technologies in Public Opinion Research." *Public Opinion Quarterly* 78, no. 4:788–794.

Sidahmed, Abdel Salam. 2001. "Problems in Contemporary Applications of Islamic Criminal Sanctions: The Penalty for Adultery in Relation to Women." *British Journal of Middle Eastern Studies* 28, no. 2:187–204.

Tsioulcas, Anastasia. 2014. "What Makes GlobalFEST So Interesting?" *All Things Considered*, NPR, January 16. http://www.npr.org/2014/01/16/263081652/what-makes-globalfest-so-interesting.

van Nieuwkerk, Karin. 1995. *A Trade Like Any Other: Female Singers and Dancers in Egypt*. Austin: University of Texas Press.

Verney, Peter. 1998. "Can't Dance/Won't Dance?" Speech, Freemuse World Conference on Music and Censorship, November, Copenhagen. http://freemuse.org/archives/5697.

Westende, Nastasja van 't. 2009. "'God Gave Me a Good Voice to Sing': Female Wedding Singers in Greater Khartoum, Sudan." In *Proceedings of the International Conference on Performing Gender in Arabic/African Theatre*, edited by Mieke Kolk, 38–63. Khartoum/Amsterdam: Intercultural Theatre, East Meets West No. 4.

Willemse, Karin. 2007. *One Foot in Heaven: Narratives on Gender and Islam in Darfur, West Sudan*. Vol. 5. Leiden, Netherlands: Brill.

Wureta, Esayas, and Anita Fábos. 2012. "Performing Ethnicity: Wedding Videos and Morality in the Sudanese Diaspora." Paper presented at the conference Digital Crossroads: Media, Migration, and Diaspora in a Transnational Perspective, Utrecht University, Netherlands, June 28.

TWELVE

# Being a Revolutionary and Writerly Rebel

SUHAIR AL-TAL

Why was I considered a bad girl?

I have always asked myself this question after each milestone or battle during which I had to take a stand in life, be it spontaneous or more deliberate. A tornado of feelings runs through me whenever I face this question—a lot of anger, a bit of grief, sometimes sarcasm, and perhaps even secret joy. Nevertheless, I have never actually paused long enough to find an answer.

My story is long, perhaps much longer than the sixty years I have been alive and burdened with experience. It is not unique; many others have faced the same accusation in their own ways. Therefore, with these words, I will only pause at some images that have formed the basis for such an accusation, one—I might add—that I do not accept. I will not defend my experience, nor will I claim heroism. I will not claim to have been extraordinarily rational in reaching the decisions that have made me who I am. I will, however, start by saying that it could have been the coincidence of birth, maybe genetics, or even the closed environment I grew up in that made me the person I am now. Once that is said, I can talk about the choices I have made in the worlds through which I have moved.

## Testimony 1: The Tomboy

Let me start with the coincidence of birth and the element of genetics. My birth played a role in my formation, which later came to be described as "bad." I was born at the edge of the desert, claimant to ambiguous Bedouin origins and an even more ambiguous craving for modernity. I was born into a relatively small rural tribe in eastern Jordan that compensated for its lack of numbers by educating sons, and it did not oppose educating daughters at a time when literacy was a rarity in the country for both men and women. This education enabled many tribe members to fill elite political positions, first in the Ottoman Empire, then in the Mandate government, reaching a level of extensive political influence that endures until this day. The tribe became a pillar of the political system in Jordan, even though many of its members have belonged to different currents of political opposition since the Mandate period.

Genetics played its role as well. I belong to a small family—rare for its time. My father was a leftist poet opposing the regime who graduated from the American University in Cairo in the late 1940s. My mother is one of the first educated women in Jordan and also joined an oppositional political party. Going further back into my roots, I will pause at my grandfather on my mother's side, who was one of the first people to obtain a university degree at the beginning of the previous century and was one of the strongest opponents of the regime since its establishment in the early 1920s. He was the loyal guardian of the poet (and my uncle) Mustafa Wahbi al-Tal, known as 'Arar, the godfather of contemporary Jordanian poetry both political and literary. This uncle likewise was a pillar of the political opposition, having established the first national party in opposition to the regime in the 1930s. His poetry is redolent of freedom. He vigorously opposed the British Mandate and the local political system and mocked "the cardboard independence" of the nascent monarchy. He was a political representative of the gypsies and their way of life, and he empathized with poor peasants and their sordid living conditions. His life was a combination of poetry, imprisonment, and exile. Therefore, it was not strange that an ethos of poetry and political opposition extended to my small family, placing me in a situation to experience exile, the imprisonment of my father, and the isolation of my mother early in my childhood.

I should mention that my uncle, the poet who was raised and lived under the wing of my maternal grandfather (who also happens to be *his* uncle), was rejected by his own father—my grandfather on my father's side. Mustafa Wahbi al-Tal was the bad boy who opposed the Jordanian regime, which was born under the shadow of the Mandate. This paradox imprinted itself on me; on the one hand, my father's side of the family is very supportive of the regime. Among them is the former Prime Minister Wasfi al-Tal, who was assassinated in Cairo in the 1970s. He ruled during one of the most politically dangerous stages in Jordanian history, the 1970 civil war known as Black September. On the other hand, members of my mother's side of the family belonged to different groups on the spectrum of political opposition, from the extreme Right (the Muslim Brotherhood) to the extreme Left (the Communist Party). At times I have felt stranded between the two grandparents in the middle of this familial-political paradox; I remember my father spending a year as a political prisoner while his nephew, Wasfi al-Tal, was prime minister.

Amid these contradictions, I found myself returning to my grandfather's home in 1964 after years of exile during which I only remember the word "refugee." My father had escaped to Damascus, along with other men of the opposition, during a 1957 revolt against the newborn Jordanian democracy to avoid serving a fifteen-year prison sentence. I returned to find myself in a huge house where many of my cousins lived. The house consisted of rooms whose doors opened onto a wide courtyard planted with a large mulberry tree as well as other fruit trees and colorful flower beds. This house was built based on the Damascene style in honor of my beloved grandmother. That is what my grandfather said, and I believed him. From that home, which is now a museum called the 'Arar Cultural House, I miss two things: my grandfather's desk and the mulberry tree.

My paternal grandfather was one of the first lawyers in Jordan, one of the very few who received a degree in law in the early years of the twentieth century. I remember his room, or what used to be his office, as Ali Baba's cave. The dim atmosphere, rich with the scent of time and memories and books stacked on the shelves all the way up to the wooden ceiling, were all part of a magical world into which I wanted to dive. My desire to enter the room was fed by the family women's insistence on closing the room and not allowing us entry even to help clean it. This Ali Baba's cave was my refuge when I needed to escape the large family's noise after years of a quiet childhood in Damascus. I did not know how to read well, but my gazing at the bookshelves and the stacked memoirs was enough to calm me. In the darkness of this room I recalled the image of my father being taken away from me in handcuffs, escorted by strangers toward the Jordanian borders, only to learn later that he was imprisoned. I recall the image of one of my uncles whom I dearly loved and dreamed of meeting again, only to have the dream snuffed out by news of his suicide for the sake of a beloved who was killed according to tribal traditions. In that cave I gazed at bookshelves and wondered if they would ever lead me to the meaning of prison, freedom, love, death, suicide — such large words that I kept hearing but was yet to understand.

I remember sneaking into the room at sunset one day; they had forgotten to lock the door. My short frame did not allow me to reach the first shelf. I tried to climb but fell, and they found me, ending my small adventure and musings with a round of firm strikes to my behind with a cane, all because I had dared to invade the world of the family elder. The room was locked after that, and I never stepped foot in it again.

A real tragedy happened in 1965, when my majestic grandfather stepped down as family patriarch due to age (he was more than one hundred years old). My father was still imprisoned for being a member of the banned Communist Party. On a sweltering summer day, under the instructions of one of my cousins, the women of the family cleaned out the office and threw away most of its contents. I remember a raging fire in the middle of the yard, the children running around carrying piles of dusty books to throw into it. They were like cannibals surrounding their elder, the cousin who undertook the mission of going through the books, keeping a few and throwing the rest to the children. They yelled for more, dancing diabolically around the fire, bragging about who could carry the biggest pile, making the fire roar louder. Because of my young age and small size, I could not stop the tragedy. They did not hear my screams, so I climbed to my sanctuary at the top of the mulberry tree with tears staining my young face.

That large mulberry tree in the middle of the yard was the most important part of the elegant property. It grew in a strange way, its trunk rotating around itself like a python standing on its tail. It broke into the sky, its branches rising about the roof. For the boys, climbing that tree and picking the fruit was a hobby, while the girls watched from the sidelines, waiting for the boys to grace them with a few of the berries. For me, the image of the girls waiting provoked me. That is why one day, while the boys were competing to see who could reach the highest branch, I decided to join in. I did not ask for permission, and I climbed. I paid no attention to my skirt, which was torn, or to my underwear, which was exposed, until the boys laughed, and the girls whispered while I hung on the highest branch. I climbed down carefully, to be received by slaps from any of the adults who could reach me, but I kept yelling, "I beat them! I beat them!" The following day I was mortified by my bruised face, so I sneaked into the boys' room and borrowed a pair of pants. I climbed the tree all the way to the top, and when they realized that I was up there, I only climbed down when I got my mother's word that I could climb it whenever I wanted. Even though my adventure became the talk of my peers, earning me the nickname "Hasan Sabi" (tomboy), climbing trees remained my favorite hobby, and for years, the highest branch on that mulberry tree was my sanctuary.

It pains me that I received beatings — literal or figurative — on two occasions, the figurative being after the burning of my grandfather's office belongings and the literal/physical after the tree incident, an incident that was followed by name-calling, the most prominent being "tomboy," which, to some extent, means "bad girl." I wondered if I was indeed a bad girl. I did not care about the answer as I ran toward my teenage years — years I might have lost or that may have been stolen from me. I am not sure which.

## Testimony 2: The Swamp of Politics

The irony about the coincidence of birth is that sometimes it becomes a fate directing what follows in life. I will be honest and say that I never tried to intervene and change this fact, knowing that I could. This coincidence burdened me with the words "refugee" and "girl," which were both directly associated with the concept of "taboo." I carried these two terms within myself as I reached my teen years while stepping into the world of politics after the tragic June 1967 war against the Zionists. Being called a "refugee" gave me a different perspective on this war, making the Palestinian people and their cause my personal cause and the standard by which I measured the nationalism and seriousness of political work. It helped me destroy all the figures I had inherited from my childhood (the father, the leader, the family — and others).

I do not claim that I based my choice to join a particular party on sound information and judgment. I was greatly influenced by my young female teachers who had experienced defeat and consciously refused it. This influence was deepened by my initial readings about Marxism and the Bolshevik Revolution, as well as some world literature. My father's rich library, which was rebuilt after the burning of my grandfather's books, played a major role in shaping my experience. My generation observed the work of the New Left movements in their diverse forms in Europe and the

Americas—the student revolution in France, the civil rights movement in the United States, and the armed struggles and revolutionary violence in Latin America, notably in the life and death of Che Guevara, who was a role model for the Arab commando in general. I decided to join one of the commando units of the New Left, the Democratic Front for the Liberation of Palestine.

In reality, I never carried a weapon, but being exposed to even primitive training courses was enough to ignite a familial and social clash that brought back the terms "girl," "taboo," and "forbidden," words that loomed over my head like the blade of a sharp sword. My leftist parents, who were burned by the pain of imprisonment and exile, did not strongly disagree with my involvement, but they feared that I would lose my chance at higher education—I was an excellent student in high school. They wanted to give me a chance at a bright educational future. The rest of the family saw my behavior as betraying their support for the Jordanian regime, which was preparing to go to war against the Palestinian commandos and to exile them from Jordan by mobilizing tribal members to be the social base of the regime's side in this war. The simple acts of joining a march or participating in a student strike were enough to incite rumors and social isolation or to result in my confinement to my own home, outcomes that I met at times with silence and solitude and at times with heated debate that was not empty of offensive words that I now regret. For my family, the solution to my behavior came once I received my high school degree: I was sent out of the country right before the crucial battle in September 1970 between the army and commandos. I experienced my own exile after being dubbed "the bad girl" by the tribe.

My destination was Belgrade in former Yugoslavia. I was not intrigued by the Danube or the wonders of the ancient city or even the promises of a bright future in the world of engineering. These did not offer me the solace I needed to dedicate myself to studying. Even with a bit of student political work, I lived a struggle that I had not expected or prepared for, in the form of cultural and sociopolitical alienation. I struggled through new battles with the same weapons—the girl and the taboo—since the open-mindedness of my comrades did not go past their political slogans. In these battles I faced the replacement of the paternalism of the father with that of the comrade and the crushing of the tribal authority by that of the organization. Worse still was the transformation of the little girl with braids into a young woman desired by every leftist passing by under the name of liberation. My freedom, according to the understanding of most of those I dealt with, was limited to the freedom of accepting their sneaking into my bed.

So I screamed at the top of my lungs the loudest "NO" I had ever yelled, and I left Belgrade and a strict commitment to political organization forever. In their eyes I was once again the bad girl, followed by their rumors of what they desired to have but never obtained.

I did not return to Amman, since my return was preceded by the destruction of the commando organizations and their exile from Jordan. Many of my peers were imprisoned there, and I was wanted by the authorities due to my past affiliations, a matter that embarrassed many of my tribe members and increased the chance that they would seek revenge. I had one option: Beirut.

I fell in love with Beirut. It has become a home that never leaves my being, a city to which I travel with my imagination when I cannot physically be surrounded by its warm embrace. To me, Beirut was never a coffee shop on the side of the road or a bar or a beach where adventure seekers go. It was not the office of a commando organization in the Fakhani neighborhood, overflowing with the remnants of meaningless correspondences, ashtrays stuffed with cigarette butts, the scent of sweat and stinky shoes. To me, Beirut is a university, a library, a theater, a cinema, and great friends who took my hand and helped me walk steadily toward awareness and the rebuilding of my cultural being.

I moved between my university in the Fakhani neighborhood, where I lived, and Hamra Street, which pulsed with culture and art in the heart of Beirut. I participated in public work through the Democratic Front for the Liberation of Palestine and the Jordanian Student Union in Lebanon in support of freedom, democracy, and human rights while maintaining beautiful friendships with some of the great people who continued working with both the old and new Left organizations but who were not afraid to critique them.

In such movements, I realized that the tribe is not a blood faction but a patriarchal structure that seeps into the strongest institutions and most discussions about modernity and development. I was assured that those belonging to the revolution, men and women of different nationalities, are split into two groups, the first dedicated to giving their lives to the cause and the second dedicated to profiting from poverty and death and destruction. I dedicated my efforts to learning; I listened deeply to the experiences of political figures, authors, poets, and artists—most of whom belonged in one way or another to the national and communist movements—and I studied their work.

In Beirut I also learned about journalism, which later became the career that saved me from the evil of sitting down at tables with villains. Still, I was never far from the sporadic internal Palestinian-Lebanese struggle or Zionist attacks on Lebanon leading to the long civil war, with all its pains and sins. I looked death in the eye more than once and became acquainted with it while volunteering in rescue missions in support of those fighting against the Zionist enemy as well as fighting alongside partners for a cause. In these instances, I came to know people more deeply and appreciate them more fully. I came to know the value of life.

My preoccupation with studying, learning, and training to become a journalist detached me from student life, which irritated many of my female colleagues at the dorm. There, among all the young female activists, I became the bad girl who used her beauty and work as a journalist to have relations with the young commandos and perhaps even spy for the security authorities. Back home in Jordan, where the tribe continued to be the social and political center of male patriarchal authority, I was once again the bad girl because I refused to leave Beirut, and only God knew the nature of the sins I indulged in there. Later I was told that I had received a new nickname: "the commandos' slut."

Was I?

## Testimony 3: Flying in the Realms of Writing

Let us say that my profession as a journalist was a mere coincidence. After I left Belgrade and settled in Beirut, I worked on compensating for what I had missed as a university student by enrolling in the Faculty of Accounting, but my interests did not lie there. Therefore, I compensated for the boredom of studying with reading, which I came to reflect on in humble writings that I published anonymously in the student magazine. That occupied me until I met a young Lebanese journalist who spoke of a beginners' workshop in journalism run by a Lebanese magazine. I enthusiastically applied and was accepted, and after an apprenticeship, I ended up dedicating my time to investigative reporting. Fifteen years later, I was a professional in Jordanian journalism after a long tour among many major Arab newspapers.

I grew attached to this career, and I held onto it such that it became my outlet for expressing my political and social interests. Thanks to this profession, I moved a lot and learned even more. Through journalism, I sneaked into the world of literary writing, specifically short stories, and from there to academic writing and scientific research.

I will not claim that I faced difficulties in the beginning of my professional journey as a journalist. The environments in which I worked outside of Jordan were friendly and accommodating. People accepted the presence of women in such a profession. I also will not deny the care of the mentor I honor, my husband, my friend, and my colleague, who sponsored my professionalism until I was experienced enough to spread my own wings and develop a distinctive style and language of my own. The problems began when, out of a desire for stability, I returned to my country to permanently settle down in the early 1980s, after many years abroad.

When I returned to Amman, I was received by my family and tribe like the prodigal son who had returned at last. Many others did not forget, even if they had temporarily ignored, my social and political identity. I was received with a deathly silence, and I felt as if I were walking in a minefield where anything could explode at any second. My intuition was right. The first altercation happened in my workplace. I was reluctantly accepted, given my expertise in Arab journalism, on the condition that I supervise a social column targeting women, the main topic of which was "How to Cook for Your Husband."

Like a house of cards, I saw my professional career crumble before my eyes—the interviews, news reports, investigations, long trips to deserts and villages and cities, working during war and peace and anything that came in between, working at conferences at five-star hotels and in refugee camps and poorhouses. How could I give it all up to sit behind a desk supervising a page that exemplified all that I had rebelled against since I was a child, a page that promoted and endorsed stereotypes of women? I stood my ground and fought for my right to work in my area of expertise. Eventually I found a position in a humble newspaper whose writers were leftists and who all bet on my capability of surviving in an environment of macho backwardness.

My mission was never easy. Being a journalist was difficult enough on its own, but I had to tolerate holes dug deliberately in the road of my achievements. I had to fight daily battles with men who saw me only as a beautiful woman hired to decorate the office. But I insisted on competing with them and sharing the glory of having a byline. I moved across more than one Jordanian newspaper, and the situation never changed.

My colleagues reveled in creating new ways to harass me, ways that were mostly despicable, starting with hiding the keys to the women's bathroom during my night shift when I was the only woman working at the newspaper at the time and ending with sabotaging my articles and at times my name, in character assassination that did not exclude my personal life and reputation.

I will never forget my bitter experience while covering one of the Arab summits in Baghdad. I was the only reporter sent from my newspaper in a group of almost twenty representing the different Jordanian media. This was a chance to prove my professional worth, even though it was fraught with difficulties that were compounded by the humble tools of pen, paper, and the rare tape recorder I was using. Nevertheless, through much hard work I managed to obtain more than one scoop. On the last day of work, we were called late at night into a press conference with Yasir 'Arafat, the chairman of the Palestinian Liberation Organization (PLO), who arrived jubilant over the financial and moral support he had received. As is customary, I presented my questions after stating my name and the paper I worked for. I did not react when the chairman, who recognized me, made a joke at my expense that I will not deign to repeat here. I sent out my last report and returned home happy with my achievement, only to meet a whirlwind of rumors that spread across the media to land in the middle of my tribe, especially rumors of the joke made by 'Arafat. The leaders of the tribe were still discussing the social and political crisis caused by a previous mission of mine when I spent time in the western African desert with members of the Polisario liberation movement in the Arab Maghreb. The venture was not accepted by the security authorities, who in turn banned the publication of all remaining investigations and articles I had prepared about this Saharan revolution.

My union activism after returning home only added insult to injury. I was a member of the Journalists Union, Women's Union, and Writers Association. All served as political platforms during the twenty-two years of martial rule in Jordan (1967–1989) that banned all forms of direct and open party activism. Each organization offered a platform for different opinions in a society that does not acknowledge the value and necessity of a variety of opinions. This caused more than one altercation in various organizations, and in my country when two people argue and one is a woman, the reason for the altercation is presumed to be the bad behavior of the woman.

I spent nine years working as a journalist in Jordan, nine years of vicious battles that were exacerbated by an impenetrable glass ceiling. People who joined the profession years after I did, some of whom I personally mentored and trained, preceded me, and I became one of their employees, while they exerted authority over me; these battles were intensified by my vigorous defense of my rights and professional position and by my complete rejection of surrender to those who oppressed me. The hardest oppression came when my passport was confiscated, preventing me from leaving the country for a number of years.

During my years of working in journalism in Jordan, I was dubbed a "bad girl" but also "the Playmate of Jordanian Journalism," a demeaning reference to *Playboy* magazine.

In the middle of so much conflict, writing short stories became the crack in the wall that allowed light into my darkened life, allowing me an escape from the fast pace and shallowness of journalism. I gravitated toward the short story for its potential for symbolism and linguistic creativity, its capacity to absorb my personal experience and interactions with people and surroundings.

I am not ashamed to admit that my literary writings reflect part of my personal experience, which is rich with characters, events, and symbols. They gave me an incentive to break through the wall of female silence. I wanted to speak of my pains and joys, my weaknesses, anger, strength, nostalgia, and sadness. I wanted my stories to scream for me and say, "I am a woman who loves life and who deserves to live it the way any human should."

I did not know that my writings would, once more, open the gates of hell before me.

In a patriarchal tribal system, a woman who breaks her silence by writing opens the door for the masculine imagination to see her in a strange form. It gives men the chance to picture her as the devil who has lost her mind and must be punished and banished back into hell. By writing, I broke taboos and overcame punishment, character assassination, social isolation, and seclusion. I stepped over the red line defined by this patriarchal system, and I received the harshest punishment possible. I was prosecuted for offending public morals and ethics under Jordanian penal law because one of my stories, titled "Al-Mashnaqa" (The noose), included the term *udwun tanassulī* (penis). The ostensible reason for this trial, sentencing, and conviction was my use of an obscene word—that is, the story was considered pornography. The unannounced reason was to teach me, as well as other women of the country, a lesson. Once again, this time under a judicial ruling, I became a bad girl.

As I appealed this ruling, I stood alone. The patriarchal system was able to wreak havoc around me as soon as the charges were pressed and the trial began. I was threatened, should the charges stick, with the loss of all my civil rights, including the custody of my only daughter, who at the time was only two years old. I was also threatened with social isolation within media, cultural, academic, and even feminist circles. I remember how the leaders of the feminist movements, the Journalists Union, and the Writers Association abandoned me and my cause. So I fought with the support of my parents and just three friends who found justice in my cause and righteousness in my choices. With the help of these loved ones I was able to stand tall and continue fighting. Unfortunately, I lost the case, was convicted of the charges pressed against me, and was sentenced to a year in prison, which was later reduced to fifteen days in jail. However, the Royal Pardon of 1989 included my case, and therefore all judicial rulings against me were cancelled. Nonetheless, the social ramifications of the trial still reverberate today.

After the ruling, and with the increasing pressure from security forces against newspapers, I was unable to continue my career as a journalist. I took a humble job at the Ministry of Culture. I never stopped writing, and in an obvious challenge to the trial and the ruling, I published the story that led to the trial in a collection of short stories under the same title. After obtaining my master's degree in philosophy, I published my most famous research to date, *The City of Rose and Stone: A Study of Sex Crimes in Jordanian Society* (1998). Its publication came after long battles with government institutions that tried to ban it.

My battles have never stopped; what I thought would be a less aggressive work atmosphere in government turned out to be more vicious. The bureaucracy as well as the administrative and social corruption forced me to go through struggles that I never sought, especially when my reputation for being a daring, combative, bad woman preceded me.

From my position, which only improved due to the civil service system and my education, I combatted financial and administrative corruption at the ministry. Due to my experience and my somewhat advanced age, I was able to combat the social corruption in the form of sexual harassment of young female employees by exposing attempts of harassment against myself first and then others, who then found strength in my outspokenness and came forward themselves. The result of that was an attempt to hit me where it hurt most. In 1998 the minister of culture obtained a cabinet decree, signed by the prime minister, banning me from publishing my writings in Jordan. However, neither the culture minister nor the prime minister understood that the only way to prevent me from writing would be to cut off my fingers.

They did not cut off my fingers, and I continued to write and publish abroad. The truth is, I have not written many new short stories. However, I obtained a PhD in philosophy and improved my research skills, specializing in feminist causes. I could not overcome the barriers that stood in the way of my teaching at the university level, but I continue to write.

I am now a little over sixty years of age, but I feel as though I have lived much longer. I often seclude myself in my small apartment in one of Amman's neighborhoods, spending most of my time between my books, my plants, and my research, alone except for my loyal dog. Every once in a while I meet men and women of my tribe at social events, and I wonder if I am still the bad girl to them. I honestly cannot answer that because we are a hypocritical society. I do not fall prey to words of praise and am not fooled by respectful terms of address. I know that there are people who forbid their daughters from reading my work; the Ministry of Education has banned my books from school libraries. As for the cultural and media circles, they have abandoned me.

I will not deny my happiness at seeing a new generation of female writers and journalists who are following in my footsteps, fighting their own battles in their own ways, and occupying positions suitable to their cultural standing. I will not claim credit for anyone else's success, and no one, except my leftist parents, can take credit for mine. I will not claim sainthood or nobility, because the fierceness of the battles I have fought have taught me to use the same methods my adversaries use. I have responded to each attack with worse and with a level of audacity that could border on rudeness. I do not deny that on many occasions I feared for myself from myself, nor do I deny that I miss the calm, romantic girl I could have been.

I miss her noble vulnerability and her need for a shoulder to cry on. However, and in all cases, I never saw myself as a bad girl. I only saw a rebel who stepped away from the social, political, and intellectual rules of the tribe, a girl who fought battles to prove her existence and won, and with that success, she survived.

Yes, dare I say, she survived.

# Afterword

## LAILA AL-ATRASH

After examining the array of experiences of Arab women in the chapters of this volume, each with its own significance, circumstances, and distinctiveness, I was faced with a number of puzzling and painful questions:

What were we doing all these years? We, women who have dedicated our careers to women's liberation and changing societal perceptions of women's issues.

How did our plans for enlightenment crumble against the tidal waves of dark fundamentalism that continue to drown out woman's reason and willpower such that she submits to roles others fashion for her? And to the utter supremacy of male over female? In the United Nations Development Programme's *Arab Human Development Report on Women* in 2005, I was cited among a handful of Arab female writers who had left a mark on their society. There were others who came before me, pioneers like Nawal El Saadawi, Fatima Mernissi, and countless other women. I wonder how it is that we are still leading, decades later, the same fight against this attack on women and their accomplishments. How has our role, past, present, and future, been eroded in the onslaught of politicized religion?

The "bad girl" label brings back sad memories. By her society's and family's standards, my mother was a bad girl because she claimed her inheritance rights from a feudal father who, upon her refusal to relinquish her share, had reassigned hundreds of dunums of land to his only son. Her three sisters had agreed to give up their shares so as not to be stigmatized as bad girls.

The rift with her family continued for years. When she insisted on marrying my father without her family's consent, they accused her of having had a relationship with him before marriage. I asked my father when I grew up whether my mother indeed loved him and saw him before marriage, as her family said. He was outraged: "Her family is insane! All because she asked for her inheritance? Would I have married her if she had allowed me to hold her hand? Would I marry a bad girl?"

I remember my father once preventing me from going out with my girl-friends because I was wearing a sleeveless dress, and I refused to change out of it. My mother stood by me: "Don't create a scandal in front of her friends. All the girls dress like her." He spat in my face. I wiped it away and went out anyway with the conviction that rights are taken, not granted.

Now I understand my father's position; if you want to go against your society's norms, you must be prepared to face them head on. In my home-town of Beit Sahour, a village near Bethlehem in the West Bank, people's stares at my bare arms implied that I was a bad girl. Still, many other girls followed my lead in the early 1960s.

But my father stood by me when I was attacked by a fundamentalist teacher following the publication of my first article on "honor crimes" and the unhealthy socialization of girls. This was in 1965, and I was a first-year university student. Mine was the first article on this topic to be published in Jordan and Palestine. The issue is as contentious today as it was back then.

I began writing for Jordanian newspapers in 1966. In the 1980s my articles began to highlight the impending threat posed by madrasahs (centers for teaching the Qur'an), training camps for youth in remote areas of Jordan, young Jordanian men traveling to Afghanistan to join the ranks of what had universally become known as the Afghani mujahi-deen in the showdown between the United States and the Soviet Union in the Afghani mountains, and the growing threat from Islamic fundamen-talist groups. I noticed that most of my articles were not being printed, so I stopped writing for the paper.

In 2005, another experience demonstrated to me the extent of Arab publishers' fear of fundamentalist groups. I first published my novel *Elu-sive Anchors* in Lebanon. A later edition was published in Palestine, and I could not help but notice that the Palestinian version was much smaller, with a large portion of a dialogue between a main character and a Taliban leader deleted. I asked the publisher about it, and to my shock he said, "I deleted it. Do you want them to burn down my publishing house and everyone in it? If you are not scared, I am!"

In 2010 much fuss was raised over the printing of another of my novels, *Desires of That Autumn*. The art designer for the book lodged a formal com-plaint with the minister of culture accusing me of promiscuity and offend-ing religion in my writing. I was the bad girl who would corrupt the morals of the younger generation, and this designer said that he would not allow his five daughters to read my work. Printing of the novel was halted under the pretense that I distorted the meaning of the Quranic verse "Your wives are yours to plough; so approach your women when and as you wish" (Al-Bakara, 224) because it was used by one of the characters as a justification for sodomizing his wife.

The novel posed the following question: Can poverty and social injustice lead to fundamentalism and terrorism? I believe the printing was stopped because the novel touched on issues that were not discussed publicly in Jordanian society: the bloody events of September 1970 between the PLO and the Jordanian army, a taboo subject in Jordan. This topic was only briefly mentioned in the novel, but I was publicly criticized for many months. Finally, and with the support of the Writers Association, the novel was published in Jordan and then Lebanon with no protest from any readers.

Following the Arab Spring, the fall of Muhammad Mursi, and the decline in support for the Muslim Brotherhood that accompanied the rise of ʿAbd al-Fattah Sisi as president of Egypt, the newspaper's editor-in-chief asked me back again. I refused. I had become more provocative in the eyes of the Islamists, and I did not want to cause the paper any problems with my "daring" views. Instead, I turned to social media; Facebook became the place where I engage with my nearly thirty thousand followers without fear of being labeled. This is where informed dialogue can happen.

What Rawan Ibrahim writes about Yasmin, who was raised in an orphanage, is a harsh reminder of the cruel shortcomings of our legal systems and how the law penalizes the victim. Yasmin became the bad girl because in society's eyes her mother had sinned, an issue that few Arab writers and columnists have been moved to write about. Many critics mentioned this when discussing my novel *Children of the Wind*, the story of a young doctor who had been raised in an orphanage, only to be taken out and cared for by a relative, mainly out of guilt for having had a hand in the so-called honor killing of his mother. The doctor refuses to admit he ever lived in an orphanage for fear of the stigma it carries. When his wife becomes pregnant, he is plagued by fear of his own death, and the thought that if he dies his child would also be raised in an orphanage. So, he returns to the area where he grew up looking for the children with whom he was raised. Each of their stories illustrates the injustice of the law that cast them onto the streets with ID numbers that set them apart from other children.

I ask again, how is it that we are still leading, decades later, the same fight against this attack on women and their accomplishments?

Regrettably, in many Arab countries Islamists have demanded control over ministries of education, and governments have granted such positions to appease them. In doing so they have contributed to the spread of reactionary thought, including discrimination against women. Curricula at all levels have further solidified gender, religious, and sectarian discrimination.

Thus, the issues for which we fought decades ago are still controversial and perhaps even more acute now, despite improvements in the education levels of girls and women. Girls are being brought up as mere bodies and cannot escape this role. They are taught to satisfy those around them by being "the fairest of girls" and "sisters of men."

Rula Quawas and her students, most of whom wear the hijab, wanted to raise their voices in protest against sexual harassment at the University of Jordan. From the 1960s through the 1980s, this same university epitomized women's liberation and understanding of their roles. What has happened since that time is a regression.

Change and enlightenment require a battle, and I believe that fighting ideology with rational thought is possible as long as platforms for such a fight are available. That is why I decided to start writing for the theater—a direct form of communication with the audience. I have so far completed four plays, including one for children, because real change starts there, and real acceptance of change has to begin at a young age.

I am fully aware that I have at one time or another been labeled the "bad girl," even when I thought I was being good, trying to do good, or fighting to change misconceived notions that prevented society from moving forward. But I know that we are only bad girls as long as there is bad surrounding us, as long as our differences are used against us. Once the bad is gone, so will the label that follows all those who fight it.

# Afterword

MIRAL AL-TAHAWY

TRANSLATED BY SAMIA HISSEN DOANY

As an Arab girl drilled in obedience, I was never allowed to go near girls with bad reputations. This did not prevent me from eyeing them with helplessness and envy, for I could not emulate their beauty, their boldness, and their ability to commit little taboos that I did not dare to contemplate. "Bad girls" do not peer fearfully around themselves, nor do they give great importance to their images in the mirrors of others; they do not consider red lines too seriously because they are more tolerant of their own faults and trained in toughness. They easily reply to scorn with scorn and are able to live life as a succession of tense scenes or short adventures that may or may not end dramatically. I carry bad girls in my memory like deep-rooted icons because they have succeeded, in their brief passage through my life, in depositing profound impressions of guilt and sin.

I explored my childhood with a bad girl who built houses of sand with me, exchanging pieces of candy for bits of junk to construct doors and cushions and imaginary children's rooms. She was called Amal. Amal knew how to escape during siesta and arrive carrying in her lap her cotton dolls, stacking these children among the sand heaps. She would spread her hair, which her mother did not braid, and say, "Come on, let's play." In my exuberant storytelling, Amal becomes the fairy, the gypsy, and the street girl on whom I project all my longings. Amal grew up before me, and she would show me the burn marks on her thighs, punishment for frequently running away. She cried as they tried to circumcise her for the second time because of her rebellious history. Sometimes Amal was tied to a bedpost and left to bark like a puppy out of her family's fear of the shameful acts she had not yet committed. Later, she disappeared to play the roles she constantly practiced while playing: she was married off at age twelve to fill a passerby's house with offspring.

The only bad girl I never dared approach in friendship was Nahi, who was the first to exhibit the signs of womanhood in our class at school. Nahi knew that she was like forbidden fruit: beautiful, desirable, and a potential object of lust, jealousy, and rage. She encountered rumors regarding her behavior and written messages from lovers with her confident, sarcastic smile, but she never tried to prove that she was a good girl. Nahi would reveal her chest a bit to allow her breasts to move discreetly, while we girls, her classmates, regretted our girlish absence of womanhood.

Often bad girls are the ones who have allowed their bodies to be bared, exposed, raped, or harassed. We avoid describing them as victims because that would contain an implicit condemnation of society, while society strives to remove that stigma and place the burden of transgressing the public order on women's shoulders. A woman's crime is her gender; if she is raped, she must have paved the way for the crime, perhaps summoned and incited it—just as the first Eve instigated eating fruit from the forbidden tree, resulting in the emergence of the idea of the sin of human nakedness and the ensuing expulsion from paradise.

Ever since Eve's discovery of men's dread, even terror, of exposing their own or women's shameful nudity and her realization that her body had the power to seduce and instigate, women have used their bodies as social and political weapons. Even before Lady Godiva rode her horse naked through the streets to protest taxes that her feudal husband had levied on the common people, women have invented naked protests in political and social spheres. In ancient Bedouin societies, too, women used nudity to incite revenge or valor in war. By merely tearing her robes or baring her breast or face, a woman could cause long wars of revenge in both Islamic and pre-Islamic times.

Bad girls are not embarrassed to use their bodies to express their dissatisfaction. They flee, give up their virginity, or commit suicide when illtreated or forced into marriage, pour kerosene and burn themselves, all to resist authority at its worst.

In Egypt in recent years the participation of young women in political movements has been on the rise and has broadened to include women, from both the right and the left, beyond those who had been active before the Arab Spring—young journalists, university students, and so forth. As a result, harsher methods of suppressing protests have been employed since 2011. The Arab Spring gave rise to exceptionally ugly practices to curb the presence of women in the public sphere—virginity checks, stripping, sexual harassment—all employing humiliation to dissuade women from participating in the revolution.

Political authorities were not the only parties who deployed the female body within the conflict; female activists themselves referenced the violation of women's bodies in order to incite action. They goaded men into action by using the violations against women as challenges to the masculinity of Egyptian men. Asma Mahfuz, for instance, used a video circulating through Facebook to urge men of honor to protect the bodies of protesting women from harm.

Women's protest through nudity constitutes a challenge to patriarchal society and to the rising religious discourse that incriminates the female body. It is a dissent that parallels the extremism of religious discourse and its control over how people picture the female body as shameful nakedness. These protestations also focus on the physical aspect of women as a source of seduction, sedition, and incitement to sin. The growth of religious radicalism and its fanaticism regarding the female body have led to correspondingly dramatic acts of resistance; the more that this discourse is used, the more extreme women's bodily responses become.

On a parallel track, bad girls populate the history of literature as dissolute and fit for the bedroom and for appeasing male desires. Wasn't Shahrazad the protagonist of the most permissive of famous Arabic books in history? As for Wallada bint al-Mustakfi, she was the only poet at whose mention Arab sources balked because she wrote on her own robes,

> By God I am fit for the lofty—I walk my way and strut with vanity
> I avail my lover the dish of my cheek—I give my kiss to those who covet it

In a number of traditional texts, writing is linked to dishonor. Women's writing was understood to be limited to love letters to seduce men. Thus writing became a symbol of deceit and lewdness and aroused admonitions forbidding women from taking up the pen. This idea has survived into modern times, connecting women's writings to the female body, linking it to unveiling, exposure, nudity, and taboos. I myself would hide under my pillow the memoirs of Dr. Nawal El Saadawi, and when my father caught me in the act, he exchanged his long, silent scowl with an affectionate smile as he presented me with a copy of *The Prophet's Daughters* by Bint al-Shati'. The bad girl inside me flung aside this didactic volume and continued to gobble up in secret the works of Laila Baalbaki, who was tried for pornography, and to succumb to the fiery gaze of Ghada al-Samman, who adorns the book covers of her published stories with a photograph of her pencil eyebrows and challenging stare. I would memorize her rhetorical phrases that could not hide her obsession with defiance and determination. I recorded in my diary her replies to the question she is repeatedly asked: Why do you write about such thorny subjects? I dreamed of images filling books that I had not yet written, and I nursed my desire to become a writer under the pretext of reading. Arab women's writing was never detached from protests for the liberation of women's bodies, and it has accompanied the deployment of the nude female body as a weapon to express defiance. The body has been these writers' enduring obsession and an axis around which women's agony has been wrapped.

In women's writings, the celebration of the body has developed from shy claims for rights to unabashed expressions of sexuality, lust, and natural desires that should not be concealed because they are an integral part of life. In the early 1990s, critics observed the emergence of a new type of Egyptian feminist novel that celebrated the woman's body differently and, for some readers, shockingly, a form termed by the Egyptian writer Edward al-Kharrat as the "girls' tale" and "novel of the body."

In fact, this phenomenon was not limited to Egypt but extended to the rest of the Arab world. It included the works of numerous respected writers whose works were translated into several languages, such as Ahlam Musteghenimi, *Dhakirat al-jasad* (*Memory in the Flesh*); Salwa al-Neimi, *Burhan al-ʿasal* (*The Proof of the Honey*); Fadila al-Faruq, *Taʾ al-khajal* (The stigma of shame); Samar Yazbek, *Raʾihat al-qirfa* (Cinnamon); Alia Mamdouh, *Al-tashahhi* (Lust); Amal Jarrah, *Al-riwaya al-malʿawna* (The cursed novel); Siba al-Haraz, *Al–akharun* (*The Others*); and Warda ʿAbd al-Malik, *Al–Awba* (The return), as well as other works that broke down prohibitions that society imposes on the female body. This new writing confronts practices of excessive romanticizing, self-monitoring, conservatism, and use of symbols and metaphors to address taboo subjects that characterize much earlier writing. In fact, women's sexuality has become one of the basic pillars of the Arab feminist novel.

Criticism directed at these bold novels has focused on the idea of exposure and nudity, expressed as uncovering the unmentioned in Arab society or as lifting the veil, revealing the concealed, or baring reality. Together these texts constitute a rebellious body that has stripped society bare. Through their narrators these writers have dropped their masks of fear and emphasized nakedness and exposure. For many critics, they represent a kind of seduction designed to solicit popularity, while for others they have signified an uncovering of the self and a tradition of taboos that has necessitated concealment and suppression.

In this framework, I would try, as an Arab girl drilled in obedience, to prove to my tribe that I did not belong to this new generation of writers. I would strenuously deny any relationship with my protagonists of ill repute who defied traditions. I would try to dismiss from my writings the sin of revealing and to escape into imagined, folkloric realms where fairies would open forbidden doors and where I could continue to watch my heroines who, I insist, bear absolutely no resemblance to me! My protagonists fall in love and wallow in the ecstasy of rebellion while I watch them with hunger.

Caution and excessive self-monitoring have not protected me from accusations that I am a rebellious girl of ill repute—the daughter who left her home, removed her hijab, and deserted her traditions. In truth, I could not be what my mother desired me to be when she taught me the laws of existence: "An Arab girl is like a pliant camel—that is, a camel trained in obedience." I would often disregard her and run away to distant streets with Maha and other bad girls who taught me the pleasures of defiance.

I write in my novels about the journey of the blue eggplant—the girl who rebelled and fled, loved and was shattered, and left in her papers a summary of her long history of failure. I try to use indirection, metaphors, and symbols, consoling myself as I remain helpless before the horror of knowing that bad girl narratives usually end tragically. The protagonists may end up in mental hospitals, like the poet Mayy Ziyada did, or commit suicide by jumping from high-rise buildings, as did the scholar-activist Durriya Shafiq, the first Egyptian woman to earn a doctoral degree in philosophy from the Sorbonne University, who was nonetheless refused an appointment as a professor at Cairo University because she was a woman. Shafiq threw herself from her balcony to her death in the mid-1970s, as the leftist activist Arwa Salih did in the mid-1990s, leaving behind a small book entitled *Al–Mubtasarun: Dafatir wahidah min jil al-haraka al-tullabiyya* (The premature: Notebooks from the student movement), published in 1996, thus incriminating through her death the movement that failed in its own liberation. In one chapter, "The Intellectual in Love," she offers one of the most important personal and literary testaments on the contradictory attitudes of the cultured elite to the female's body and its sexual freedom.

Salih committed suicide to condemn the Arab Left. Several years later, the Egyptian activist Zaynab al-Mahdi committed suicide to condemn the Arab Right and its practices regarding the woman's body. Following the military breakup of the 2013 demonstration in Rabiʿa al-ʿAdawiyya Square and forced evacuation of Tahrir Square through systematic sexual harassment, there occurred a spate of suicide protests. Zaynab al-Mahdi hanged herself at her home, leaving behind a number of questions about the kidnapping, torture, and rape of women activists. She also left information regarding her relationship with the Muslim Brotherhood and the electoral committee for the Islamist presidential candidate Abd al-Mun'im 'Abu-l-Futuh. She wrote of mental harassment after her decision to remove the hijab. Beside her hanging body the twenty-year-old left a confession of her powerlessness to continue living, a few tweets that reveal the despair of a generation of women who found the land of freedom still far out of reach, and a video in which she talks about her experience with circumcision as an act of physical violation. So, between the wearing and rejection of the hijab, female circumcision, collective harassment, and politically systematic sexual violence against women that accompanied the events of January, Zaynab al-Mahdi gave her life to use her body to condemn the deteriorating situation of women at a time of collective failure and general decline.

Thus have the beautiful, bad girls engraved meaningful imprints in the history of social liberation, imprints denoting the ferocity of the conflict, the harshness of tradition, and the dominance of social constraints. They have revealed, through their literary and physical exposure, the social hypocrisy and fragility of the liberal climate. They have uncovered the shameful faults of society that are concealed behind supposed virtue. Bad girls are heroines because life is a ripe fruit to be desired without guilt and not a dishonor to pluck.

# Contributors

**Diya Abdo** is associate professor of English at Guilford College in Greensboro, North Carolina. Her work centers on Arab women writers, autobiography, Islamic feminism, comparative literature, and postcolonial translation. She is author of articles in *Frontiers: A Journal of Women Studies*, *Image and Narrative*, *Women's Studies Quarterly*, *Eugene O'Neill Review*, *Journal of Lesbian Studies*, and the MLA's *Approaches to Teaching the Works of Assia Djebar* (2017), among other publications, as well as poetry, fiction, and creative nonfiction. Her public essays have appeared in *Jadaliyya*, *Feminist Wire*, and *Electronic Intifada*. Abdo is founder and director of Every Campus a Refuge, an organization that advocates for housing refugees on campus grounds and assisting them in resettlement. She has a PhD from Drew University.

**Amal Amireh** is associate professor of English and world literature at George Mason University. Her research focuses on Palestinian literature, gender, sexuality, nationalism, and Islam and Arabic literature in postcolonial contexts. She is the author of *The Factory Girl and the Seamstress: Imagining Gender and Class in Nineteenth-Century American Fiction* (Routledge, 2000) and coeditor of *Going Global: The Transnational Reception of Third World Women Writers* (Routledge, 2000) and *Etel Adnan: Critical Essays on the Arab-American Writer and Artist* (McFarland, 2002). Her essays and reviews have appeared in publications including *South Atlantic Quarterly*, *Signs*, and *Critique: Critical Middle Eastern Studies*. She founded and writes the blog *Improvisations: Arab Woman Progressive Voice*. Her PhD in English and American literature is from Boston University.

**Laila al-Atrash** is an award-winning writer and prominent media figure in the Arab world whose work portrays the experience of Arab women and dimensions of their human rights activism. Her television programs and written work, including nine novels, four plays, and a short-story collection, have received various awards. She also is the recipient of Jordan's State Appreciation Award, the highest honor granted for excellence in the arts, and the *Arab Human Development Report IV* named her as one of the Arab female writers who have had a distinct influence on their societies. Her novels have been translated into nine languages, and her work is taught as part of the curricula at various universities around the world.

**Jan Bardsley**, professor of Asian studies at the University of North Carolina at Chapel Hill, received her PhD in 1989 (East Asian Languages and Cultures, UCLA). She specializes in Japanese humanities and women's studies. With Laura Miller, she has coedited two books, *Manners and Mischief: Gender, Power, and Etiquette in Japan* (University of California Press, 2011) and *Bad Girls of Japan* (Palgrave, 2005). She is also the author of *Women and Democracy in Cold War Japan* (Bloomsbury Academic, 2014) and *The Bluestockings of Japan: New Women Fiction and Essays from Seitō, 1911–1916* (University of Michigan, Center for Japanese Studies, 2007), which was awarded the 2011 Hiratsuka Raichō Prize by Japan Women's University.

**Anne Marie E. Butler** is a PhD candidate in global gender studies at the State University of New York at Buffalo. In her dissertation she explores sexuality in contemporary Tunisian art. Her research interests include contemporary art and visual studies, specifically Middle Eastern art and culture, gender and sexuality studies, and postcolonial and decolonial studies. She received her master of arts in politics from New York University.

**Patricia Caillé** is *maîtresse de conférences* in communications at the Université de Strasbourg. She is coeditor of "Les cinémas du Maghreb et leurs publics," *Dossier Africultures* (2012); "Circulation des films: Afrique du Nord et Moyen Orient," *Dossier Africultures* (2016); and *Regarder des films en Afrique: Approches comparées* (Septentrion, forthcoming).

**Samia Hissen Doany** is an educational and languages consultant who has helped to shape Arabic and English curricula and teacher training at the Jubilee School, Amman Baccalaureate School, and King's Academy, among other schools. She has worked in Palestine, Lebanon, Jordan, the United Kingdom, and the United States and has taught literature in English and Arabic. Her own writings include a book of short stories titled *Daisies from the Desert*. She holds a master's degree in comparative literature.

**Anita H. Fábos** is associate professor of international development and social change at Clark University. Her work has encompassed ethnicity, gender, displacement, urban refugees, and refugee and citizenship policy in the Middle East. Her published works include *"Brothers" or Others? Propriety and Gender for Muslim Arab Sudanese in Egypt* (Berghahn, 2010) and "Resisting 'Blackness,' Embracing Rightness: How Muslim Arab Sudanese Women Negotiate Cultural Space in the Diaspora," *Ethnic and Racial Studies* (2012). She has led programs and taught refugee studies at the University of East London and American University in Cairo and has conducted fieldwork among diaspora Sudanese in Egypt, England, Dubai, and Canada. She received her PhD in anthropology from Boston University.

**Rawan W. Ibrahim** is lecturer in social work at German-Jordanian University's Department of Social Work. As a consultant in child and youth alternative care settings for the UNICEF Jordan Country Office, she is supporting the Jordanian government in deinstitutionalizing children through the development of Jordan's first foster care program. In addition to implementation science and the development of community-based programs, her research interests include preparation and postcare support of youth transitioning from institutional care to independent living. She has contributed to and authored several publications and book chapters, among them "Cast Out and Punished" in *Young People Transitioning from Out-of-Home Care: International Research, Policy, and Practice* (Palgrave Macmillan, 2016). She holds a PhD in social work from the University of East Anglia, England.

**Randa A. Kayyali** is lecturer in anthropology at George Washington University's Elliott School for International Affairs. She is author of *The Arab Americans*, published in English (Greenwood, 2006) and in Arabic (Arab Institute for Research and Publishing, 2007) and numerous articles and book chapters. She serves on the board of the Arab American Studies Association (AASA) and is chair of the AASA 2017 convention. She received her doctorate in cultural studies from George Mason University, where she taught classes in anthropology, cultural studies, and global studies.

**Florence Martin** is professor of French and Francophone cinema and literature at Goucher College in Baltimore, and general editor of *Studies in French Cinema*. She is author of *Screens and Veils: Maghrebi Women's Cinema* (Indiana University Press, 2011), coeditor with Patricia Caillé and Kamel Benouanès of *Les cinémas du Maghreb* (Africultures, 2013), and coeditor with Guy Austin of "French and Francophone Cinema and Contestation," a special issue of *Studies in French Cinema* (November 2013). She is coediting with Maria Flood a special issue of *Studies in French Cinema* on terrorism and migration in Maghrebi films (forthcoming in 2018). She holds a doctorate from the Sorbonne.

**Laura Miller** is the Ei'ichi Shibusawa-Seigo Arai Endowed Professor of Japanese Studies and Professor of Anthropology at the University of Missouri–St. Louis. She received her PhD in anthropology from UCLA in 1988. She has published more than seventy articles and book chapters on Japanese culture and language, including topics such as Japanese girls' slang, self-photography, the divination industry, and elevator girls. She is the author of *Beauty Up: Exploring Contemporary Japanese Body Aesthetics* (University of California Press, 2006) and coeditor of three other books, two with Jan Bardsley. Miller is currently doing research on Himiko, a third-century female ruler of Japan.

**Rima Najdi** is a performance artist based in Berlin. She focuses on the body as a tool and map of experiences and identity politics and is interested in the vulnerabilities of one's body, looking at gender politics, safety, mobility, and representation. She received a Watermill Center International Summer Residency (2011) and an artist fellowship (2015–2018) with Urban Heat, a project developed by the Festivals in Transition network of thirteen international partners and supported by Creative Europe to enable artists to engage with the invisible communities within cities. She received a residency in the Sundance Theater Lab in the Middle Eastern–North African region and a postlab grant (2016) and has been commissioned by CTM Radio Lab, Berlin (2017).

**Rula B. Quawas** is professor of American literature and feminist theory at the University of Jordan, founding director of its Women's Studies Center, and former dean of its School of Foreign Languages. Her research focuses on feminist readings of American and Arabic texts written by women writers. She is author of numerous essays and book chapters and of books, including *The Voice of Being Enough: Young Jordanian Women Break Through without Breaking Down* (Dār al-azmina li-l-nashr wa-l-tawzīʿ, 2016), *From the Speaking Womb of the Desert: Stories from Jordan* (Dār al-azmina li-l-nashr wa-l-tawzīʿ, 2013), and *Crossing Borders: A Narrative Journey into the Middle Eastern World* (Champlain, 2015). Quawas has been honored for her work for the empowerment of Jordanian women and was nominated in 2013 for the International Women of Courage Award. She received her PhD from the University of North Texas.

**Hanadi al-Samman** is associate professor of Arabic language and literature in the Department of Middle Eastern and South Asian Languages and Cultures at the University of Virginia. Her research focuses on contemporary Arabic literature, diaspora, and sexuality studies, as well as transnational and Islamic feminism(s). She is author of *Anxiety of Erasure: Trauma, Authorship, and the Diaspora in Arab Women's Writings* (Syracuse University Press, 2015) and articles in *Journal of Arabic Literature*, *Women's Studies International Forum*, *Alif: Journal of Comparative Poetics*, and the edited collection *Mapping Arab Women's Movements* (American University in Cairo Press, 2012). She is coeditor of the *International Journal of Middle East Studies* special issue "Queer Affects" (2013) and *The Beloved in Middle Eastern Literatures: The Culture of Love and Languishing* (I. B. Tauris, 2017). She received her PhD from the University of Indiana.

**Adania Shibli** is visiting professor in cultural studies and visual culture at Birzeit University in Palestine. Her research focuses on visual arts, cinema, and other visual practices within the context of Arabic culture. She was a lecturer at the School of Critical Theory and Cultural Studies at the University of Nottingham and at L'École des hautes études en sciences sociales in Paris and a postdoctoral research fellow at Wissenschaftskolleg zu Berlin, EUME Programme. Shibli earned her PhD from the University of East London with the doctoral thesis "Visual Terror," on British and French television networks' visual compositions of the 9/11 attacks compared to major attacks in the "war on terror." Shibli also has written fiction and narrative essays on visual arts and politics and twice won the Qattan Young Writer's Award, Palestine. She was born in Palestine.

**Miral al-Tahawy** is an award-winning Egyptian novelist and short-story writer and an affiliated member of the Virginia G. Piper Center for Creative Writing at Arizona State University in Tempe, where she is associate professor of modern Arabic literature and head of Classics and Middle Eastern Studies at the School of International Letters and Cultures.

**Suhair al-Tal** focuses her research on feminist studies and human rights. She is a longtime activist in union movements through the Jordanian Writers Association, Jordanian Press Association, and Jordanian Women's Union, among other organizations. She is author of fiction and nonfiction in Arabic. Her works include *City of Rose and Stone: Study in Sex*

*Crimes in Jordanian Society* (Community Center Jordan, 1997) and *History of the Feminist Movement in Jordan 1944–2008* (Dār al-azmina li-l-nashr wa-l-tawzīʿ, 2014), both in Arabic. She was born in Irbid, Jordan, and received her PhD from St. Joseph University in Beirut.

**Nadia Yaqub** is associate professor of Arabic language and culture in the Department of Asian Studies at the University of North Carolina at Chapel Hill. She is the author of *Pens, Swords, and the Springs of Art: the Oral Poetry Dueling of Weddings in the Galilee* (Brill, 2006) and numerous articles and book chapters on gender and women in Palestinian visual and literary arts. She received her PhD from the University of California, Berkeley.

# Index

Note: page numbers in *italics* refer to figures.

of badness, 44; "girls" as term and, 7–8; the "good bad girl," 168, 172, 181n1; inheritance rights and, 212; in literary history, 218; Madame Bomba and, 51; *maw'ūda* and, 163; meaning of, 21; Muslim Americans and, 70; *nushūz* (female disobedience in the intimate sphere), 171; Palestinian mothers and, 92–93, 100–108; pleasure and, 168–169; Prouty and, 65, 69; "reel bad Maghrebi girls," 167–168, 181; reluctant bad girls, 7; scapegoats and survivors, 15–17; sexual harassment student video, 25–26; Sudanese musicians and, 186–187; in Syria, 148; al-Tahawy on, 216–217, 220; al-Tal and, 199–200, 204, 209; transgression and, 6–8; *wa'd* practice and, 146; Yazbek and, 146. *See also* Second Intifada and "bad Palestinian mothers"; *specific case studies*

Badran, Margot, 29–30

"Bahiyya's Eyes" (Rifaat), 32

Baker, Ahmed, 107

Barakat, Hoda, 151

Bardsley, Jan, 3–4, 7–8

Bashir, Omar al-, 188

Baudelaire, Charles, 160

*Bawabat ard al-'adam* (*The Crossing*) (Yazbek), 158–163

"begging the question," 105

Beirut, 49–51, 205–206. *See also* "Madame Bomba: The TNT Project"

Beirut 39, the, 147

Benjamin, Walter, 160

Ben Mabrouk, Néjia, 172

Berryman, John, 38

"Between Secular and Islamic Feminism/s" (Badran), 29–30

Bin 'Ali, Zin al-'Abidin, 113, 115–116, 118, 141, 180

Bint al-Shati', 218

Bizet, Georges, 173–175

bodies and embodiment: as always political, 134–135; Arab spring and deployment of female bodies, 217–218; celebration of, in women's writings, 219; discursive and flesh-and-blood bodies and, 114–115; Egyptian "novel of the body," 219; Hamdi's transformed body, 119; masculine space, disruption of, 113–114; *maw'uda* and the buried corpse, 156–158; ownership of bodies, 137; raped body speaking (Iman al-Obeidi, Libya), 120–126; Sboui's topless self-portraiture, 132–144; self-marking, 135–143; suicide and, 221; transgression embodied, 3; virginity tests, 3, 18n4, 114, 126n, 180, 217. *See also* nudity; sexual assault and rape

body language, 135

British Broadcasting Corporation (BBC), 99, 102–103

Brown, Laura, 156–157

Bu'azizi, Muhammad al-, 113–119, 126, 127n3, 127n8, 127n10

Bu'azizi, Salim al-, 115

Bulu-bulu, Hanan, 188

burial alive. See *wa'd* practice and archetype

*Buried Secrets/Les secrets* (Amari), 177–181

Burqiba, Habib, 144n1, 171

Butler, Judith, 30

Caillé, Patricia, 169

care, residential. *See* group homes, residential care, and transition to adulthood

*Carmen* (Bizet), 173–175

cemeteries, 133, 141, 160–161

Central Intelligence Agency (CIA), 65–66, 71–75

Certeau, Michel de, 160

Chahine, Talal, 65, 73

children: of absent fathers, in Qur'an, 81; Palestinian, deaths of, 92–109; personal status laws scapegoating, 16; second wives and, 87–88. *See also*

assassination of, 123; regulation of Sudanese musicians and, 189; Sboui's images and, 132–133; as site for public performance, 11; Sudanese diaspora musicians and, 186, 189, 195

intersectionality, 64–65

Intifada. *See* Second Intifada and "bad Palestinian mothers"

Iranian Revolutionary Guards, 154

Iraq, US war in, 109n2

"Is Feminism Relevant to Arab Women?" (Golley), 29

Islam: colonialist mindsets and, 143; disavowal of, to prove loyalty to US, 70–71; Femen's critique of, 134; Orientalist understandings of gender and, 13; political, rise of, 8; Prouty and, 67, 70–75; Salafis, 152, 155, 188; Sboui and, 134; *wa'd* outlawed in, 10; Wahhabi, 188; Western gender narratives and Islamophobia, 14; Yazbek and, 155

Islamic State (IS), 3, 67, 112, 161–163, 164n8

Israel and Palestine. *See* Second Intifada and "bad Palestinian mothers"

Israeli Broadcasting Association (IBA), 94–99, 110n5

Izanami, 158

Jacir, Annemarie, 169–170

*jāhiliyya*, 149–151, 153

Jamahiriya 2 (Libya), 122–123

James, Henry, 25

Jarrah, Amal, 219

Jawarish, Mu'ayyad, 104–106

Jelloun, Taher Ben, 127n10

*Jerusalem Post*, 101, 106

"Jihad Jane," 66–67, 75n2. *See also* Prouty, Nada

Johnson, Penny, 9

Jordan: "badnessism" in, 21; British Mandate, 38, 200; firstborn daughters and golden reputation in, 37–38; patriarchal family and cultural system as collective society, 79–80, 90n1; personal status laws in, 16; sexual harassment in, 21–22; student dormitories in, 82, 90n3; women's political gains in, 18n7; women's public speech in, 9. *See also* Feminist Theory class, University of Jordan; group homes, residential care, and transition to adulthood; Tal, Suhair al-

Jordanian Student Union, Lebanon, 205

Journées Cinématographiques de Carthage (Tunis Film Festival), 171, 182n8

Jullier, Laurent, 172

Kahf, Mohja, 73

Karaman, Tawakkul, 112

Kassab, Maria, 49

Kazoun, Rayya, 49

Kharrat, Edward al-, 219

Kilani, Leila, 176

Kinda tribe, 150

language, as receptacle for cultural heritage, 10

LaRose, Colleen, 75n2

Lebanon: Palestinian-Lebanese struggle, 203–206, 214; in Prouty autobiography, 68; suicide bombings in, 49–51. *See also* "Madame Bomba: The TNT Project" (Najdi)

Leites, Nathan, 168, 181n1

*Let Me Be* (Rasha), 193

Liberman, Hillel, 103

Libya, 120–126

*Libya on This Day* (Jamahiriya 2), 122–123

Lucas, Marie-Aimee Helie, 39

*Mabat* (IBA), 94–99

Macdonald, Andrew, 126

"Madame Bomba: The TNT Project" (Najdi): background of, 49–50; and definitions, 51; letters in response to, 50; about Madame Bomba, 51–53;

monologue of a stranger, 61–62; monologue of Madame Bomba, 59–60; personal diary of Madame Bomba, 53–59; suicide bombers, Beirut history of, 50–51

Maghrebi directors, female. *See* films by female Maghrebi directors

Mahdi, Zaynab al-, 220–221

Mahfuz, Asma, 218

Mahmood, Saba, 6, 18nn5–6

Malik, Saadia, 192

Malkki, Liisa, 163

Mamdouh, Alia, 219

Manbi, Faraj, al-, 124

marking and self-marking, 135–143

Marks, Laura, 178

marriage: arranged, 175; child marriage, 118; and patriarchal responsibility for women, 83; to redeem rape victim, 123; second wives, 87–88; suicide and, 217

martyrdom (*shahādā*), 107

masculinity and masculinist discourse: "badnessism" and, 21; becoming masculine, 116; construction of badness, challenging, 34; demarcation of public spaces as masculine, 127n4; feminist education and, 34; heterosexual norms of, in cinema, 168; masculine space disrupted by women's bodies, 113–114; nation embedded in, 41; slap by a woman as emasculation, 115–116, 127n11; walking and, 160. *See also* honor and dishonor; patriarchy

"Mashnaqa, Al-" (The noose) (al-Tal), 209–210

master power narrative, 66–67, 74

*maw'ūda* (daughters that fathers wanted to suffocate), 150–151, 163. See also *wa'd* practice and archetype

*mayyita al-akthar ḥuḍūran, al-* (the living dead), 157

McGuiness, Frank, 40–41

Mernissi, Fatima, 171, 212

microrebellion, 2

Miller, Laura, 3–4, 7–8

Mitchell, Juliet, 34

mobility of women in Syria, 162

Monroe, Marilyn, 181n1

Morin, Edgar, 181n1

Moroccan film. *See* films by female Maghrebi directors

Mosteghanemi, Ahlam, 219

mothers, "bad." *See* group homes, residential care, and transition to adulthood; Second Intifada and "bad Palestinian mothers"

Mousely, Yousef El-, 188

Mubarak, Husni, 113

*Mubtasarun, Al-* (Salih), 220

Muluhi, Tall al-, 147

Musrati, Hala al-, 122–123

Mustakfi, Wallada bint al-, 218

*My Body Belongs to Me* (Sboui), 133, 137–139, 138, 142–144

naming, 7, 23

Nasri, Assala, 148

Nasri, Basma al-, 117

nationalism, 39, 114, 203. *See also* patriotism

Neimi, Salwa al-, 151, 219

Nejjar, Narjiss, 173–175

New Left movements, 203–204

*New York Post*, 66

9/11. *See* September 11, 2001

"novel of the body," Egyptian, 219

*Nuba of Women on Mount Chenua, The* (Djebar), 170–171, 172, 182n6

Nubatones, 190, 193

Nubian "songs of return," 193

nudity: in Amari's *Buried Secrets* (film), 178; Bedouin women's use of, 217; as challenge to patriarchy, 218; Elmahdy photos, 1–3, 114; racial privilege and, 133–134; Sboui's topless self-portraiture, 132–144; as weapon of defiance, 219

nushūz (female disobedience in the intimate sphere), 171
Nusra front, 159, 162–163

Obeidi, Iman al-, 114, 120–126
objectification: Grosz on the body and, 135–136; "human furniture," 25; Sboui and, 135; sexual harassment as, 21; student video and, 27, 32, 33; subjecthood vs. objecthood, 21, 27
Orientalism, 13–14, 64–65, 68, 70
orphans. *See* group homes, residential care, and transition to adulthood

Palestinian-Lebanese struggle, 203–206, 214
Palestinian Liberation Organization (PLO), 208, 214
Palestinian mothers. *See* Second Intifada and "bad Palestinian mothers"
patriarchy: abandoned children and, 78, 79, 83; anarchy and, 142; feminist education and, 33–34; Prouty and, 67, 68; Sboui, Femen, and, 143; Sudanese musicians and, 187; al-Tal on, 209–210; tribal preference for male children and, 164n2. *See also* honor and dishonor; masculinity and masculinist discourse
patriotism, 64–65, 69. *See also* nationalism
Pelley, Robert, 67
Peres, Shimon, 101–102
Perjovschi, Dan, 142
Perjovschi, Lia, 142
Personal Status Code (Code de Statut Personnel, CSP), Tunisia, 144n1
piety movement, 6, 18n5
pleasure, film viewer and, 168–169, 172
Polisario liberation movement, 208
political engagement and activism. *See specific case studies*
*Politics of Piety, The* (Mahmood), 6
prayer, right to lead, 18n6

pregnancy, 45, 70, 81, 87–88, 214. *See also* group homes, residential care, and transition to adulthood
privilege, 14, 133–134
Prouty, Nada, 63–65; back story of, 65–66; as bad Arab girl and good American woman, 68–70; badness and, 17; break with natal community, 13; Druze heritage and "slipperiness" of, 71–72; ethnic politics of Detroit and, 72–74; "Jihad Jane" label, 66–67; strategic media recuperations, 67–68; strategic religious identities, 70–71

Qadhdhafi, Mu'mar al-, 114, 120
Qadhdhafi, Sa'di al-, 122
Qashush, Ibrahim al-, 157
Qays ibn 'Asim al-Tamimi, 149
Qur'an, 81, 150–151, 214

Rabi'ah tribe, 149–150
*Ra'ihat al-Qirfa* (Cinnamon) (Yazbek), 147, 219
rape. *See* sexual assault and rape
"Rape of Iman al-Obeidi, The" (video), 128n22
Rasha, 189–195
re-authenticity, Arab, 169–170, 182n4
"refugee," 203
reputation: golden, 37–38, 42; threats to, 40–41
residential care. *See* group homes, residential care, and transition to adulthood
resistance vs. transgression, 7
revolution and the revolutionary: bad-girlness and, 146; bodies of women as sites of contestation, 114; changes in gender and sexuality and, 113; feminist fiction, exposure to, 31; "the longest revolution," 34; nationalism vs., 114; Sboui and, 139, 141; seeing body as revolutionary, 119; Tawakkul Karaman as "mother of," 112. *See*

DISPLAY